7.50

SENSE AND NONSENSE
IN PSYCHOTHERAPY

THE CHALLENGE OF HYPNOSIS

Other Pergamon titles of interest

J. C. ANCHIN & D. J. KIESLER
Handbook of Interpersonal Psychotherapy

F. CAMPBELL & G. SINGER
Brain and Behaviour

J. D. KEEHN
Origins of Madness

W. LAUTERBACH
Soviet Psychotherapy

S. RACHMAN
The Effects of Psychological Therapy, 2nd Edition

VAN DE RIET *ET AL.*
Gestalt Therapy

PERSONALITY AND INDIVIDUAL DIFFERENCES

An International Journal

Editor-in-Chief: H. J. Eysenck

Publishes articles which aim to integrate the major factors of personality with empirical paradigms from experimental physiological, animal, clinical, educational, criminological or industrial psychology, or to seek an explanation for the causes and major determinants of individual differences in concepts derived from these disciplines.

Free specimen copy supplied on request.

SENSE AND NONSENSE IN PSYCHOTHERAPY

THE CHALLENGE OF HYPNOSIS

BY

LÉON CHERTOK

translated by R. H. AHRENFELDT
and revised by the Author

PERGAMON PRESS

OXFORD · NEW YORK · TORONTO · SYDNEY · PARIS · FRANKFURT

U.K.	Pergamon Press Ltd., Headington Hill Hall, Oxford OX3 0BW, England
U.S.A.	Pergamon Press Inc., Maxwell House, Fairview Park, Elmsford, New York 10523, U.S.A.
CANADA	Pergamon Press Canada Ltd., Suite 104, 150 Consumers Road, Willowdale, Ontario M2J 1P9, Canada
AUSTRALIA	Pergamon Press (Aust.) Pty. Ltd., P.O. Box 544, Potts Point, N.S.W. 2011, Australia
FRANCE	Pergamon Press SARL, 24 rue des Ecoles, 75240 Paris, Cedex 05, France
FEDERAL REPUBLIC OF GERMANY	Pergamon Press GmbH, 6242 Kronberg-Taunus, Hammerweg 6, Federal Republic of Germany

First English edition 1981
Previously published in French, 1979, under the title *Le Non-savoir des psy*

British Library Cataloguing in Publication Data
Chertok, Léon
Sense and nonsense in psychotherapy.
1. Hypnotism — Therapeutic use
I. Title
616.8'916'2   RC495   80-41755
ISBN 0-08-026793-9 (Hardcover)
ISBN 0-08-026813-7 (Flexicover)

Printed in Great Britain by A. Wheaton & Co. Ltd, Exeter

"It is not easy to over-estimate the importance of the part played by hypnotism in the history of the origin of psycho-analysis. From a theoretical as well as from a therapeutic point of view, psycho-analysis has at its command a legacy which it has inherited from hypnotism." (Sigmund Freud, 1923, *A Short Account,* S.E. XIX, p. 192.)

"Hypnotism is quite dead (...) until the day of its resurrection." (Pierre Janet, 1925, *Psychological Healing,* vol. I, p. 203.)

Contents

Prologue

On December 28th, 1949, I was starting upon my psychiatric career (delayed by the war) and my psychoanalytic training, and the Center for Psychosomatic Medicine at the Villejuif Psychiatric Hospital had only just been opened. A patient was referred to me. Although she described herself as a spinster, aged 22, she was, in fact, a married woman and mother, 34 years old. The last 12 years of her life were quite simply wiped from her memory. In the course of two interviews I was able to establish a good contact with her and to arouse a few remnants of memory. Nevertheless, the case remained a difficult one. I thereupon thought of hypnosis. Some 13 years earlier, I had had the opportunity to witness the use of this technique by one of my professors in Vienna. I told the patient to lie down, to fix her gaze on two of my fingers, and to relax. She did this, then closed her eyes and seemed to be asleep. I asked her her age. She replied without hesitating that she was aged 34 and the mother of a son. I suggested to her that when she awoke she would once again recall the last 12 years of her life. That is what occurred.

I was, of course, astonished, without fully realizing the significance of what had just taken place. This case brought to my mind Charcot's famous experiments. But in France, 60 years later, the terms hypnosis and hysteria had, as it were, an anachronistic ring. Charcot's pupils, Babinski in particular, had erased their master's teaching. The very term hysteria had been replaced by that of "pithiatism," suggesting the idea of a kind of simulation. It was the period when, to prove that hysterical anesthesia was produced by the will, researchers stoically submitted to torture. Until 1952, when Montassut, Gachkel and I presented our communication before the Société médico-psychologique, no paper on hypnosis had been submitted to that Society since 1889 — and that had dealt with the dangers of hypnotism (the author was Dr. Lwoff, a psychiatrist also at Villejuif).

Psychoanalysis, which was starting to gain impetus, had reinstated hysteria. But, so far as hypnosis was concerned, the taboo had in fact been reinforced still further since Freud had abandoned it. The very next day after this episode, I confessed to my analyst the deed of which, in my own eyes, I had been guilty in using this "barbaric" technique. Did he absolve me? I never knew. What had occurred during this lifting of this woman's amnesia remained an enigma to me. What had happened? What psychophysiological processes had been induced by those gestures which I had made, to such a degree that the function of memory suddenly became accessible to manipulation? And this, without the gaining of insight, interpretation of the transference, or working-through – in short, in the absence of all that I had learned to regard as the motive force of psychotherapeutic action. Psychoanalytic concepts seemed to me incapable of resolving this mystery. But in my idealization of my own analyst, I remained convinced that he on his part knew what had happened and that one day, having myself become an analyst, I would also know it.

The years went by. First a student, then a trainee analyst, I buried myself in the works of the Master and his disciples: first topic, second topic, egopsychology, and, later, the Kleinian, Lacanian and other theories. I was becoming expert in all the subtleties of clinical psychoanalysis. However, I still had no answers to my questions.

While continuing in analytical practice, I began occasionally to employ hypnosis. I inquired into current research. I tried to interest my psychoanalytical colleagues in this subject. My attempts brought no support: on the contrary, they aroused reproval. I recall a memorable interview with the representative of a psychoanalytical institution who warned me against this diabolic temptation and the dangerous path upon which I was venturing. I still think of this quaint scene with some amusement, my interlocutor assuming the airs of an operetta-inquisitor and I playing the part of Galileo repeating that yet the Earth does move.

On the other hand, I met with an encouraging welcome on the part of Raymond de Saussure, one of the founders of the Paris Psychoanalytic Society, who himself practiced hypnosis from time to time, and was greatly interested in preanalytical history. We published jointly *The Therapeutic Revolution – From Mesmer to Freud*, where we attempted to show how hypnosis had been the central nucleus around which the discovery of the unconscious and of relational psychotherapy had taken place. As a psychobiological phenomenon, hypnosis seemed to me all the more a field of choice in that, in my psychiatric practice, I had become more oriented toward psychosomatic medicine. Unfortunately, psychosomatic specialists also showed little interest in hypnotism.

For two decades my contacts in the field of research in hypnosis were thus essentially confined to foreign authors, whether in the United States or the Soviet Union, the German Federal Republic or Eastern European countries. In France, apart from occasional encounters with psychiatrists from Strasbourg, I had for a long time only one contact, an anesthetist, Dr. Jean Lassner. About 1970, however, I was joined by some experimental psychologists. I then established a laboratory for the study of hypnosis at the Dejerine Center for Psychosomatic Medicine, of which I was the director. A few psychoanalysts joined us subsequently, which enabled us to initiate a dialogue between experimenters and clinicians.

It so happened that, a few years ago, two of my former patients, who had proved to be good subjects for hypnosis, were in need of surgical treatment requiring general anesthesia. I thought that it might be possible to replace chemical anesthesia by anesthesia suggested under hypnosis. The operations were carried out accordingly, and in both cases most successfully. I then proposed to my two "subjects" that they submit to a further experiment, that of blistering (i.e. the production of a blister by hypnotic suggestion), which also produced results of considerable interest.

It was not without some hesitation that I decided to undertake these experiments. I had hitherto practiced hypnotism in the quiet (and secrecy) of the consulting room, in the form of a relationship which remained in my view, if not in that of my colleagues, one of an analytical kind. However, to appear in public in an operating theater, to abandon the "pure gold" of analysis for a trivial organic procedure, represented for my analytical superego one more step towards heresy. In the case of a surgical operation I could at least claim a therapeutic alibi. But to make use of subjects for purely experimental ends . . . ! With my knowledge of the persons involved, I was convinced of the completely harmless nature of the experiments. However, I could easily foresee the indignant comments that would be voiced in some quarters.

Nevertheless, my scientific inquisitiveness prevailed. It seemed to me that an analyst should have the necessary freedom and adaptability to confront a variety of relational situations. These experiments could not but be productive. Far more than that, they were an opportunity to gain true insight. Certain questions notwithstanding, I, like all analysts, shared the illusion that we possessed a wide knowledge of psychical activity and the interpersonal relationship. This illusion was supported by the never-ending stream of new books, articles, and congresses devoted to the most diverse subjects. I now saw taking place before my own eyes processes whose nature, I was forced to recognize, remained completely enigmatic. I suddenly came up against reality. I observed that the Emperor had no clothes. Our knowledge was minimal in comparison with all that we did not understand.

It is that realization which motivated the decision to write this book. It seemed to me that there was today an urgent need to draw up a balance sheet of what we know and what we do not know. Moreover, it seemed perhaps the best service that could be rendered to psychoanalysis, as well as to psychotherapy in general.

Hypnosis is situated at the crossroads of many fields. It was not my intention to write an exhaustive and erudite work which would examine in detail every problem raised. Such an undertaking would have required several volumes. My purpose is to give the reader a preliminary outline of the range of questions which arise today with regard to hypnosis. Let each one then select that aspect of the subject which he wishes to examine further.

Deauville, May 1980.

Introduction

It was two centuries ago (in 1778) that a Viennese doctor, Franz Anton Mesmer, arrived in Paris. He rapidly gained notoriety, creating a scandal in the scientific circles of his time. He claimed that human beings were linked by a specific energy, "magnetic fluid," and that by means of this fluid it was possible for one subject to produce in another subject important psychic and somatic changes. This was how he accounted for phenomena such as possessions, exorcisms and miraculous cures which had previously been thought to emanate from divine or evil influence and had been the preserve of priests, sorcerers, and healers. For Mesmer [1971] there was nothing supernatural about the magnetic fluid, which represented a material force which could be explained by natural laws, was subject to scientific experiment, and could be used for therapeutic purposes. It was, in a way, the manifestation in the human domain of the principle of gravitation. Hence the term animal magnetism as opposed to the magnetism of minerals.

In practice, the method perfected by Mesmer consisted of submitting the subject to a series of bodily manipulations (passes), intended to produce "crises" which were thought to perform a curative function by achieving a harmonious redistribution of the fluid. Indeed, Mesmer considered that most illnesses were due to a faulty distribution of the fluid through the whole organism.

Mesmer's successors observed that the crises were but an epiphenomenon and that the nub of the matter lay elsewhere. When the subject was "magnetized" in this way, certain phenomena were produced, indicating that he or she was plunged into a specific state. This state was characterized by, amongst other things, a particularly powerful submission to the will of the operator.

The theory of animal magnetism was to be the object of numerous controversies before it was finally abandoned in favour of other hypotheses. The state induced by the operator was successively called "magnetic sleep," "somnambulism," and "hypnosis." The induction techniques similarly took many forms, but this development will not be traced in detail here. The main point is that, with Mesmer, relational phenomena, which had hitherto been the concern of morality or religion, were for the first time defined as objects of scientific investigation. Two questions were posed which have not to this day received a definitive answer: What was the nature of hypnotic influence and, more generally, of any psychotherapeutic relationship? The influence took effect both at the psychic level and at the physiological level. What was the relationship between these two fields?

From the outset, Mesmer's theories met with fierce opposition from scientific circles in general and from doctors in particular. It was to take more than a century, marked by impassioned debate, reports of commissions and counter-commissions, and the efforts of many investigators such as Puységur (1784–1785), Braid (1843), Liébeault (1866), Richet (1875), and Bernheim (1884) before hypnosis was recognized, with Charcot's work (1882) as a subject for scientific research.

During this period numerous research projects were undertaken, leading to an unprecedented exploration of mental life and the accumulation of a considerable amount of experimental material. It was thus that the notion of a psychological unconscious came gradually to be developed. The development of psychoanalysis represents the outcome of this process.

It is unnecessary here to recall the role played by hypnosis in this discovery. Let it merely be said that Freud, in showing that the Unconscious was structured according to a certain number of fundamental drives and in elaborating the notion of transference, was the first to throw light on relational phenomena in general and the hypnotic relationship in particular. He enabled us to understand that the power of the hypnotist was linked to the fantasies of his subject.

But the relationship between psychic and biological aspects of the Unconscious has remained one of the obscure points of psychoanalytic theory. This theory rests entirely upon the hypothesis of the fundamental unity of the human person, conceptualized as an indissociable psychobiological whole. This postulate is indispensable to an exploration of how fantasies and unconscious representations can act upon the most elementary physiological functions. Certain of the most important psycho-analytical concepts – the libido, affect, and the drives – are, moreover, key concepts stationed at the intersection of the two realms. However, this interaction remains ill-defined insofar as these terms retain a speculative nature and are devoid of any strict scientific validation. One of the consequences of this state of affairs is that, to a large extent, psychotherapeutic processes elude our understanding. This lacuna is more and more obvious. Thus, we are witnessing today a veritable proliferation of psychotherapeutic techniques, all of which claim to produce positive results, without adducing in support any rigorous theoretical justification – and for a very good reason.

It can be seen that the questions raised in Mesmer's day are far from resolved. Hypnosis constitutes an enigma even today, to the extent that it reveals the relationship between the psychic and the somatic in a particularly forceful way. In this sense it constitutes a route of choice – it is tempting to say an indispensable detour — towards the understanding of the areas of psychic functioning which still remain obscure.

The form of this book is unusual. It is composed in fact of two dissimilar parts. The first of these contains a description of the two series of experiments which the author has had occasion to carry out, which illustrate most particularly the psychophysiological character of hypnosis. Hypnotic analgesia shows, in fact, how a psychological, interpersonal process can act upon cerebral structures so as to modify the integration of information at the cortical level, inducing a transformation of bodily experience and behaviour. In the case of blistering, the representation is registered directly in the material body, entailing changes of an organic nature. In order to give the reader a glimpse of the evolution of research into hypnosis, it was, in both cases, thought useful to preface the description of the author's experiments with a brief historical review of previous experiments.

The content of this first part may at times seem forbidding, due to the very nature of the material discussed. It deals, in fact, with concrete data which must be precisely controlled and submitted to rigorous methodology. The impatient reader may, if he so desires, proceed directly to the second part of the book, but in the author's opinion it was important to describe some of the facts underlying our theoretical questions.

In the second part, a much more flexible approach is adopted in exploring various areas which apparently have no direct connection with the experiments reported. The present state of our ignorance about hypnotic phenomena does not permit a truly scientific explanation of the experimental material. However, it seemed of interest to draw up a sort of inventory of the questions which are being asked today about hypnosis insofar as they are relevant to psychotherapy as a whole. The author has attempted to define in what respect hypnosis represents an altered state of consciousness, which leads us to consider the problem of the relationship between hypnosis and suggestion. An outline is given of the various therapeutic uses of hypnosis. The much-debated question of the relationship between hypnosis and hysteria is also considered. It is shown that the concept of transference is insufficient to account for the specificity of the hypnotic relationship. This leads to an analysis of the uncertainties which are prevalent today in the field of psychotherapy. We shall see that the central problem is that of affect, of the psychobiological dimension of the interpersonal relationship. The question of hypnosis and affect is examined in the light of the more general problem of the interaction between the psychological and the physiological aspects of the Unconscious, such as it presented itself in the evolution of psychoanalytical theory. Finally, a survey is made of contemporary perspectives in research in hypnosis.

A third part (Appendixes) presents two studies intended to demonstrate the present state of experimental research.

It can be seen that hypnosis has rich potential for expansion in many directions. However, it still arouses considerable resistance, particularly in France. It is still surrounded by an "aura" of irrationality, magic, and even charlatanism both for the general public and in scientific circles. This prejudice constitutes an epistemological obstacle which hinders the development of systematic research. That is why it is necessary to continue to carry out new experiments, without allowing our endeavours to be obstructed by the scepticism which arises almost automatically in the face of phenomena which cannot as yet be explained. Even the most committed investigator sometimes feels the need to "see" in order to "believe." The author in the early days himself has experienced this. He had some knowledge of psychological analgesia, having undertaken research into painless childbirth, but had never witnessed a surgical operation under hypnotic anesthesia. He knew, of course, that such operations had been performed in the past, but this was purely book knowledge. As far as blistering is concerned, his knowledge was even less precise. He was unaware of the literature published on the subject.

As far as he knew, it consisted of one experiment carried out at the end of the nineteenth century, which had not been reproduced since then. It was necessary to conduct these two experiments himself, so that this abstract knowledge could become a living reality.

It is hoped that this work will inspire other research in its turn. It is worth the effort. It is still not recognized that hypnosis, which for some people evokes little more than the flashiness of the music hall, highlights problems which actually touch upon the very root of human consciousness.

PART I

EXPERIMENTS

1

Hypnotic Analgesia

Historical Background

The use of psychological means for the suppression of pain has long been attested.[1] Its origins may be traced back to practices derived from magic, such as those which are encountered in certain ethnic groups. Similar practices were also known in Antiquity and the Middle Ages.

This account, however, concentrates more precisely on the history of the relief of pain without the use of drugs, since it first became the object of an experimental approach with the development of the theory of animal magnetism at the end of the eighteenth century. In fact, Mesmer's successors came to the conclusion that magnetic sleep could sometimes produce in the subject more or less total analgesia. For more than half a century, the question of analgesia was thus to be intimately linked with controversies about whether or not the fluid existed.

HYPNOTIC ANALGESIA IN SURGERY

The first experiment reported in the literature took place on November 7th, 1820, at the Hôtel Dieu Hospital, on an 18-year-old girl, Miss Samson. She was magnetized by Baron du Potet (1796–1881), a well-known magnetist of the day, working in the Department of Dr. Husson (1772–1853), in the presence of Récamier (1774–1856), a famous surgeon at the time. Récamier "lifted her several times from her chair, pinched her, opened her eyes, and she felt nothing" (Foissac, 1833, p. 276).

Récamier was later to submit two other patients to the test of moxa.[2] On

[1] Cf. Chertok (1957) for a more detailed account.
[2] Method of cauterization.

3

January 6th, 1821, in collaboration with the magnetist Robouam, he put to sleep a man calles Starin. He then applied a moxa "to the anterior part of the right thigh, slightly supero-laterally, which produced a scab seventeen lines long by eleven wide." The patient "gave not the slightest sign of any sensation, either by crying out, movement or alteration in pulse rate" (Foissac, 1833, p. 280). It was only on waking that he felt severe pain.

The second experiment was performed on Lise Leroy and proceeded in a similar manner. The moxa was applied to the epigastric region and resulted in "a scab fifteen lines long by nine wide" (*ibid.*, p. 281).

Eight years later, on April 12th, 1829, Jules Cloquet (1790–1883) performed the first surgical operation under hypnotic analgesia. The patient was a 53-year-old woman with asthma, magnetized by her physician, Dr. Chapelin, who made the suggestion that she undergo the operation without fear. It is worth noting that in the waking state the patient was dreading the operation. But throughout the operation itself, "the patient continued to converse calmly with the surgeon and did not give the slightest sign of sensation" (Cloquet, 1829, p. 132).[3]

The operation was for "the removal of a cancer of the breast during magnetic sleep." It was under this title that Jules Cloquet presented a report to the Royal Academy of Medicine on April 16th, 1829. During the course of this meeting, a passionate debate took place as to whether the fluid did or did not exist, as usually happened whenever animal magnetism was mentioned. Hippolyte Larrey (1766–1842), formerly chief surgeon to the Grande Armée, regretted that Cloquet "should have allowed himself to be taken in by such tricks." "Who can tell," he added, "the lengths to which men will go, out of self-interest or fanaticism, to disguise the pain they feel, and the patient is nothing but a crony of the hypnotists" (*ibid.*, pp. 133–134).

Larrey quoted the example of soldiers who had been able to withstand painful treatment without any apparent signs of sensation, an attitude

---

[3] It is interesting to note that Cloquet, a well-known surgeon and anatomist, was apparently attracted to unorthodox methods. He was one of the first people in France to experiment with acupuncture as a method of treatment. In a book published in 1826 by de Vannes, one of his assistants, there is a description of ninety cases treated by Cloquet by this method. For the most part they were painful cases of neuralgia (which today we would call "psychosomatic"). However, de Vannes makes no mention of the use of acupuncture for analgesic purposes in surgery (de Vannes, 1826).

which he attributed to their courage. He referred likewise to the case of Kléber's assassin, who is known to have sung whilst under torture.

In effect, the opponents of animal magnetism refused to admit the validity of this experiment, because the existence of magnetic fluid seemed to them inadmissible from the physiological point of view. Cloquet replied that, without claiming to explain anything, he was reporting an undeniable fact, and "the truth, however incredible, is nonetheless true, and it must always be told" (*ibid.*, p. 134).

A similar debate took place at the same Assembly on January 24th, 1837. The first case to be presented there concerned a patient of Oudet (1788–1868), on whom he had performed dental extractions under magnetic anesthesia. Oudet was assured that he had been "tricked" like Cloquet. In this connection, the various motives were cited which can induce a patient to feign insensibility. Once again the discussion turned to the reality of the fluid (Oudet, 1837).[4]

In Great Britain, du Potet had been able to win over to the cause of animal magnetism Elliotson (1791–1868) of the University College Hospital, London, an eminent physician who had been one of the propagators of the stethoscope invented by Laënnec. This had already earned him the hostility of his colleagues. As a result of his belief in animal magnetism, Elliotson was obliged to resign all his official positions. In 1843 he published a number of cases of surgical operations under hypnosis (Elliotson, 1843). In the same year he founded the journal *The Zoist* in which there is an account of all the operations performed under hypnotic anesthesia at that time, not only in England but in other countries as well (Elliotson, 1846).

---

[4] It is remarkable that even today the fact of hypnotic anesthesia meets a wall of astonishment and even irony. Reservations and resistances which, in varying degrees, have lasted 200 years always invoke the same argument that "hypnotic analgesia is inexplicable on the neurophysiological level, and its mechanism has no theoretical foundation." An eminent colleague of the author exemplified this approach in a friendly but mocking reproach, when, happening to see on television the film of one of the experiments to be described later, he compared the scenario to a badly produced parody of science fiction. When hypnosis is not likened to cinema, there is apparently a need to find some fallacy in it at all costs, the secret ingredient whose discovery would once again throw everything into doubt. Witness the remark made, again after the film was shown, by an anesthetist become analyst, even though he was sincerely convinced of the reality of hypnosis: "What drug did you give him to get him to come round like that?"

Following on from Elliotson's work, Esdaile (1808–1859) carried out 315 operations in India under magnetic anesthesia, including 200 for the removal of scrotal tumours. Esdaile did not magnetize his patients himself, but called upon young people from 14 to 30 years of age, both Hindu and Moslem, mostly assistant surgeons and pharmacists at the hospital at Hoogly. Hypnosis was induced by passes of one or both hands in front of the face. It was repeated several times in a dark room before the operation (Esdaile, 1846, 1852).

In the same period, several operations were performed in France by, for example, Ribaud and Kiaro (1847),[5] Fanton (1845),[5] Loysel (1846a,b), etc.

Shortly after 1840, an event occurred which was once again to call in question the theory of animal magnetism. Braid brought about a veritable revolution by discontinuing the use in induction of the magnetic passes which were thought to ensure the transmission of the fluid, replacing them with fixation of the gaze on a bright object, to which he later added verbal suggestion. This change in technique was generally considered as proof of the non-existence of the fluid. The term hypnotism introduced by Braid replaced that of animal magnetism (Braid, 1843). It should be noted, however, that hypnotism and animal magnetism existed side by side for a while, each theory having its supporters. As early as 1813, Abbé Faria (1756–1819), who denounced the "fluid" theory, had already used verbal suggestion to put his subjects to sleep. *The Zoist* for its part remained faithful to the term mesmerism long after the development of Braid's work in England and France. The book by Binet and Féré, published in 1887, was still entitled "Animal Magnetism."

Moreover, the discovery of ether (1842–1846) renewed doubts about the use of magnetic anesthesia, and this at a time when Elliotson and Esdaile were envisaging its coming into general use. Pharmacodynamic anesthesia seemed to be more easily obtained.

Hypnotic analgesia, however, continued to be used essentially for experimental purposes. In his book on hypnotism, Braid had reported several surgical operations performed under hypnosis (dental extractions, the lancing of abscesses, orthopedic operations, etc.). Braid's work was known in France through Azam (1822–1899) of Bordeaux. The latter carried out several experiments over a 2-year period without ever

---

[5] Quoted in Charpignon (1860, p. 14).

publishing his work. In 1859 he spoke about it to Broca (1824–1880)[6] who, in collaboration with Follin at the Necker Hospital, carried out the removal of an extremely large and painful peri-anal abscess. He was to deliver an account of this operation to the Academy of Science and the Surgical Society on the 5th and 7th December 1859 (Broca, 1859, 1860).

It may seem surprising that Broca should take an interest in hypnotic analgesia when he already had an arsenal of anesthetizing agents at his disposal, including chloroform. In fact the use of this type of anesthesia was only in its early stages and accidents were still frequent. This was why Broca declared, "Any safe method which works successfully on just one occasion is worthy of study" (Broca, 1860, p. 248). Nevertheless, he had no illusions about the general use of hypnotic procedures in surgery. "But," he added, "however strange they may appear, they deserve the full attention of physiologists, even if they are not consistent enough to serve as the basis for a regular method of surgical anesthesia" (*ibid.*, p. 253). "There can be no doubt whatever that the study of hypnotism is destined to enlarge our sphere of knowledge in physiology" (*ibid.*, p. 258).

Mention must also be made of Liébeault who introduced a factor which was to have important consequences, both theoretical and practical. It concerned the possibility of obtaining the suppression of pain by post-hypnotic suggestion, enabling the operation to be performed with the patient awake. In a study published in 1885, he mentioned nineteen cases of dental extractions performed painlessly or with reduced pain between 1882 and 1883 (Liébeault, 1885).

Charcot's presence at the Salpêtrière and Bernheim's as head of the Nancy School coincided with the great period of work on hypnosis. Several operations were performed under hypnotic analgesia at about this time, particularly in France by Pitres (1886), Mabille and Ramadier (1887), Bernheim (1886, pp. 270, 370), Fort (1890), Mesnet (1888), and Liégeois (1889, p. 265 seq.); in Switzerland by Forel (1889); in the U.S.A. by Wood (1890); in Sweden by Velander (1890); and in Cuba by Auard Martinez Diaz (1892).

On Charcot's death (1893), interest in hypnosis diminished considerably, as much in France as in other countries. Thus, this period saw few

---

[6] The same Broca (1861) who, 2 years later, was to initiate a new stage in the problem of cerebral localization (see Hecaen and Lanteri-Laura, 1977).

publications devoted to hypnotic analgesia in surgery. It was only after the Second World War that such publications once again became more numerous, principally in the United States. Hilgard and Hilgard (1975) compiled a list of these which is reproduced in Table 1.

Hypnotic Analgesia in Obstetrics [7]

Attention should likewise be drawn to the role played by hypnotic analgesia in obstetrics. As early as 1831, Husson had drawn attention to the fact that hypnotic techniques could be used to lessen pain in childbirth (Foissac, 1833). Several attempts were made in this direction during the nineteenth century, particularly by Cutter (1845) in the United States, Saunders (1852) in England, and in France by Lafontaine (1860, p. 197) and Liébeault (1866, p. 387 seq.; 1885; 1887). From 1885 onwards, these attempts became increasingly numerous. In France, mention may be made of Dumontpallier (1892), Auvard and Secheyron (1888), Mesnet (1888), Grandchamps (1889), Luys (1890 a, b), Edwards (1890), Journée (1891), Le Menant des Chesnais (1894), Lugeol (1893), and Voisin (1896). In other countries: in Austria, Pritzl (1885); in Holland, De Jong (1889); in Germany, Sallis (1888), Schrenck-Notzing (1893), and Tatzel (1893); in Spain, Ramon Cajal (1889); in England, Kingsbury (1891); in Russia, Dobrovolsky (1891), Botkin (1897), and Matveev (1902); and in the United States, Lichtschein (1898).

The observations they made are for the most part very detailed and contain a wealth of clinical material. They show experimentally the various modalities of analgesia. The subject may be aware of the contractions of the uterus without experiencing the slightest feeling of pain; the pain may be diminished; it may be felt without being manifested in the behavior of the parturient; on the other hand, she may show autonomic signs of pain, whilst declaring that she is not suffering; or else she may forget the whole experience, etc. Moreover, observers have noted the influence of verbal suggestion on physiological functions, such as uterine contractions, lactation, and so on.

After the First World War, attempts were made in Germany and Austria to use hypnosis on a larger scale. This tendency was in part due to a reaction against the abuses of analgesia by drugs (Dämmerschlaf) produced with the aid of opiates (morphine, scopolamine). This movement was represented by von Oettingen (1921) at Heidelberg, Schultze-Rhonhof (1922, 1923), Heberer (1922), Kirstein (1922), Franke (1924), and von Wolff (1927). During this period, techniques became more varied: the use of hypnosis during childbirth or only during the preparatory phase (the delivery in that case being rendered painless by post-hypnotic suggestion); the use of hypnotic suggestion in combination with drugs; the use of suggestion in the waking state, etc.

---

[7] On this subject, cf. Chertok (1957) and Chertok *et al.* (1966).

TABLE 1

Operations under hypnotic analgesia or anesthesia without chemical adjuvant

Type of operation	Reference
Abdominal surgery	
Appendectomy	Tinterow (1960)
Caesarean section	Kroger and DeLee (1957)
	Taugher (1958)
	Tinterow (1960)*
Gastrostomy	Bonilla, Quigley, and Bowers (1961)
Breast surgery	
Mammaplasty	Mason (1955)
Breast tumor excision	Kroger (1963)
Breast tissue excision	Van Dyke (1970)
Burns	
Skin grafting, debridement, etc.	Crasilneck, McCranie, and Jenkins (1956)
	Tinterow (1960)
	Finer and Nylen (1961)
Cardiac surgery	Marmer (1959)
	Tinterow (1960)
Cateract excision	Ruiz and Fernandez (1960)
Fractures and dislocations	Goldie (1956)
	Bernstein (1965a)
Genitourinary	
Cervical radium implantation	Crasilneck and Jenkins (1958)
Curettage for endometritis	Taugher (1958)
Vaginal hysterectomy	Tinterow (1960)*
Circumcision where phimosis present	Chong (1964)
Prostate resection	Schwarcz (1965)
Transurethral resection	Bowen (1973)
Oophorectomy	Bartlett (1971)
Hemorrhoidectomy	Tinterow (1960)*
Nerve restoration	
Facial nerve repair	Crasilneck and Jenkins (1958)
Thyroidectomy	Kroger (1959)
	Chong (1964)
	Patton (1969)
Venous surgery	
Ligation and stripping	Tinterow (1960)
Miscellaneous	
Removal of tack from child's nose	Bernstein (1965b)
Repair of lacerated chin in child	Bernstein (1965b)
Removal of fat mass from arm	Scott (1973)

*Some non-analgesic medication used during pre-operative or surgical procedures.

This expansion, however, remained relatively limited in scope. The usual resistances against hypnosis made a rapid appearance. Furthermore, hypnosis itself implies conditions which render difficult its use on large groups of people. That is why, with the improvement of pharmacological methods in the meantime, 1925 onwards saw the progressive abandonment of hypnosis in the Germanic countries.

Thanks to Pavlov's influence, which gave hypnosis a physiological explanation, the resistances against it were less pronounced in the Soviet Union than anywhere else. From 1923 onwards, there began a period of intense experimentation. Hypnotariums were even established in Leningrad (Vigdorovič, 1938) and Kiev (Syrkin, 1950). These were units in which women were prepared for childbirth in sessions of group hypnosis. One of the principal researchers was Platonov (Platonov and Velvovsky, 1924), who was a pupil of the great Russian neuropathologist Bekhterev and worked in collaboration with Shestopal (Platonov and Shestopal, 1925), Nicolaev (1927), Kalašnik (1927), Postolnik (1930), Shlifer (1930), and Zdravomyslov (1930, 1938).

The experience accumulated by these authors made it possible to demonstrate that labor could be made more or less painless by psychological means. On this basis, the psychoprophylactic method was developed in the Soviet Union. In this approach, hypnosis was replaced by "educational" methods: teaching the anatomical and physiological aspects of childbirth, using techniques of persuasion designed to convince the pregnant women that labor pains were not inevitable, and to eliminate the associated fear. "Pain-reducing" procedures (rhythmical breathing, effleurage of the abdomen during the uterine contractions), etc., were also employed with this method.

The proponents of the psychoprophylactic method were of the opinion that, in contrast to hypnosis which put the woman in a state of *passive* dependence, it had the advantage of allowing her to participate *actively* in the process. They considered that labor pains were not organically determined, but constituted a conditioned reflex, acquired over the centuries as a result of sociocultural influences. An appeal to the active side of the woman stimulated an "activation" of the cortex. A new conditioned reflex was created which effaced the old one. Thus, this method had a prophylactic role, while hypnosis, based on cortical inhibition, had only a *curative* effect.

This theory of "cortical activation" is not, in fact, founded on any experimental basis. It corresponded to the tendency then predominant in the Soviet Union, to attempt to explain everything in terms of Pavlovian physiology. It was challenged by some practitioners in the 1950s, including some who were themselves using the psychoprophylactic method, and today it has been practically abandoned.

The psychoprophylactic method has nevertheless played an important role in the humanization of childbirth. It was to spread rapidly throughout the world. First introduced in France by Lamaze and Vellay in 1952 (Lamaze and Vellay, 1952, 1956), it was initially used by a minority of women and doctors politically involved in Leftist organizations. But its sphere rapidly expanded, and in 1956 it even received the official approval of Pope Pius XII (Childbirth without Pain,

Papal Speech, 1956). In the United States it made slow progress under the name of the "Lamaze Method." Elsewhere hypnosis continues to be used from time to time in childbirth (Abramson and Heron, 1950; August, 1961; Kroger, 1962, 1963; Cheek and Le Cron, 1968).

What conclusions can be drawn from this brief history? The perfecting of pharmacological analgesia in surgery and the spread of the psychoprophylactic method in obstetrics have relegated hypnotic analgesia to the background. It is hardly used any more except when, for one reason or another, the patient cannot tolerate pharmacological analgesia. However, from a theoretical point of view, this work has produced important experimental material which remains fundamental to our understanding of the phenomenon of pain. It has shown that the latter cannot be reduced to a series of mechanical reactions to noxious stimuli, but that it involves a global organismic dimension, linked to some extremely complex factors: socio-cultural attitudes, relational factors, etc.

The Experiments

The very expression hypnotic analgesia is sufficient to suggest the idea of a crossroads; we are dealing with the "meeting point" between hypnosis and pain. No more is known about pain than about hypnosis, and the complexity of the phenomenon of pain becomes apparent as soon as the noxious stimuli are examined. It is true that the pathways adopted by the algogenic impulses are unknown. Likewise, the reality of the central control of sensory-sensorial impulses is generally accepted. But the precise details of the mechanism, unexplained to this day, remain in the forefront of the theoretical and patho-physiological debates on the subject of pain.

The value of presenting the following two observations lies not in the area of surgery, nor in the mode of anesthesia employed. They represent two operations performed under hypnotic anesthesia. It must be stressed that these are by no means the first performed under hypnosis. However, they were marked by two incidents to be described later, and led the author to perform an experiment which, curiously enough, seems never to have been attempted previously, namely the recall of the operation experience under subsequent hypnosis.

It should be mentioned that every stage (pre-operative tests, operations, and recall) was recorded on film and tape.

THE OPERATIONS[8]

These were performed in 1974 and 1975, the first by Professor Raoul Tubiana at the Ambroise Paré Hospital at Neuilly.

For some years the author has known the two patients to be particularly suitable to deep hypnosis with spontaneous amnesia upon waking. They had normal reactions to pain and have had surgical operations under general anesthesia on several occasions. They underwent a series of pre-operative tests: a pinprick, the application of artery forceps and Kocher forceps, with the aim of "evaluating" the depth of anesthesia. No drugs were administered before, during or after the operation.

First case

Mrs. D. underwent her operation in October, 1974, at the age of 49. She is an anesthetist nurse, who had suffered for some years from retention of urine, presumed to be psychogenic, which up to this time had not responded to treatment. This complaint, the onset of which followed a hysterectomy, required catheterizing twice daily.[9] The operation was for the removal of a ganglion of the left wrist and a foreign body in the pulp of the right index finger. These operations normally require a general anesthetic.

At the appointed time, she came on her own from her room to the operating theater. Hypnosis was induced by means of the procedure to which she had long been accustomed (counting up to 10 at the most). Then the following suggestion was made: "You feel as if there is a leather glove on your right forearm[10] and you will not feel any pain there." We talked with her throughout the operation which was marked by an incident which occurred whilst the surgeon was at work in the radial groove: bradycardia (a sudden

---

[8] A preliminary account of these experiments was published by Chertok, Michaux, and Droin (1977).

[9] Since then, an operation on her sphincters has allowed Mrs. D. to gain partial recovery of micturition. She can now empty her bladder by exerting manual pressure upon it, but she has not regained her vesical sensitivity, and has no feeling of the desire to urinate. On the other hand, her bladder does not *empty* completely and residual urine always remains. The possible psychological origin of her complaint remains an open question to which there is still no answer.

[10] This was an error on our part, since the operation was to be on her left arm, an error which Mrs. D. herself rectified (see below, p. 20).

drop in the pulse rate from 90 to 60), a fall in blood pressure from 140 to 90 mm, and sweating—all indicating a definite state of stress. However, the patient showed no withdrawal reaction and no change of expression. She merely asked for a drink. The episode lasted about 10 minutes, but the anesthetist in attendance did not consider that any action was necessary (cf. Fig. 1).

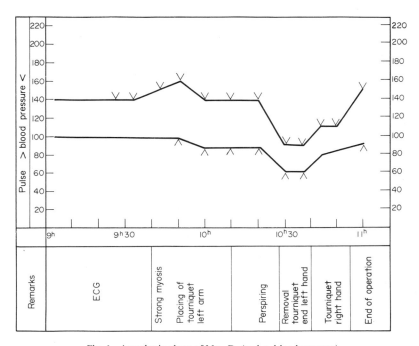

Fig. 1. Anesthesia chart of Mrs. D. (pulse, blood pressure).

Once the ganglion had been removed, we suggested to Mrs. D. complete analgesia of her right hand, in order to operate on the index finger. The foreign body was removed.

Upon waking, the patient felt fresh and in good spirits. She drank a cup of coffee and returned to her room on her own. No effort was made to lift her amnesia.

That evening, the author paid her a visit and she informed him that she felt none of the usual post-operative pain or itching. She had tried to take her own pulse, but could not feel it. Moreover, one of the anesthetists, informed of the situation, had already verified the persisting analgesia by pricking Mrs. D. with a pin. The author repeated the same test and ascertained that the "leather glove" effect on the left forearm persisted, as well as the local anesthesia in the right hand. The author then recalled that he had forgotten to lift the suggestion of anesthesia at the end of the operation. However, Mrs. D. refused to have it lifted, on the grounds that it would avoid the administration of post-operative analgesic medication. Three days after discharge from the hospital, she returned to the Laboratory, where her hypnotic anesthesia, which was found to have persisted up to that time, was finally lifted.

Second case

Mrs. T. underwent her operation in April, 1975, at the age of 55. She holds an advanced postgraduate degree in German. (When she came to see the author some years previously, she also presented with psychogenic urinary retention following hysterectomy, like Mrs. D. It was possible to cure this condition by hypnosuggestion.)[11] As she suffers from a coronary condition, chemical anesthesia would present some problems in her case, although they would not be insoluble. The operation involved the extraction of five teeth from the lower jaw, along with a pulpectomy (an operation performed upon a live nerve and therefore extremely painful).

As in the preceding case, she needed no assistance on her way to the operating theater. She received no premedication and was hypnotized by means of the technique to which she was conditioned. As well as the analgesia, we obtained the inhibition of salivation and bleeding by the following suggestion: "You will feel no pain. You will feel a slight tickling sensation. You will not salivate and you will not bleed."[12]

---

[11] What may appear to be a strange coincidence is due merely to the fact that the author was then acting as a psychosomatic consultant to a urological department (Professor Pierre Aboulker).

[12] Of course, the author knew, but only theoretically, that suggestion could check bleeding and salivation during dental extractions. Faced with the situation in practice, he tried to find some *expressive* phrase which might be addressed to the patient in order to prevent her bleeding. It was a stomatologist, present at the operation and familiar with these problems, who, seeing the author's embarrassment, provided the solution: "But, look here," he said, "simply tell her not to bleed or salivate. That is enough." And indeed, this proved adequate.

Nothing untoward occurred during the operation. When she woke, Mrs. T. asked: "Is it all over? Have you done everything?" She stated that she could remember nothing about the operation.

RECALL UNDER HYPNOSIS OF OPERATIVE EXPERIENCES

The course of this experiment, to be retraced in detail for each patient, was conducted according to a set pattern. It was an attempt, in both cases, to revive the experience of the operation by means of subsequent hypnosis. This was to be achieved by presenting in stages to each subject a series of three suggestions which may be summarized as follows:

1. You are back in the operating theater. You are aware of what is going on around you. You will tell me about it.
2. You are aware of your bodily sensations during the operation. You will describe them to me and tell me what you were thinking at that moment.
3. Even if it now seems to you that you are not aware of these bodily sensations, a part of you is aware of them. That awareness will come to you and you will be able to describe the sensations. [13]

Here is the essence of the memories recounted (and recorded on tape).

Mrs. D., operated on October 21st, 1974, was hypnotized again on January 9th, 1975, more than 2 months after the operation.

In reply to the first suggestion, Mrs. D. recalled the presence of many people, getting up on to the operating table, her conversation with us, and asking for a glass of water during the incident described.

"And then they operated on me. I know . . . I did not feel anything. I could not feel what they did to me. I know what goes on. I see it every day. But I know I was very hot, and then I was thirsty. I asked if I could have a drink. They brought me a glass with a pipette."

All Mrs. D.'s memories corresponded to what had happened.

In response to the second suggestion, she replied: "My arms—I could not feel them at all for several days. I was completely numb. I did not feel as if

---

[13] The formulation of this suggestion was inspired by the work of Hilgard (1974). It is, however, questionable whether it is really necessary to present the patient with this concept of "a hidden part of himself," or whether the same result would not be obtained merely by repeating with emphasis the previous suggestion.

it was my hand they were operating on. I did not look, but if I had looked it would have seemed like an operation on someone else, not me."

In an attempt to revive a more precise memory of the bodily experience, the third suggestion was given.

She said: "My whole body was numb, but where they were operating it burned to start with . . . as if they were cutting with a knife. It didn't last long. Afterwards it burned. It was so hot . . . I don't know if it was the thermocautery . . . I didn't see . . . or if it was when the cyst was removed. It was burning . . . it was agony . . . as bad as the incision. . . . But it was bearable. It was as if . . . it was like hot flushes. It got stronger and stronger, and then went away. It didn't last. Then I felt nothing. I don't know what was causing it . . . I didn't see."

We then asked Mrs. D. what she was thinking about during the operation. She was on holiday at St Jean-de-Luz with her husband and daughter. She was on a pedal-craft. The sun was shining.

The question was made more precise. "What were you thinking about when the hot flushes came?" "I thought my heart was packing up . . . and then I said, 'If it stops, too bad' . . . I thought I would, you know . . . peg out . . . but I am not scared of that. One doesn't notice it . . . and then there were enough people around to start it going again."

Mrs. D. also remembered that at that moment we mopped her brow.

In the case of Mrs. T., who had her operation on April 21st, 1975 (dental surgery), there were two separate experiments in recall.

(a) Awakened after the operation, she was hypnotized again half an hour later. We gave the second suggestion and she stated: "I did not think about anything. At first I heard the noise of a sort of engine in front of my face. I don't really know how to describe it. The noise of an engine that kept stopping from time to time and then starting again. I think that was about all. That was all at first. It lasted quite a long time all the same. And then . . . the noise of an engine coming towards my face but . . . well it was annoying but wasn't . . . there was no pain . . . And then after that I heard you talking. . . ."

We insisted, repeating the same type of suggestion, but Mrs. T. gave no new information. We then moved to the third suggestion to which she responded as follows: "Because I was relaxed, I was not at all afraid of the operation . . . I cannot say that I felt any pain . . . I am trying but . . . If there was any . . . two or three slight sensations of . . . not even pain . . . like a slight tickling sensation on my jaw, but I cannot begin to call it pain."

(b) A second attempt was made to revive Mrs. T.'s memories of the operation under hypnosis 3 days later on April 24th, 1975.

On the first suggestion, Mrs. T. recounted her morning in detail, waking up at home, her journey to the Lariboisière Hospital, being settled in the operating theater, the preparation and so on. She asserted that she was calm and confident.

Upon the second suggestion she immediately declared: "I can hear the sound of an engine. An engine running, running, keeping on running; stopping sometimes but then running again and that is when, I think, that is the moment when I felt the sensation of burning, of heat."

We stressed the point: "You feel the burning?" "No, no, like, like . . . well it's as if there was burnt flesh. . . . The sensation of heat, I felt it in my face, but I don't know if it was in my mouth, and then after a moment the engine . . . the drone of the engine stopped.

"I don't know, I don't know anymore. There were slight . . . I felt sort of slight twinges three or four times. Yes, maybe three or four times – I'm not sure. Like slight twinges in the jaw, and then I think I woke up after that and then you said it was over. . . .

"I felt something. I felt someone putting something in my mouth. It reminded me of when my dentist took impressions of my jaw to make my dentures, but not so unpleasant, in any case it didn't hurt. Then after that, I think I woke up. Only I woke up and I had just one thought in my head: 'When are you going to start so that we can get it over with?' And you replied: 'It's over.' "

Then we gave the third suggestion, to which she replied: "Yes, that bit about the engine, it wasn't in front of my face, come to think of it, it was in my mouth and the engine was the . . . was the drill, or whatever it's called. So she began to deal with my tooth, but it was as if the tooth belonged to someone else and not me. I wondered which tooth she was treating . . . then I said to myself: 'After all, I'd like to know which tooth she is treating so that I can follow what's happening and then I shall know whether it's hurting me or not' . . . But I didn't feel a thing."[14]

She added: "I tried to understand why I felt that this was all happening to someone else. It was as if she was working on some other person, but someone inside me all the same. So I was almost like a spectator."

On the subject of the dental extractions, Mrs. T. said: "I know that

---

[14] "She" refers to the dental surgeon who operated, who is also Mrs. T.'s regular dentist.

afterwards she took some teeth out, but perhaps that was done much more quickly because I didn't have time to realize it. I wasn't at all aware of the extractions, as I had been aware of the other work, the pulpectomy she performed. So I think that it must certainly have happened very quickly. I had no time to react or to wonder about it. As it didn't hurt and I didn't feel a thing, I had no reason to worry. I was asleep."

Up to this point, the interviewer was the same person who had hypnotized the patient. However, the following question was put to her by his assistant.

"Just now you referred to another person being treated. You knew something was happening, but you could not feel anything. What was this other person feeling?"

The patient replied: "Of course she was saying: 'It hurts! You're hurting me!' "

After this reply, the assistant gave the following suggestion: "I am going to count up to 5, and at 5 you will no longer be the Mrs. T. who was speaking just now, but that other person who was in pain."

Mrs. T. then said: "Oh, it hurts a bit, but it's not that bad. Occasionally you touched a sensitive spot with the drill and it hurt, but it didn't last.[15] Oh, I think I was exaggerating when I said that you hurt me. It was sensitive but not painful. . . . It's a tooth on the right that you treated, but it's not at all the same as when you give me dental treatment at your place, in your surgery . . . you can't even compare the pain . . . it's like a pain but rather far away, which doesn't reach anything . . . it doesn't really seem to reach the body, one's own body . . . I think that, all in all, things went very well."

POSSIBLE INTERPRETATIONS

From the raw data furnished by the two operations described, one might conclude without further ado that hypnosis offers a means for the suppression of pain. Indeed, evidence to that effect is provided by the absence of manifestations of pain, such as the spinal withdrawal reflex, or the facies which usually indicates the perception of pain.

The author's experiments with recall show, however, that the problem is probably more complex, and the most important finding seems to be that, under hypnosis, the perception of information about pain and its recognition

---

[15] She confused the assistant with her dentist.

as such by the subject persist but seem to undergo a qualitative change.

This brings us to the problem of the mechanism of attenuated emotional acceptance, as described by some physiologists.

This mechanism is characterized by a feedback relayed from the cortical structures, back to the centers of pain integration. The nociceptive information is registered at the cortical level, but the accompanying emotional response varies according to the meanings which are attached to it and according to its intensity.

The permanent regulation, however, is limited by the noxiousness of the stimulus and the subject's earlier learning patterns (personal attitude to pain, and socio-cultural background).

Hypnosis permits the modification and alteration of the significance normally attached to the information. The hypnotic relationship brings into play two relatively distinct and complementary mechanisms.

The first process consists in an adaptation by the subject to the demands of the situation, in a manner relatively independent of the hypnotist's specific suggestions. This process may be described as a response to internal needs rather than to external requirements. To some extent it implies the assimilation of the actual threatening perception to an analogous but non-threatening perception. Such is the case with Mrs. D., who likens the burning of the incision to the burning of the sun, and the discomfort of perspiration to a hot flush.

The subject may also have recourse to rationalization, as when Mrs. D. tells herself that she is in the hands of competent professionals and denies that she is liable to react emotionally when faced with a dangerous situation: "Me? I'm not afraid of dying. . . ."

The second mechanism consists in conforming to the letter of the suggestions made by the hypnotist. When the hypnotist says "You feel no pain," his words completely determine the subject's perception.

Thus, Mrs. D. uses essentially the first mechanism and Mrs. T. the second, which might explain the differences which appear during the recall sessions.

Mrs. D. talked to the experimenters fairly readily about her experience of a certain amount of pain and the associations which accompanied it, whereas Mrs. T. remained more reticent, doubtless because of her greater submission to the suggestion of analgesia, but also perhaps because her associations were confined to those proposed by the hypnotist.

From this point of view, the incident which occurred during Mrs. D.'s operation may be explained as a fluctuation in the hypnotic relationship, an explanation based on what the author knows of the personality of Mrs. D., who has always had a more active attitude and has shown herself less dependent in her relationship with the hypnotist. To sum up, the incident would indicate that for the space of 10 minutes, Mrs. D. doubted the hypnotist's word, during which time the manifestations of pain partially reappeared. However, her recourse to rationalization enabled her to overcome this passing difficulty.[16]

Two other facts will serve to illustrate the distance which Mrs. D. maintained in respect of the suggestions given to her.

At the beginning of the operation, an error was made in the formulation of the suggestion by demanding analgesia of the right arm instead of the left, an error which Mrs. D. herself corrected. In addition, when the operation was over, the experimenters failed to lift the suggestion of analgesia. This time Mrs. D. did not put it right herself, but seems to have engaged in skillful manipulation; while still conforming explicitly to the suggestion which the author had omitted to lift, she made use of this omission for the purposes of her "post-operative comfort." On the whole, she conformed *as she herself pleased* to the hypnotist's suggestion, whether it was explicit or implicit.

DISCUSSION

The author's results do not correspond to the currently accepted ideas about analgesia, which are based on two facts:

1. The absence during an operation of behavioral reactions normally associated with the perception of pain.

---

[16] Ernest and Josephine Hilgard (1975) observe that, in the course of their experiments in hypnotic analgesia, a painful stimulus generally produces reactions (of a cardiovascular nature), whether during the course of the hypnotic analgesia or in the waking state: acceleration of the heart rate and rise in blood pressure. In rare cases (when the subject is very deeply hypnotized), the authors observed that these reactions can be considerably attenuated. The only indices of autonomic nervous reaction which the present author was able to observe were a drop in blood pressure and bradycardia, occurring during this very brief period in Mrs. D.'s operation.

2. The absence of awareness of pain on the part of the subject, to be inferred from the fact that on waking he never mentions having experienced any pain whatever.

However, it must be noted that in the case of general chemical anesthesia, and in employing central analgesics, the potentials produced indicate the arrival at the cortex of the nociceptive stimuli applied to the subject, without their pain-producing character becoming evident.

Of course, there are justifiable grounds for questioning the authenticity of experience reported under hypnosis. Does it correspond to a real experience of pain during the operation? Or, when a subject under hypnosis recalls certain bodily sensations experienced during an operation and describes them as painful, is it on the basis of prior knowledge which classifies them as sensations which are normally painful, even though they were not experienced as such at the time? In the final analysis, may the memory not be merely a reconstruction?

The answer is by no means straightforward. However, in the author's view this hypothesis of a reconstruction must be abandoned for three reasons:

1. It is clear, as we have seen, that during the recall session each of the two patients gave sufficiently precise details after suggestion No. 1 to exclude any notion of fabrication pure and simple.

2. Access to memories has been shown to be relatively difficult. It must be noted that, in both cases, what the patients said had the object of denial. This could be seen as indicating a conflict, induced by the fact that the suggestion of analgesia, on the one hand, and the subsequent demand that the painful experience be recalled were formulated by the same hypnotist, thus putting the patient in a "double-bind." Confirmation of this might be seen in Mrs. T.'s declaration to the experimenters a few days after the recall: "I remember your asking me several times if I was in pain. But I couldn't be in pain since you had told me that I wouldn't feel any."

In Mrs. T.'s account of what she recalled, the memory of an experience which she described as painful was followed by an immediate disclaimer or denial of the pain. These two versions in rapid succession hardly suggest a reconstruction, but seem, on the contrary, like the manifestation of a conflict between the real sensation of pain and the desire to conform to the suggestion of analgesia.

3. Finally it must be noted that, even during chemical anesthesia, the

subject seems to retain the capacity to absorb a certain number of facts which can be recalled under hypnosis. Cheek (1959, 1964 a, b, 1966) used thirty-seven subjects who had undergone surgery under general chemical anesthesia to demonstrate that the patient can in fact hear the conversational exchanges between the surgical team and, under subsequent hypnosis, give an exact account of these even several years later.

The facts reported by Cheek seem to be confirmed by the experiment conducted by B. W. Levinson (1967) on ten hypnotizable volunteers, aged 21. The subjects were put under general chemical anesthesia (Fluothane, nitrous oxide, oxygen and Flaxedil). Once they were anesthetized, some statements were made that were calculated to induce stress. These same subjects were later hypnotized. The following results were obtained. "Of the 10 subjects used, 4 were able to repeat practically verbatim the traumatic words used by the anesthetist. A further 4 patients displayed a severe degree of anxiety while reliving the operation. At the crucial moment, they woke from the hypnosis and refused to participate further. The remaining 2 patients, though seemingly capable of reliving the operation under hypnosis, denied hearing anything" (p. 202).

It therefore seems difficult to challenge the possibility that a painful experience can be recalled under hypnosis, and that a certain integration of nociceptive information takes place during an operation under hypnotic analgesia.

The experiments undertaken by Hilgard (1974) on a significant number of subjects confirm this hypothesis. Having been given the suggestion of analgesia, the subjects in these experiments declared that they were not conscious of any pain. However, when asked to take cognizance of a hidden part of themselves which remained aware, the subjects tended to give an estimate of the pain close to that given without the hypnotic analgesia. We will return to these experiments at greater length in the second part of the book (pp. 69-71).

CONCLUSION

Hypnosis appears to provide the subject with the capacity to modify the mechanisms of emotional regulation by means of a relational process.

The integration of information about noxious stimuli in the field of consciousness is not totally suppressed, but there seem to be modifications in the way in which it is processed. It is still perceived, but is no longer accompanied by suffering.

Of course, the experiments reported here refer to only two cases, so that our results cannot be generalized and their validity is open to challenge.

However, as has been mentioned, the investigations of Cheek, Levinson, and Hilgard confirm this interpretation. Furthermore, it should be said that researchers in this field have formulated the hypothesis of a double dimension to the phenomenon of pain: the dimension of information (sensory pain) and that of suffering (suffering pain) (see below, p. 71).

The hypnotic state therefore appears as a modified state of consciousness, by means of which the hypnotist can induce distortions in the areas of volition, memory, and sensory perception—in this case, in the interpretation of the algogenic information.

The distortions produced under hypnosis have never been satisfactorily explained on a neurophysiological basis. The process involved seems inexplicable in terms of what has so far been established in neurophysiology, reasoning as it does in quantitative terms of "more" or "less" excitation and inhibition, or "blocking," whereas the mechanism in question here, while certainly seeming to have a quantitative aspect (the diminution of the intensity of the perception controlled by a "feedback" mechanism) is more specifically concerned with altering the quality of the information.

Whatever the case, hypnosis thus appears to be a privileged instrument of research in the study of the experience of pain.

2

Blistering

Can one produce somatic effects by purely psychic processes without the action of the will? The answer is yes, and the whole modern psychosomatic movement takes this principle as its starting point. The action can take place either at the functional level or at the level of tissue structure. Specialists in psychosomatic medicine have thus studied the existing correlations between traumatic events, conflicts, personality structure and functional or organic disorders (asthma, hypertension, peptic ulcer, ulcerative colitis, etc.).

But experimental study has generally been limited to the observation of the physiological concomitants of one or another emotion (whether suggested or spontaneous). One of the interesting features of hypnosis is that it allows the production of somatic phenomena "at will" by *direct* verbal suggestion.

A prime example of this type of experiment is that of blistering (the production of "burns") by hypnotic suggestion, which constitutes a curious chapter in the history of medicine. Although the phenomenon has been known for close on a hundred years and has been observed on several occasions, it is still called in question time and again, so inexplicable does it appear in the light of our physiological concepts.

Before describing the author's own experiments, it seems of interest from the epistemological point of view to show the obstacles which can arise in research of this kind.

A Century of Hesitation

The first experiment to be published was that performed by Focachon in 1885 in collaboration with Liébeault and Bernheim (in Beaunis, 1886, pp. 70–84). Similar experiments were subsequently carried out in the German-speaking countries (Krafft-Ebing, 1889; Doswald and Kreibich, 1906; Kohnstamm and Pinner, 1908; Heller and Schultz, 1909; Schindler, 1927); in Hungary (Jendrassik, 1888); in Russia (Rybalkin, 1890; Podiapolski, 1909; Smirnov, 1912; Sumbaiev, 1928; Finne, 1928); in England (Hadfield, 1917); and in Sweden (Wetterstrand, 1891, 1903 cited by Alrutz, 1914). The most recent experiments are those of Ullman (1947) and Johnson and Barber (1976) in the United States, and Borelli (1953) in Germany.[1]

From the beginning, these experiments gave rise to impassioned debate. Many writers have even cast doubt on the reality of the phenomenon observed, alleging that it was simulated. Such suspicions have been expressed all the more often because the persons used for these experiments were highly suggestible subjects, mostly hysterics, whom a whole trend of medical opinion has always been inclined to regard as malingerers. Thus the controversy centered upon the methods of control. The following episode illustrates the importance of this question. In 1896, the famous neuropathologist from Munich, Schrenck-Notzing, succeeded in inducing by suggestion an erythema in a 20-year-old girl. As the experiment was carried out under insufficiently controlled conditions, he decided to repeat it. A dressing was placed on the subject's arm. The girl was caught scratching herself through the dressing with the aid of a needle. When a new attempt was made using a plaster, nothing appeared. Schrenck-Notzing concluded that the phenomenon was not authentic and thereupon contested the experiments previously reported (Schrenck-Notzing, 1896, 1898).

In Berne in 1907, the doctors attending the Congress of the German Society of Dermatology received with great scepticism a report by Kreibich, a celebrated dermatologist of the day, who presented a series of histological sections of vesicles produced by hypnotic suggestion (Kreibich, 1907). Kohnstamm and Pinner (1908) came up against the same incredulity at the next Congress held in Frankfurt in 1908.

Kreibich's experiments, published in collaboration with Doswald (1906), not to mention other experiments, nevertheless met all the requirements of rigorous control (the vesicle having, in fact, appeared barely 10 minutes after the suggestion was made, without the subject having been out of sight for one

[1] Only those experiments conducted with a minimum control and cited most frequently in the literature are mentioned here. Moll has published a review of the literature in which other experiments, more or less well controlled, figure alongside those quoted above, some of them dating from the beginning of the nineteenth century (Moll, 1924, p. 125).

moment). But, as mentioned above, the phenomenon in question seemed totally incomprehensible from a physiological point of view. This accounts to a large extent for the minimal impact made by these investigations.

The discussion which took place in 1908 at the Paris Neurological Society (Société Neurologique de Paris, 1908a, b) illustrates clearly this aspect of the problem. In the context of general consideration of the nature of hysteria, the question arose as to whether it was possible to produce by suggestion changes in trophic state, reflex activity, and temperature. There was a confrontation between two positions on this issue. Babinski excluded the possibility entirely, while Raymond, in a more flexible way, accepted it within limits. For Babinski, suggestion could not, as a psychic process, be applied to physiological functions which were not subject to the voluntary system. The so-called somatic symptoms in hysteria were, therefore, either the expression of some unrecognized organic illness or the product of deception on the part of hysterics.[2] The majority of those present took Babinski's view. This amounted to a denial of the phenomenon of blistering.[3]

Babinski's attitude bears witness to the reluctance of many experts of the period to admit the possibility that the psychic can act directly upon the somatic. One can measure the strength of this resistance by the reaction, 30 years later, of Pattie, an American psychologist who, having reviewed the experiments which have been mentioned here and having recognized that on the whole they were credible, nevertheless asserts: "The writer, after all this evidence, still finds himself in an attitude of suspended judgment, an attitude due mostly to his inability to understand by what physiological processes suggestion – or the central nervous system – could produce *localised and circumscribed* erythemas or blisters" (Pattie, 1941, p. 71).

These reservations are far from having entirely disappeared. In 1962 an American writer, Gordon Paul, undertook a systematic critique of the

---

[2] Babinski did not know of, or chose to ignore, the experiments of his master Charcot, and in particular the experimental production and suppression by suggestion of peripheral cyanotic edema, involving circulatory and thermoregulatory changes independent of voluntary control. This experiment had been carried out without any deception and had been perfectly controlled, since the disappearance of the edema occurred within a quarter of an hour before a large audience. An account will be found in the notes of Guinon (1892) and in an article by Levillain (1890).

[3] It was following this debate that Podiapolski (1909) conceived the idea of carrying out an experiment which would exclude all possibility of trickery. He succeeded in producing a vesicular lesion under rigorously controlled conditions.

observations compiled by Pattie, in an attempt to show that the results obtained were due not to hypnotic suggestion, but to accidental causes (Paul, 1963). It is not possible here to enter into the details of the various experiments (see Table 2, pp. 31–36). Suffice it to say that, whilst it is of course necessary to submit the experimental conditions to serious examination, in this area as in all others, it is sometimes better to leave well alone. A careful examination of Paul's arguments reveals that in the process of anticipating every eventuality, he ends by resorting to hypotheses which stretch the limits of credibility, presupposing so many different coincidences that they are even more difficult to credit as explanations than hypnotic suggestion.

The causes which Paul puts forward to explain the formation of the blister are of four types:

1. A deliberate action on the part of the subject. In several cases every precaution would not seem to have been taken to exclude the possibility of trickery.
2. A mechanical stimulation. In almost every case, the experimenter applied to the area in question an object supposed to be the agent of the suggested burn. The simple act of maintaining pressure for several minutes on certain particularly sensitive skins might suffice to cause a blister to appear.
3. Dermatitis produced by contact with some irritant. Paul thus impugns all the experiments carried out with a metal object, as metal can sometimes produce reactions of this type. For the same reason, he rejects those in which a dressing was applied as part of the experimental control, inasmuch as certain adhesive dressings were equally liable to act as an irritant to the skin.
4. Finally the dressing could have given rise to edema by compressing the blood vessels.

As far as the first point is concerned, in six out of eleven observations reported by Pattie,[4] the subject was under constant supervision. In four other cases a sealed dressing was applied, or alternatively a dressing specially devised to prevent any manipulation. It is difficult to see how, under these conditions, the subject could have engaged in any deception. Only the experiments carried out by Focachon and Rybalkin can really be considered suspect in that respect, insofar as the experimenter was content to apply a simple unsealed dressing. On the other hand, in Rybalkin's experiment, an erythema appeared whilst the subject was still under surveillance, which tends rather to lend credibility to the authenticity of the experiment.

Moreover, even supposing that prolonged pressure can result in an erythema, it is certainly very rare, if not impossible, for it to produce a true blister. Furthermore, when someone has a skin which is prone to such unusual reactions, the fact is generally already known.

---

[4] Note that here the author is not taking into account the many preliminary experiments carried out by the various writers, for the most part in the absence of any controlled conditions.

The same is true of any irritation caused by a particular substance. There are thousands of occasions when people have coins (or other metal objects) in contact with their skin for several seconds. If the subjects used in these experiments had possessed a skin prone to irritation from such objects, it is hard to see how the experimenter could not have known when, in most instances, he had treated the patient in other contexts and was therefore well placed to know his or her physiological characteristics. But, out of the eleven subjects, only three are reported as presenting or having presented in the past particular dermatological reactions. There again, in two instances it was not a question of reactions which could produce blister formation but of dermagraphism (Heller and Schultz) and "a labile vasomotor system" (Doswald and Kreibich, first experiment). Only the subject in the second experiment carried out by Doswald and Kreibich can really be considered suspect, since he had previously suffered, in the writer's words, from "neurotic gangrene of the skin."

The hypothesis that an irritation was produced by an adhesive plaster seems even more improbable. While it is true that certain adhesive plasters can act as an irritant, it is hard to see why this should happen precisely and exclusively at the site of the suggested burn and not in the surrounding area[5] unless it is supposed that this precise spot alone was covered by an adhesive dressing, which is unlikely. Where experiments on cutaneous phenomena are concerned, it is normal to avoid any contact with substances which are liable to interfere with the progress of the experiment.

The explanations suggested by Paul seem even less convincing when the experiments are examined in closer detail. He contests, for example, the results obtained by Hadfield, attributing them to the dressing applied to the subject's arm. Although the subject was kept under constant surveillance, a dressing was in fact applied to reinforce the effectiveness of the control. But on rereading Hadfield's account, it is seen that a similar result had already been obtained with the same subject in an earlier attempt, when no dressing had been applied. This experiment is not taken into consideration in Paul's paper, because it was not controlled. However, it does demonstrate the absence of any causal relationship between the formation of the blister and the dressing. Thus, the validity of the second experiment is seen, unless it is supposed – as Paul apparently assumes – that in the first experiment, conducted without the application of a dressing, the result is due to simulation, and that in the second experiment, in which simulation is ruled out, it is attributable to the dressing.

In his desire at all costs to cast doubt on the authenticity of the experiments, Paul even goes so far as to commit some inaccuracies. Again in connection with Hadfield's observations, he claims that it is not impossible for the blister to have been produced by the stimulus, insofar as Hadfield did not specify the precise nature of the stimulus employed. But reading the account makes it abundantly clear that the stimulus in question is quite simply the experimenter's finger.

---

[5] The same objection can be made against the argument that the blister could have resulted from compression of the vessels caused by the dressing.

In conclusion, it must be said that it is not impossible for one of the elements mentioned by Paul to have contributed to the blister formation in one or two cases. But this can in no way call into question the validity of the observations taken as a whole.

It will not escape notice, moreover, that, in the end, Paul comes to acknowledge the reality of the phenomenon.[6] The fact is that three of the experiments mentioned by Pattie defy all his criticisms: "On the basis of the three remaining reports, we must tentatively conclude that a positive skin reaction, bullae, or related skin anomaly can be produced by hypnotic suggestion" (Paul, 1963, p. 241). This testimony is invaluable coming as it does from such a sceptical mind.

If Paul's paper is given such emphasis, it is because, in the author's view, it illustrates an approach which, without actually denying the reality of the phenomenon, minimizes its importance. This attitude also emerges from a study published by Johnson and Barber (1976). Returning to Paul's arguments about the failure to apply proper controls in the past, they maintain that blistering by suggestion can, in any case, be produced only in subjects highly susceptible to hypnosis and that, therefore, no general conclusions can be drawn. It is as if hypnotizable subjects constituted some sort of race apart, whose characteristics were of no relevance to the rest of humanity.

The observations reported in the literature on blistering have hitherto been examined exclusively from the point of view of experimental control. The question has been whether or not they could be considered authentic. This approach has neglected everything else which they might have taught us about the phenomenon itself which, for all that it is more or less generally accepted today, remains nonetheless an enigma. Only an in-depth study of the existing experimental material, together with the accumulation of new data, will enable certain aspects of the phenomenon to be elucidated.

It seems worthwhile, therefore, to draw the conclusions which emerge from these observations taken as a whole. The author's own experiments will then be presented. Finally, in the light of present-day psychosomatic research, the author will indicate how the problem may be envisaged today.

---

[6] Many writers on the subject have referred to blistering as an indisputable (albeit inexplicable) fact. Among them are Jaspers (1923) and more recently the Soviet neurophysiologist (and philosopher) Bassin (Bassin and Platonov, 1973). It must, however, be recorded that a specialist in hypnosis, in a book published in 1976, still maintained that blistering by hypnotic suggestion "has never been demonstrated in a strictly controlled experiment that precluded the use of artifice and deception" (Frankel, 1976, p. 14).

A New Look at the Literature

Table 2 assembles all the experiments mentioned by Pattie (1941),[7] as well as a certain number of observations carried out since the publication of his study. In most cases, the authors have conducted several trials, often without any form of control, before achieving their main experiment. These preliminary attempts are included in this table, on the grounds that the success of the later experiment provided *a posteriori* proof of their authenticity. Insofar as they appear to throw an interesting light on the problem, certain negative experiments are also mentioned.

The data are sometimes difficult to interpret as they have not always been recorded in a systematic and rigorous fashion. For example, when an observation makes no mention of any pain experienced by the subject, it is hard to know whether it means that he felt no pain or that the author has not considered it worthwhile to make a note of the fact. It also happens that the presentation of the data varies in its degree of precision. It is therefore advisable to exercise a certain amount of caution in interpreting this table.

CHARACTERISTICS OF THE SUBJECTS

Depth of hypnosis

Out of the fifteen subjects who produced a favourable response, ten were true somnambulists, i.e. susceptible to deep hypnosis with spontaneous post-hypnotic amnesia (I, II, III, IV, VI, VIII, IX, XI, XII, XIV).

In two cases, a reading of the report reveals that, before waking, the subject was given a suggestion of amnesia, but it is impossible to tell whether that means that amnesia did not usually occur spontaneously or whether it simply represents a precautionary measure on the part of the experimenter (VII, XIII). In experiment VII, the subject is presented as quite accustomed to hypnosis, and as having already taken part in numerous experiments (slowing of the pulse rate, post-hypnotic suggestion, etc.). In experiment VIII, he is simply described as "highly suggestible."

---

[7] For further reviews of the literature on this problem, see Dunbar (1935) and Weitzenhoffer (1953).

TABLE 2

Abbreviations: S = subject; E = Experimenter.

N.B. This table comprises only data explicitly recorded in the original observations. The absence of data concerning any particular aspects of an experiment (e.g. the pain experienced by the subject) does not necessarily imply that such aspects were absent during the experiment. It is merely attributable to the fact that a given author did not consider them sufficiently important to be mentioned.

Subject	Content of suggestion	Real stimulus	Length of hypnosis control	Subject's reactions
1. *Focachon* (France, 1884–85) Eliza F., 47 yr Hysteric. Somnambulist. Treated by E.	(A) Burn between shoulders		Several hours. Surveillance until appearance of pain	Several hours after suggestion: burning sensation and itching. Appearance of blotch. Next day: vesicular erythema
Previously used by E. for experiments	(B) Burn behind left shoulder	Official notepaper	Almost continuous until next day (about 21 hr). Surveillance not continuous (S unsupervised during night). Dressing intact when result checked	21 hr after suggestion: yellowish-white epidermis with redness and swelling. Later a blister
2. *Jendrassik* (Hungary, 1888) Female hysteric (with anesthesia of right arm). Somnambulist. Treated by E.	(A) Burn on right forearm with a hot iron	Piece of cardboard	Wakened soon after suggestion	Great pain at time of suggestion. NO pain on waking. 5 hr after suggestion: red stripe, and shortly afterwards a blister the shape of the cardboard, surrounded by blotches
Previously used by E. for experiments.	(B) Burn on upper part of left arm with hot ring	Ring	Wakened soon after suggestion. Continuous surveillance	5 hr after suggestion: ring-shaped blister, *at suggested site, on opposite (right) arm.*

SNP - D

TABLE 2 – *continued*

Subject	Content of suggestion	Real stimulus	Length of hypnosis control	Subject's reactions
Jendrassik—continued	(C) Burn on left shoulder with a hot iron	Letter K in metal	Probably continuous surveillance	A blister the shape of an inverted K, *at suggested site, on opposite (right) shoulder*
3. *Krafft-Ebing* (Austria, 1889) Hysteric. Somnambulist	Burn on left shoulder	Letter K in metal	Sealed dressing. Suggestion not to scratch	Next day: a burst blister in the centre of an erythematous area
4. *Rybalkin* (Russia, 1890) Boy, 16 yr. Hysteric (attacks of major hysteria, anesthesia of almost entire body). Somnambulist	Burn on right forearm on contact with hot stove. Pain, a blotch and blister		Surveillance for 3½ hr, then dressing applied	Pain at time of suggestion and throughout experiment. A few min after suggestion: a blotch; 3½ hr after suggestion: swelling and papular erythema; next day: 2 blisters
5. *Doswald and Kreibich* (Germany, 1906) (a) Young doctor. Somnambulist. Sensitive skin. Labile vasomotor system	(A) 2 burns on right forearm with a lighted match	Matchstick	Probably wakened after suggestion	Withdrawal movement during suggestion. Burning sensation on waking; half hr after end of hypnosis: erythema at both sites; next day: blisters
	(B) 2 burns on right forearm, on contact with a lighted match and with a poultice respectively	Matchstick Zinc plaster	Same	Withdrawal movement during suggestion. On waking: itching and burning sensation. Hyperemia at both

(c) Appearance of a blister on left forearm as quickly as possible	Matchstick	Wakened after suggestion. Continuous surveillance	Withdrawal movement during suggestion: itching and burning sensation on waking; 3 min after suggestion: a blotch; 6 min after: a sloughing of epidermis; 9 min after: a blister	
(b) Young man. Previously suffered from gangrene of the skin of neurotic origin. Easily hypnotizable	Burn with a lighted match on inner aspect of left arm. A blister, as quickly as possible	Matchstick	A stiff dressing, incapable of being moved without its being apparent	No sensation of pain. 1 hr after suggestion: a blotch with edema of the papillary bodies; after 24 hr: same condition, but more pronounced
6. *Kohnstamm and Pinner* (Germany, 1908) Female, 29 yr	Burn and production of a blister on left forearm	Matchstick	Dressing with a glass lens (window), incapable of being moved without its being apparent	Next day, some 12 hr after suggestion: intense pain and appearance of 2 erythematous blisters, one of which had already burst
7. *Heller and Schultz* (Germany, 1909) Carpenter, 19 yr. Susceptible to suggested post-hypnotic amnesia. Previously used by E. for experiments. Delicate skin, but no dermatological affections	(A) Hot coin placed on back of left hand. A blister. No pain	Coin	No control	A blister several days after suggestion. No pain
	(B) Same. Production of a blister within the next 6 hr	Same	Wakened after suggestion. Sealed dressing. Continuous surveillance	No pain. A blotch when coin removed. 6 hr after suggestion: vesicular erythema
8. *Podiapolski* (Russia, 1903) Peasant woman. Somnambulist: Hysteric. Treated and cured by E. of hysterical mutism	(A) Burn on wrist with a hot coal, reminder of a real burn previously	Coin	Wakened after suggestion. Continuous surveillance	Pain and erythema on waking. Next day: a blister 2 mm in diameter

TABLE 2 – *continued*

Subject	Content of suggestion	Real stimulus	Length of hypnosis control	Subject's reactions
Podiapolski – continued	(B) Same on the back	Coin		Pain as soon as coin was removed. No erythema. Next day: a blister
	(C) 2 hr on the back, in a position unreachable by S. Reminder of a real burn previously suffered	Coin. Thermometer	3 hr continuous surveillance	7 hr after suggestion: blotch close to suggested site. Some 11 hr after suggestion: sensation of pain. 20 hr after suggestion: a blister
9. *Smirnov* (Russia, 1912) Young woman, 19 yr. Cook. Treated and cured by E. (toothache). Somnambulist	(A) Hot butter placed on upper part of arm. A blister. Reminder of a real burn previously suffered at this site	Butter	10 min – no control	Next day: a spot, with sloughing of epidermis
	(B) Same	Same	15 min continuous surveillance	Less than 15 min after suggestion: a blotch, *a little higher than the suggested site.* 30 min after suggestion: a blister
	(C) Same on back of left hand	Same	1 hr continuous surveillance	1 hr after suggestion: a blotch *at site of previous real burn;* then, a 2nd blotch *closer to the suggested site,* giving rise 2 hr later to a blister

	Procedure		Control	Result
10. Wetterstrand (Sweden, 1903) Female, 55 yr. Hysteric	Burn on inner aspect of right forearm, with a drop of hot wax		4 hr. Sealed dressing with a glass lens (window)	25 min after suggestion: itching and increasing burning sensation. Some 4 hr after suggestion: blotch. 48 hr after suggestion: blisters
11. Hadfield (England, 1917) Soldier. Somnambulist. Suffering from combat neurosis. Treated by E.	(A) Burn on forearm with red-hot iron	Finger	No control	Pain at time of suggestion and throughout experiment. Half hr after termination of hypnosis: a blister
	(B) Same	Same	Less than 3 hr. Surveillance for first 3 hr; then, a sealed dressing	Pain for 5½ hr after suggestion. 6 hr after suggestion: a blister
	(C) Same on upper part of arm	Same	Several hr. Continuous surveillance and a sealed dressing	Pain throughout experiment. 24 hr after suggestion: a blister
	(D) Same with suggestion of feeling no pain	Same	Same	No pain. No reaction
12. Schindler (Austria, 1927) Rosa, 38 yr. Somnambulist, hysteric (hysterical fits, psychogenic ecchymoses) Treated by E. and previously used by him for experiments (production of ecchymoses by suggestion)	(A) Ecchymosis on upper part of arm. Suggestion that it will burn S.	Pencilled line around site of experiment	Plaster applied immediately after suggestion	Ecchymosis with burn. Exp. repeated several times with same result, until finally *a burn without ecchymosis* was obtained
	(B) Same		Plaster with glass lens after suggestion	5 min after suggestion: a blister

TABLE 2 – *continued*

Subject	Content of suggestion	Real stimulus	Length of hypnosis control	Subject's reactions
13. *Wells* (U.S.A., 1944) Psychology student. Pupil of E. "Very good hypnotic subject." Impossible to tell whether the post-hypnotic amnesia was spontaneous or suggested	Burn on right forearm as from contact with a hot iron	Coin	No control	Pain at time of suggestion, increasing in intensity throughout exp. (several hr). A momentary blotch observed by S., but which had disappeared when examined by E.
14. *Ullmann* (U.S.A., 1947) Soldier, 47 yr. Suffering from hysterical blindness after a bomb explosion. Treated by E. Somnambulist			About 30 min. Surveillance until appearance of the blister	Pain on waking (30 min after suggestion). 20 min after suggestion: a blotch. 1 hr after suggestion: beginning of a blister. 4 hr after suggestion: a blister 1 cm in diameter
15. *Borelli* (Germany, 1953) Male, 47 yr	A blister the following morning on back of right hand	Coin	No control	A blotch and swelling

In the three other cases, no details are given in this respect (V:2, VI, X). The account of experiment VI merely describes the patient as "easily hypnotizable."

It therefore clearly emerges that these experiments have all been conducted with *highly hypnotizable* subjects, including a very large proportion of true somnambulists. Inversely, there is not a single known case where a blister has been produced without the subject having been deeply hypnotized beforehand. No doubt this explains why Barber and Johnson, although experimenting with forty subjects, only succeeded in producing an erythema in a single case. The forty subjects had not been selected and there were no true somnambulists amongst them. The subject who presented a positive reaction was, however, one of the most highly hypnotizable (11 points out of 12 on the Harvard scale). Another subject produced an erythema a few minutes after the suggestion, but it very rapidly disappeared. This subject had scored over 5 on the 12-point Harvard scale.

It is true that patches of urticaria have been successfully produced experimentally in some subjects in the waking state, simply by evoking past traumatic situations (Graham and Wolf, 1950). However, no one has ever succeeded in producing a blister by these means. Moreover, the urticaria was not, in this case, the result of a *direct* suggestion. Recall of the trauma produced stress, which brought about the formation of a patch of urticaria. In blistering by suggestion, the blister is the direct materialization of the suggestion.

Menzies (1937, 1941) obtained significant variations in skin temperature, by suggesting to his subjects images of cold or heat. Here it was certainly a question of direct verbal suggestion, accomplished in the waking state. But these experiments involved no change in the tissues.

On the basis of the foregoing, it would be tempting to conclude that the depth of hypnosis is a necessary condition for the success of the experiment. It is as if, by means of the hypnotic relationship, the representation is invested with such affective intensity that it triggers the mechanisms which normally contribute to blister formation.

It is advisable to exercise caution, however. Very few experiments have actually been conducted. It is possible that one day it will be successfully shown that blistering can be produced in the waking state. The lack of results in this area is perhaps due solely to the fact that insufficient experiments have been carried out. Yoga adepts, for example, can produce a large proportion of the phenomena classically induced by hypnotic suggestion, such as a slowing of the pulse rate. But are they then really "awake"? Are they not in a state approaching hypnosis? Is it possible to speak of hypnosis in the absence of a hypnotist? Here we run into some most obscure questions, since no one knows of what hypnosis consists, nor even whether it constitutes a specific state.

Personality of the subject

Of the fifteen subjects who produced a positive reaction, seven were hysterics (I, II, III, IV, VIII, X, XII), several of whom presented or had previously presented conversion symptoms, and two were suffering from traumatic hysteria (XI and XIV). In three cases there was no information in this respect (VI, IX, XIII). In two other cases the subjects were considered "normal" (VI and VII). Finally, the account of experiment V:2 is not clear on this point; the subject was presented at the same time both as "non-hysterical" and as having suffered from gangrene of the skin of neurotic origin.

Thus there is a high proportion of hysterics to be found among the total number of subjects. Moreover, this fact has long contributed towards maintaining an aura of mistrust around these experiments, because of the general tendency to regard hysterics either as malingerers or as a race apart with reactions too abnormal and incomprehensible to be considered representative.

These figures should not invite false conclusions. They can be explained partly by the fact that, because the experimenters were all doctors and often specialists in the treatment of mental illness, it is not surprising that it was from amongst their patients that the selection was principally made.

But it is equally certain that hysterics are particularly liable to produce this type of phenomenon. Without entering here into the complex problem of the relationship between hypnosis and hysteria, it may be said that the same psychosomatic "plasticity" is to be found in hysterical conversion as in hypnosis. Reversing Charcot's proposition, it is very tempting to say that hysteria produces spontaneously what hypnotic suggestion produces experimentally.

Schindler's observation (1927) illustrates the kinship between the two mechanisms in a particularly striking way. The subject was a hysteric whose principal symptom was the appearance of ecchymoses which constantly formed spontaneously on all parts of the body. Several experiments were conducted resulting in the formation of a blister under the influence of hypnotic suggestion. A few days later it was observed that similar blisters began to appear *spontaneously all over the subject's body in exactly the same way as the ecchymoses.* Suggestion had become conversion.

THE RELATIONAL FACTOR

In many cases, it happened that the subjects were patients under treatment by the experimenter (I, II, VIII, IX, XI, XII, XIV).

Although not explicitly stated, this is no doubt equally true of experiments III, IV, V:2, VI, X.

Three exceptions are to be found: in V:1 the subject was an assistant in the nursing-home where the experimenter worked; in XIII, the subject was one of the experimenter's students; in VII, the subject was simply a good somnambulist used by the researcher in previous experiments.

As has already been stressed, there is nothing surprising in the existence of a therapeutic relationship between experimenter and subject, since all the experiments were conducted by doctors who found their subjects principally amongst their patients. This in no way implies that this kind of relationship is necessary for the phenomenon to be produced.

It is, however, conceivable that in certain cases the existence of a strong positive transference, linked to the therapeutic relationship, may have played an important part. It is certainly true that the prestige attached to the medical profession at the time when most of the experiments were performed, and the doctor's conviction of the therapeutic power of hypnotic suggestion, explain in part the extraordinary docility shown by their patients.

This is well illustrated by a detail from one of Wetterstrand's observations: "The doctor then suggested to the subject that the blister would form at 2 o'clock at the latest. After some resistance she promised to try, 'in order to please the Doctor'" (Alrutz, 1914, p. 3).

Unfortunately, the various observations carry almost no information on the relational aspect. This is easily explained as far as the experiments performed at the turn of the century are concerned, inasmuch as this aspect was then generally obscured from view. But curiously, the subject is not broached in more recent accounts either.

THE DEVELOPMENT OF THE PROCESS

This varies very much according to the experiment.

The time lapse between the suggestion and the consequent materialization varies from a few seconds to 7 hours for the development of an erythema, and from 5 minutes to more than 2 hours for the appearance of a blister.

Duration of hypnosis: Depending on the case, the subject was wakened immediately after the burn was suggested or during the subsequent half hour (II A, II B, V:1 A, V:1 B, V:1 C, VII B, VIII A, IX A, IX B, XIV); or from one to several hours after the suggestion (I A, I B, VIII C, IX C, X, XI B, XI C, XI D). There is no information on the subject in II C, III, IV, V:2, VI, VII A, VIII B, XI A, XII, XIII, XV.

At first sight, it does not look as if any correlation can be established between the length of hypnosis and the time it takes the phenomenon to appear or the kind of result obtained. No definitive conclusions can be formed, however, on this issue, since the variables at our disposal are both few and imprecise. In a large number of cases, the length of hypnosis is not even mentioned. Furthermore, information on how long it takes for the blister to form is often only vaguely indicated.

The *content of the suggestion* and the *stimulus employed* also vary greatly according to the experiment. Mostly, the experimenter suggested to the subject that he was really being burned. Sometimes the suggestion related only to the appearance of the blister, with no mention of a burn. In two experiments (VIII, IX), it comprised the recall of an earlier episode experienced by the subject. Finally, in two cases (VII, XI D) the suggestion of a burn was accompanied by the suggestion of analgesia.

Usually the stimulus employed is an object likely to be readily associated with the idea of a burn in everyday life (a metal object, a match, etc.). But this is not always so. In the experiment conducted by Schindler, the experimenter contented himself with pencilling a circle around the relevant area. In fact, it is questionable whether the presence of a material stimulus is necessary to the success of the experiment, or if a simple verbal suggestion indicating the chosen area for the experiment would not be just as effective.

Whatever the case, it can be seen that the form of the suggestion, or the use of whatever stimulus, seems to have no more significant influence on the way in which the blister appears than does the length of hypnosis. The variations which can be observed in the evolution of the process arise more from the degree of lability of the subject's autonomic system, as well as from the dermatological differences between the different zones chosen for the experiments, or from psychodynamic factors – a point to which the author will return later.

PAIN

It has often been thought that the hallucinated perception of a burning sensation was a necessary condition for the success of the experiment. This hypothesis was based on the more or less explicit conceptualization of suggested blistering as equivalent on the physiological plane to an ordinary burn, where the mechanisms which lead to blister formation are triggered by a message *coming from the periphery*. As will be seen later, this conception now seems superseded.

It remains nevertheless true that, if we consider the observation in detail, in all the experiments with a successful outcome there were fifteen in which the subject felt some pain, as against only three (V:2, VII A, VII B) where no pain was experienced. Furthermore, the absence of a painful sensation is explained in two of these experiments (VII A and VII B) by the fact that a suggestion of analgesia had been given by the experimenter concurrently with the suggestion of a burn. In the other ten cases, no details are given on this aspect.

As always with hypnosis, it is clearly difficult to know whether the pain in question is really experienced or whether it is a pretense. In a certain number of cases, however, the pain appears to have reached such an intensity that it seemed that it could be considered authentic. There is, moreover, nothing surprising in the fact that painful sensations can be induced in highly hypnotizable subjects, since it is known that, conversely, hypnotic suggestion can suppress the perception of pain.

It is necessary to distinguish between two sorts of reactions, according to whether the pain appeared as soon as the suggestion was made or subsequently. In the former case (II A, IV, V:1 A, V:1 B, V:1 C, VIII A, VIII B, XI A, XI B, XI C), it is undeniably a question of a hallucinatory sensation produced directly by the suggestion. In the latter case (I A, IV, VI, VIII C, X), and especially when it happens a long while after the start of the experiment, it may on the other hand be a purely organic pain caused by the pathological process itself. It seems, for example, to be the case in experiments VIII C and XIV, where the perception of the pain occurred only after an erythema had already appeared in the relevant area. Similarly in experiment VI, the pain seems to have appeared only after the blister had already formed. This would tend to prove that even when the feeling of pain exists, it does not play an essential role in the process.

An observation reported by Hadfield seems, however, to contradict this assertion. During one and the same experiment, he gave two suggestions of burns in two different positions, in one case with a suggestion of pain and in the other with a suggestion of analgesia. In the former case the experiment resulted in the production of a blister, while in the latter case no result was obtained. Hadfield deduced that "it was the suggestion of pain, and perhaps continuous pain, which produced the blister" (Hadfield, 1917, p. 678).

Experiments V:2 and VII, however, show that blistering can occur when the subject perceives no pain. The observation by Heller and Schultz (VII) is particularly interesting, since a suggestion of analgesia was given, as in Hadfield's experiment, but without in any way impeding the blister formation. Conversely, observation XIII shows that a very intense pain can be felt throughout the whole experiment without any significant result being obtained. It is possible that the result obtained by Hadfield can be explained by the fact that the suggestion of analgesia given by him included an implicit injunction not to produce a blister.

It can be concluded, therefore, on the basis of the existing material, that pain does not represent an indispensable link in the production of the phenomenon. The author's experiments, furthermore, confirm this hypothesis (see further below). The fact that the sensation of pain was present in the majority of cases may easily be explained: the representation of pain is intimately associated with the idea of a burn. From this point of view, it is possible that the hallucinatory perception of pain contributes to the reinforcement in the subject's mind of the suggestion of a burn, particularly as far as the localization of the phenomenon is concerned. It would be interesting to know, in this connection, what form the perception of pain assumed in those experiments where the blister appeared elsewhere than at the site suggested. Unfortunately, there is no information on the subject in the accounts of these cases. Similarly the elements at our disposal are too fragmentary for it to be determined whether the presence of the sensation of pain influences in any way whatever the time required for the blister to form.

This table had already been compiled when the author learned of the experiments conducted in the Soviet Union by Finne (1928) and Sumbaiev (1928) which are worth reporting.

Finne initially conducted his first series of experiments in 1925 in Leningrad using a woman of 32, suffering from hysterical mutism and also susceptible to deep hypnosis (hypnosis with spontaneous post-hypnotic amnesia). A coin was placed on the patient's back with the suggestion that the coin was very hot and would produce a blister, which duly formed 24 hours after the suggestion. As the experiment had been conducted without any control, it was repeated a second time with the participation of two surgeons, and a sealed dressing was placed over the area in question. The same result was obtained.

Two years later, Finne repeated the experiment with a woman of 35, Marguerite Pavlovna G., who was likewise an excellent somnambulist. A bronze 2-kopeck piece was applied to the nape of her neck, while simultaneously the suggestion of a burn was given. A blister appeared at the given spot, but once again the experiment was not controlled. It was repeated on July 12th, 1927, in the presence of Platonov, one of the pioneers of psychotherapy in Russia. A 2-kopeck piece was placed on the subject's arm, with the same suggestion delivered three times in the space of half an hour. The subject was wakened immediately after the last suggestion. An erythema appeared half an hour later, which gradually developed to the blister stage over a period of 3½ hours. The subject had remained continuously under the supervision of a doctor for the entire period.

Experiments in blistering by hypnotic suggestion were similarly performed by Sumbaiev (1928) with one of his patients, a 30-year-old hysteric who presented anesthesia over his entire body, with the exception of the left leg, and was frequently sunk in a twilight state. He was a very good somnambulist.

During the course of the first experiment, the lid of an inkpot was placed on the patient's left (non-anesthetic) leg, with the suggestion of a burn. The patient had such a strong sensation of pain that it was necessary to put him to sleep again. After he was wakened, he went home, returning a few hours later with several blisters at the site of the suggested burn.

The same experiment was performed on April 17th, with the subject on this occasion under continuous surveillance. This time, only an erythema was obtained. A third attempt ended in the same way, with one interesting variation: the suggestion of a burn having also been given in respect of the right leg, the subject nevertheless felt no pain there and the suggestion remained ineffective, while an erythema had appeared on the left leg.

On May 11th, a further attempt resulted in the formation of two blisters. Unfortunately, Sumbaiev seems not to have bothered about the control. The only certain result from these experiments was therefore the production of an erythema.

A second series of experiments was then conducted, during which Sumbaiev succeeded in inducing the development of edema several times by suggesting to the subject that his ears were frozen. (The experiment took place in Siberia.) The control on this occasion seems to have been relatively rigorous.

The Author's Experiments

The experiments to be presented were once again conducted with the co-operation of the two subjects, Mrs. D. and Mrs. T.

When the author started this study, he had no intention of undertaking an actual experimental research project. Knowing that such experiments had been carried out in the past, the author wished to conduct the same experiment in his turn. But in the beginning it was more out of a kind of curiosity than with a detailed study in mind. It was only during the course of the experiments, and having acquainted himself with all the literature published on the subject, that the author appreciated the theoretical importance of the phenomenon, as well as the precautions called for from the point of view of control.

The author had, moreover, known both subjects for a very long time. Apart from the two surgical operations already reported, he had conducted many experiments with them and had never observed any tendency whatever on their part to simulate. He was, therefore, not initially concerned about the possibility of a deception, which explains why all the experiments were not perfectly controlled.

The author has decided to publish them, however, inasmuch as they appear to complement in an interesting way certain facts gathered in the course of previous research, particularly in relation to the role played in the course of the process by intra- and interpersonal factors. As will be shown later, there are many reasons for believing in the authenticity of the results obtained by the author. Experimentation in this field is extremely difficult.

Subjects likely to produce such phenomena are rare. Moreover, these experiments turn upon such complex factors (atmosphere, the subject's psychic state, the bond between him and the experimenter, the attitude of the latter, etc.) that they do not succeed every time.[8] Thus, if he is unwilling to consider any but perfect experiments, the researcher runs the risk of being condemned to work with very restricted material.

MRS. D.

First Experiment (A.1), March 20th, 1975

Mrs. D. was hypnotized and a 5-franc piece applied to the outer aspect of her left forearm, while the following suggestion was given: "I am putting a very hot coin on your arm. The coin will burn you."

When the coin touched her arm, Mrs. D. had a withdrawal reaction as if it were really hot.

On the following day, March 21st, Mrs. D. returned to the Center, and at the spot where the coin had been applied, a crescent-shaped vesicular lesion was observed.

Mrs. D. told us that she noticed the presence of this lesion when she woke up. She had not noticed anything in particular the night before. The blister had therefore formed during the night. She also recalled having felt a smarting sensation in her arm shortly after leaving the Center. She had then thought no more of it, for she had a lot of work to do. She thought she had scratched herself during the night.

On March 24th, Dr. Buckel noted the presence of a "crescent-shaped vesicular lesion, 20 mm by 20 mm, situated on the outer aspect of the middle of the left forearm."

A biopsy carried out by Dr. Molas on *May 3rd, 1975,* was reported on as follows: "Two samples were taken from the very small biopsy specimen: they were identical. On the surface there appears to be a complete abrasion of the epidermis, exposing the dermis, which shows a moderate infiltration by a few round cells. Deeper, a slight senile hyperelasticity and a few round cells were

---

[8] This irregularity is perhaps one of the most disturbing and mysterious aspects of this type of phenomenon. It oftens elicits reservations, not to mention rejection, from scientists accustomed to the infinite repetition of an experimental fact. The parapsychologists also encounter this problem.

observed, or occasional polynuclear cells distributed around the vessels. There is no abnormality of the hair follicles or sebaceous glands. Conclusion: examination reveals no specific characteristics, and the appearance is compatible with the diagnosis of a burn."

It should also be mentioned that *as early as March 21st,* the day after the experiment, Mrs. D. declared that she did not believe that the blister was caused by suggestion. She put forward another explanation, namely that the blister was due to a watch which she had placed on her wrist before going to bed, after it had been exposed all day to heat from the lamp on her desk.

Confronted with the author's scepticism about this explanation, which seemed very unlikely, she ended by saying: "I don't want it to succeed, because if it works when hypnosis doesn't work on my symptom, it must be because I am incurable."

Second Experiment (A.2), May 29th, 1976

Although Mrs. D. was hypnotized with a view to a demonstration on hypnosis, she was given the suggestion of a burn without having been forewarned. The author gave the suggestion in the same form as in the first experiment, namely the application of a hot coin to the outer aspect of her left forearm. As on the previous occasion, Mrs. D. withdrew her arm abruptly when I made contact with the coin.

She returned to the Center the following day. There was no mark on her arm.

On June 2nd she announced that on the day of the experiment she had been annoyed to see an erythema appear on her arm and put picric acid on the blotch to prevent its development.

She was asked why she had done it. Since on the previous occasion she had thought that it was not the suggestion which produced the blister, she should have had no fear of its succeeding this time. She replied that she was not altogether positive that the suggestion had not worked the first time, and that she had preferred to take these precautions.

Third Experiment (A.3), January 22nd, 1976

A double experiment was carried out with Mrs. D. and Mrs. T. in the presence of a camera team who had come to film it.

Before the experiment started, Mrs. D. repeated that she did not wish it to succeed, for the same reasons as previously expressed (cf. Exp. 1). It was therefore decided, with her agreement, to use the inner aspect of her forearm, so that the traces, if any, would not be visible.

At 12.30 p.m., she was hypnotized and given the suggestion of a burn in the same form as before. Contact with the coin produced, as usual, a withdrawal reaction, accompanied by an expression and behavior, denoting suffering, which lasted several minutes.

At about 1.00 p.m., Mrs. D. was wakened and rejoined Mrs. T. in the waiting room, where several other people were also present, both patients and staff of the Center. Then they went to lunch with members of the team. Afterwards, they returned to the Center, where they remained together for the whole afternoon, in the company of several of the author's collaborators.

At 2.15 p.m., Mrs. D. showed triumphantly that her arm was unmarked.

Hypnosis was induced again, and the suggestion of a burn reinforced. She was wakened immediately after the suggestion. From that moment on, until 7.00 p.m. her arm was to be filmed at regular intervals (every half hour).

At 4.00 p.m., an erythematous macula was seen to appear (also visible on the film).

At 7.00 p.m., Dr. Le Goaster observed that, at the spot where the coin had been placed, there was: "A diffuse excentric erythema, a poorly marked peripheral halo, with a central pigmented area 5 cm in diameter."

From 8.00 p.m. to 9.00 p.m. Mrs. D. dined with two members of the team and the cameraman. She hoped the erythema would disappear.

At 9.00 p.m. she returned to the Dejerine Center.

At 11.00 p.m. the traces were the same as at 4.00 p.m.

Mrs. D. had not been left alone for a single moment since the beginning of the experiment.

At 11.30 p.m. she was again hypnotized. The suggestion of a burn was repeated, and she was told that she would sleep until 8.00 a.m., when she would go and wake the members of the team. Two of them had, in fact, to sleep in the waiting room. Mrs. D.'s watch was taken away from her.

At 2.00 a.m., the subject entered the waiting room in a state of spontaneous somnambulism, saying: "I've lost my kitchen." Then she returned to bed.

At. 5.30 a.m. she came to waken the members of the team, thinking that it was 8 o'clock. She looked for her watch and recovered it.

At 8.00 a.m., Mrs. D. wakened the team. There was now no mark whatever on her arm.

First recall under hypnosis, January 23rd, 1976

At 8.30 a.m. the day after the experiment, Mrs. D. was re-hypnotized and asked to relive the events of the night. She said she had thought she was at home and had remembered that before coming to the Center that morning she had baked a cake and forgotten to turn off the oven. She therefore got up to go to the kitchen, but found herself in a strange place. Hence the words: "I've lost my kitchen." She did not remember having seen the two people from the team who were in the waiting room.

She was also asked why she had agreed to undergo the experiment in spite of her reservations. She replied: "I wanted to see whether it would work. I would have been annoyed if it had. It would have meant that I was suggestible. And there is no reason why I should be for this and not for other things."

Questioned on the subject of why the experiment had worked the first time, she replied: "I was taken unawares. I hadn't thought about all that."

It will be noticed that Mrs. D. reacted here as if she was convinced that the first experiment had succeeded, which contradicts her earlier attempts to explain it.

MRS. T.

First Experiment (B.1), January 5th, 1976

Mrs. T. was hypnotized and given the following suggestion: "I am placing a very hot coin on your arm."

The coin was applied to the outer aspect of the upper arm for one or two minutes.

Questioned about her sensations, Mrs. T. declared she felt nothing. When pressed, she eventually said: "If you say the coin is hot, I should feel something, but I can't feel anything."

She was assured, nonetheless, that the coin would affect her skin and that in 2 days' time she would have a blister on that spot, "as if a very hot coin had been applied to your arm."

This suggestion was twice repeated. The second time, Mrs. T. said that she felt a slight smarting in her arm, adding more specifically: "A sensation of intense heat in my arm." The pain seemed to be located more or less in the area where the coin had been placed.

Mrs. T. said: "It is not like an ordinary burn, because an ordinary burn is a very sharp, instant sensation, which then fades away, whereas this is a sort of heat which comes gradually and grows. . . . It itches and smarts but, still, it's not too bad."

A few minutes later, Mrs. T. grimaced with pain and said it was burning her.

She left the Center.

Two days later, on January 7th, Mrs. T. returned to the Center. She had a scab on her arm, *but not in exactly the same place where the coin had been placed.*

Dr. Buckel observed the presence "on the outer aspect of the upper arm of an ovular lesion 3 mm by 6 mm in size, with an irregular edge, ochre in color, with a flat surface. There appears to have been prior localized pigmentation, but the other lesions seem to have appeared over the last 24 hours. Non-pruriginous."

During the interview, Mrs. T. said that, after leaving the Center, she had been aware of a growing sensation of inner heat all day long. The blister must have formed during the night, as she had not noticed that she had anything on her arm until the following morning.

Second Experiment (B.2), January 15th, 1976

Mrs. T. was hypnotized and given the suggestion of a burn in the same terms as in the previous experiment.

She said she felt nothing on the contact with the coin.

When she returned to the Center on January 22nd, there was nothing to be seen on her arm. She said that she had not noticed anything in particular since the day of the experiment.

Third Experiment (B.3), January 22nd, 1976

A double experiment was performed on the same day with Mrs. T. and Mrs. D., in the presence of a camera team who had come to film the proceedings, two dermatologists, Drs. Benveniste and Le Goaster, and several colleagues at the Center.

11.30 a.m. Hypnotic Induction.

The coin was applied to the back of her right forearm for 1 or 2 minutes, while the suggestion of a burn was put to her in its usual form. As in the previous experiments, Mrs. T. said that she did not feel anything when the coin touched her.

We assured her that in a few hours she would nevertheless have a blister at that site, as if she had been burned.

At 12 o'clock, Mrs. T. was wakened, and went into the waiting room (adjoining the room where the experiment took place), where she remained for a few moments in the company of several people, patients and staff of the Center.

Between 12 and 12.30 p.m., needing a glass of water to take with some medicine which she regularly took at this time, she left the waiting room for several minutes to go to the washroom. There she met Mrs. R., a member of the Center's staff. However, she was alone for 2 or 3 minutes. Then she returned to the waiting room.

At 12.30 p.m., Mrs. T. called Dr. Benveniste and told her: "My arm feels hot and I don't know what is happening. Can you tell me what is wrong?"

Dr. Benveniste observed, at the spot where the coin had been placed, the presence of a "vesicular erythema resembling a first degree burn."

The erythema was immediately filmed. From that moment onwards, photographs were taken at regular intervals (every half hour) so as to follow the process as it developed.

1.00 p.m. No observable change. Mrs. T. and Mrs. D. went to lunch with the members of the film crew. Afterwards they returned to the Center where they remained together the whole afternoon, in the company of several of the author's colleagues.

At 2.00 p.m. the appearance of blisters was noted.

At 4.00 p.m. the lesion had assumed the form of "an edematous erythematous patch, with an irregular edge, covered with small vesicular lesions, some of which had burst" (Dr. Benveniste).

At 5.00 p.m. a dressing was placed on Mrs. T.'s arm and she went home.

On her return to the Center the following morning, the lesion was in the same state as on the previous day.

Fourth Experiment (B.4), March 3rd, 1976

This experiment was carried out on the premises of Science Films, so that, if the blister were produced, it would be possible to film its formation without interruption.

Mrs. T. was hypnotized and given the suggestion of a burn in the same terms as before. The coin was applied for several minutes. Mrs. T. did not feel anything in particular when it touched her, but a little later began to feel a hot prickly sensation in her arm.

She said that she was disturbed by the change of setting, and the fact that she was not in a comfortable position. (For the purposes of filming, her wrist was actually attached to the arm of the chair.) When she woke, it was noticed that, unlike previous experiments, the session had not been entirely erased by amnesia. This was ascribed to the fact that, in Mrs. T.'s case, maintenance of the trance required the continuous presence of the hypnotist at her side. Actually, he left the room on several occasions.

After 2 hours, no mark whatever could be seen on her arm. Similarly, nothing appeared during the following days.

Fifth Experiment (B.5), June 26th, 1976

At 9.42 a.m. Mrs. T. was hypnotized and the burn was suggested in the usual terms.

After the coin had been held on her arm for several minutes and the suggestion repeated, Mrs. T. said that she felt "a very hot, sharp sensation. The coin is hot, very hot."

She remained under hypnosis until 11.30 a.m.

Between 11.00 a.m. and 11.30 a.m. she gave several indications of what she could feel.

"I can't quite localize it, but I can feel an intense irritation somewhere in my arm."

Then (without any prior questioning on our part): "Can't you remove the hot heavy object you have placed on my arm? Because it's burning me."

A few minutes later she added, "I want to scratch my arm, it's itching."

At 11.30 a.m. Mrs. T. was awakened and remained for 1 hour under the supervision of one of the author's colleagues. She repeated several times that it was burning her and that she wanted to scratch. She said that, strangely enough, the burning sensation was particularly painful around the "scar" left by the first experiment. The mark was indeed redder than before the experiment. There had, in fact, been occasion to look at it before the experiment began, when it had been discussed with Mrs. T. She was astonished that a more recent scar left by a real burn had already disappeared, while this mark remained.

CONTROL

Out of eight experiments, five produced a positive result:
  A.1: blister
  A.2: erythema
  A.3: erythema
  B.1: blister
  B.3: blister.
The first three experiments were not subject to any control, as Mrs. T. and Mrs. D. went home each time, between the time when the suggestion was given and the observation of the result.

Experiments A.3 and B.3 should have taken place under conditions of absolutely rigorous control, as the two subjects remained at the Center for the entire duration of the experiment. It had been anticipated that they would remain under the constant surveillance of one of the team. Unfortunately, due to factors arising from a lack of coordination, this was not the case.

In the waiting room, where she went immediately after she was awakened, Mrs. T. was constantly in the company of several people, both patients and staff of the Center. It is hard to see how, under these conditions, she could have executed any maneuver without attracting attention. Unfortunately, there were 2 minutes during which she left the waiting room and was alone in the washroom. From a purely objective point of view, the idea of some deliberate action on her part during this period cannot be totally excluded.

However, this seems unlikely. As already indicated, the author has known Mrs. T. for a very long time. She is a very scrupulous person, and all that we know of her runs counter to such an idea. It will not go unnoticed that, had she so wished, it would have been very easy for her to "cheat" in the second experiment, since she was allowed to return home. The fact is that she did not do so. Furthermore, the possibility of an involuntary action carried out in a moment of psychic dissociation can be set aside in her case. She has never been subject to mishaps of this kind.

Finally, Mrs. T. had already shown other evidence of her particular susceptibility to hypnotic suggestion and of what we might call her psychosomatic "plasticity." During the surgical operation that has already been reported above (including the extraction of five teeth from the lower jaw and a pulpectomy), at a given moment the following suggestion was made to her: "Do not bleed." The bleeding which usually accompanies such an operation was, in fact, reduced to a minimum.

As for Mrs. D., she was not alone for a single moment throughout the whole experiment. Once she had been wakened, she immediately joined Mrs. T. in the waiting room where, it will be remembered, several members of the Center's staff were present. There she remained seated beside Mrs. T. If she had attempted to cheat in any way, the latter would have noticed it at once. It is true that an erythema can be produced simply by rubbing, but unless the subject has a particularly sensitive skin (which is not the case with Mrs. D.), the rubbing would have to be relatively vigorous and prolonged and would hardly go unnoticed. Furthermore, when she left the waiting room, Mrs. D. remained under constant surveillance by one of the team.

There is, in addition, no reason to doubt Mrs. D.'s consistently expressed wish to see the experiment fail. The fact is that the very day after the first experiment she refused to believe that the blister formation was due to hypnotic suggestion, and she subsequently applied picric acid to her arm in order to prevent the appearance of the phenomenon, all of which is inconsistent with the hypothesis of some intentional deception.

As for the first experiment (A.1), Mrs. D.'s own explanation that the blister was produced by contact with her watch can also be set aside. The area in question is distinctly higher than the normal position of her watch.

On the other hand, Mrs. D. could have burned her own arm in a state of somnambulism. She is indeed subject to such states (and one of these attacks occurred when she spent the night at the Center during the third experiment). She was rehypnotized and asked to describe everything which had happened that day between leaving the Center and discovering the scab on her arm the following morning. (In fact, it very often happens that a subject can recall under hypnosis the events occurring during a somnambulic episode.) This recall did not reveal any memory of such an incident. Obviously that does not represent an absolute guarantee. It would have been possible for Mrs. D. to have scratched her arm while asleep under the influence of the suggestion, thus producing the blister. However, the shape of the scab (a crescent) did not suggest the effect of scratching. In any case, it appears that there are reasonable grounds for supposing that, as in the two previous experiments, the process took place in a spontaneous fashion, at least up to the stage when the erythema was formed.

Psychodynamics

MRS. D.

Mrs. D.'s case shows how psychodynamic factors can intervene in the process. From the very beginning of the experiments, Mrs. D. manifested an ambivalent attitude, agreeing to submit to the experiment while hoping that it would not work. These are the terms in which she herself interprets her scepticism the day after the first experiment: "I don't want it to work." The "watch" hypothesis as an explanation for the blister has all the hallmarks of a rationalization. The episode with the picric acid during the second experiment is significant in this respect. If she had really disbelieved that the blister was due to hypnotic suggestion, Mrs. D. would not have felt the need to take precautions against the possible effects of the suggestion.

It is in the light of this same resistance that her attack of somnambulism in the third experiment also lends itself to interpretation. Before Mrs. D. went to sleep, the hypnotic suggestion had taken partial effect with the formation of an erythema. The thought, "I must switch off the oven" (with no basis in reality, as Mrs. D. had in fact switched it off before coming to the Center) seems to have been a barely disguised application to the somatic process in action, with the oven as the symbolic equivalent of the burn. According to this hypothesis, there is a veritable counter-suggestion at work, aimed, like the picric acid in the previous experiment, at preventing the formation of a blister. This was effective counter-suggestion since, instead of developing as on the first occasion as far as the blister stage, the erythema completely disappeared. It will be noted, however, that in spite of everything something was produced. The formation of the erythema seems, therefore, like a compromise between the wish to accomplish the hypnotic suggestion and the rejection of the suggestion.

As we have seen (p. 20), Mrs. D. showed, on the whole, a far less "submissive" attitude than Mrs. T. towards the words of the hypnotist. Everything occurred as if Mrs. D. maintained under hypnosis a relative degree of independence. While executing the hypnotic suggestion up to a point, she interpreted it and manipulated it to suit herself. This is, moreover, a well-known phenomenon. Numerous writers have shown that, even when the subject was hypnotized deeply, he still retained some control of the hypnotic situation and that, for example, it was impossible to make him commit acts to which he was deeply opposed.

In this case, how can Mrs. D.'s resistance to the "burn" suggestion be explained? She interpreted it herself as linked to her symptom: "I do not want it to succeed because, if it worked now and not with my symptom, it must mean that I am incurable." An ingenious explanation. For his own part, the author is tempted to reverse the proposition: if he succeeded in producing a blister, he might also succeed in making her symptom disappear. And it may be that unconsciously she wished to retain her symptom, which represented a gratification in fantasy.

MRS. T.

In contrast to Mrs. D., Mrs. T. showed no reservations about the experiment. Generally speaking, her relationship with the hypnotist was much less ambivalent than was the case with Mrs. D. The suggestions put to her were always carried out to the letter. In particular, it was possible to cure her of her symptom. Her attitude was significantly expressed in her statement a few days after the above-mentioned surgical operation: "I couldn't have felt any pain because you had said that I wouldn't."

Mrs. T. also referred to what the hypnotist said during the first experiment, but this time in order to underline the discrepancy between the suggestion and the sensation she experienced: "If you say that the coin is hot, I should feel something, but I don't." On this point, the author's observation confirms the conclusions which he reached after examination of the literature, namely that it is not the perception of pain which triggers the process resulting in blister formation. Indeed, in the two successful experiments, Mrs. T. felt no pain on contact with the coin. On both occasions she perceived a slightly painful sensation of heat in the course of the experiment. But it will be noted that in the third experiment this sensation was more the consequence than the development of the process, since it appeared when the erythema had already formed.

There is another fact which demonstrates the absence of any correlation between the perception of pain and blistering. Although no result was obtained during the last two experiments, these were precisely the experiments during which the painful sensation was most keenly felt.

How can we explain why no result was obtained in these cases? It is difficult to answer this question. It does not appear that any particular psycho-dynamic factor can be invoked here. This observation serves more than ever as a reminder that hypnotic suggestion is still very much an enigmatic phenomenon.

In the final experiment, a faint erythema appeared where the blister had appeared on the first occasion. This is reminiscent of Smirnov's observation (IX: 2 C), in which an erythema formed on the site of a real burn suffered by the subject in the past. Thus, it seems that in certain cases the memory of a past experience can interfere with that part of the suggestion concerned with the localization of the phenomenon.

Pathophysiology

We must face the fact that in our present state of knowledge there is no means of explaining, even hypothetically, the physiological mechanism of such a phenomenon. Let us simply say that, in the light of research undertaken over the last half century, it is now possible to look at the problem in a slightly different perspective.

The writers who applied themselves to this problem at the beginning of the century attempted to explain blistering by a pathophysiological mechanism similar to that which is involved in the case of a burn caused by an exogenous noxious agent. Thus, for Alrutz (1914) it is the projection on to the area suggested by the experimenter of a hallucinated percept of pain which sets off the reflex mechanisms that normally come into play after a real application of heat.

On the one hand, as we have seen, several observations – including the author's own experiments – demonstrate that the perception of pain is not essential to the success of the experiment.[9] On the other hand, from a physiological point of view, the identification of a representation with a real exogenous stimulus, acting along an afferent path, is hard to accept. It is more plausible to suppose that the central nervous system acts along purely efferent (i.e. endogenous) pathways. That is why, in order to avoid any confusion, the term "blistering" seems preferable to the term "burn."

The progress made in immunology enables us to envisage other models which are, admittedly, equally obscure, but possess the advantage of touching upon an area familiar to psychosomatic research. The role of psychological factors in allergic disorders such as asthma or urticaria, for example, is widely recognized today. Thus, in a study published in 1950, Graham and Wolf highlighted the correlation between the onset of attacks of urticaria and certain emotional situations. Similarly they succeeded in experimentally inducing attacks of urticaria merely by evoking these situations.[10] In fact, from the pathophysiological point of view, there is no

[9] With reference to the distinction established by modern neurophysiologists between sensory pain and suffering pain, which latter represents the subjective aspect of pain (see below, p. 71), it may be said that, in the case under consideration, the pain perceived by the subject is of the nature of "suffering pain," to the exclusion of any strictly organic dimension. (We do not here refer to the pain following the blistering, which is, for its part, clearly organic in character, reflecting as it does the lesional process in action.)

[10] Mention may be made of the work done by Stephen Black and his colleagues (Black, 1969) at the Laboratory of Human Physiology of the National Institute for Medical Research in London. They were able to diminish and even suppress, by direct suggestion under hypnosis, cutaneous reactions normally produced by the injection of allergens. Other research in this field is summarized in an editorial in the *British Medical Journal* of May 2nd, 1964, entitled "Suggestion and allergic responses." Knowing the importance that is increasingly attributed to the breakdown of immunological defences in the genesis of certain illnesses, we can appreciate the role that this type of experimentation could play from the point of view of basic research. It is interesting to note that Medawar (1977), Nobel prizewinner in medicine and a celebrated immunologist, cited Black's research (carried out in the laboratory of Humphrey, one of the world's greatest immunologists) with reference to cancer. Criticizing the approach of Leshan (1977), who basing himself on case studies attempted to establish the correlation between a certain type of stress and the onset of neoplastic disease, Medawar stated that Black's work seemed to him to speak more in favour of a psychological factor in the etiology of cancer. In this connection, the author cannot resist relating an anecdote which seems significant. One of his American friends, whose knowledge of hypnotic phenomena is certainly beyond all doubt, sent him Medawar's above-mentioned article, asking whether the research to which the latter referred was really to be believed. This is yet another proof of the incredulity such phenomena arouse even in those who are indeed best placed to believe in them.

fundamental difference between the development of a blister and that of a patch of urticaria.

Another hypothesis can equally well be adduced from the problem of the localization of the lesion. Here, perhaps, we should call upon another concept which has progressively come to the fore – the absence of any precise separation between the nervous control of the communicating functions and the neuroendocrine control of the automatic behavioral functions. There is a constant interaction between them, and each adjusts its activity in relation to the other. One may therefore take the view that the elaboration of a painful sensation directly at the cortical level in the suggested receptor area could induce an autonomic response in the cutaneous field.

However, it is advisable to exercise caution with regard to these two hypotheses, which are unsupported by any real experimental verification. Perhaps there exist other neural pathways as yet unknown to neurophysiology.

Whatever the case, the fact that it is possible to produce, by means of words, tissue, humoral and indeed immunological changes is in itself extremely significant.

Psychosomatics

Following Alexander (Alexander and French, 1948), specialists in psychosomatic medicine have, generally speaking, distinguished two types of action of the psyche on the soma: hysterical conversion, in which the symptom is the direct realization of psyche content, i.e. of a representation, and the somatization proper, in which it is the somatic result of a state of emotional tension, while not possessing in itself any predetermined psychological meaning. Such, for example, is the process which results in the development of an ulcer. A conflictual situation invokes tension, which stimulates a gastric secretion, which, by repeated action, finishes by producing a lesion. Here the symptom is the result of the conflict, but not its expression.

The description of the mechanism of somatization varies according to different schools. But, with a few exceptions, most writers agree in thinking that hysterical conversion, to the extent that it presupposes the involvement of the representation, can be produced only in the framework of the voluntary system and striated muscle. Truly somatic and autonomic disturbances are, on the other hand, conceived as signs of a deeper regression, in which the conflict does not even attain psychological representation. In contrast to the conversion symptom, the psychosomatic symptom would seem to be asymbolic.

Of course, specialists in psychosomatics recognize the existence of diseases which involve both mechanisms. This is so, for example, in the case of asthma, which involves at the same time both striated muscle and smooth muscle, conversion (the asthmatic attack possesses a symbolic meaning) and somatization. Both mechanisms are nonetheless described as distinct.

The experiments which have been reported above tend to contradict this dichotomy. The mechanism which we are dealing with here is incontestably of the conversion type, since it concerns the direct materialization of a representation (the suggestion of a burn). The development of a blister necessarily presupposes some action on the autonomic system. Similarly, it is known that it is possible to act by suggestion on hemorrhages. It has already been mentioned above that, in the course of a surgical operation under hypnosis, the author succeeded in stopping the bleeding of his patient (Mrs. T., p. 14) in this way.[11] Admittedly, a psychofunctional phenomenon is involved here and not an organic one. It will nevertheless be noted that it owes nothing to the voluntary system. Some interesting experiments have also been conducted by Seitz (1951, 1953) using somnambulists. He sought to verify Alexander's hypotheses about conversion by showing that it was possible to substitute one symptom for another by means of suggestion, provided that it would lend itself to the same symbolic meaning. He succeeded with one subject, for example, in replacing bulimia with onycophagia, a depressive reaction, vomiting, urticaria, shingles, etc. If he thus confirmed that conversion had a symbolic significance, he rather invalidated the idea that "psychodynamic" equivalents were confined to the voluntary system, as some of these symptoms derive from the autonomic system.

The position adopted on the problem by specialists in psychosomatic medicine is in some respects reminiscent of Babinski's views. As we have seen, the latter allowed hysterical symptoms no organic reality. They were either

---

[11] The influence of psychic and nervous factors on bleeding represents another chapter in the history of medicine, little known today. Abundant literature exists, especially German and French, on ecchymoses and other hemorrhages induced by suggestion or appearing spontaneously in hysterics. The Munich doctor, Rudolf Schindler, presented a review of the literature devoted to this subject together with his personal observations in a short work published in 1927: *Nervensystem und spontane Blütungen* (Schindler, 1927).

the result of imitation and autosuggestion (the famous "pithiatism"), clearly resting upon functions subject to voluntary innervation, or else they were due to a truly organic disease – or to a deception. Of course, the parallel carries only so far. Babinski denied any action of the psychic on the somatic; this is obviously not the case with the theorists of psychosomatic medicine. Moreover, no one defends Babinski's theory of "pithiatism" nowadays. By introducing the concepts of the unconscious, conversion and repression, psychoanalysis enabled us to understand that hysterical symptoms were the product not of a more or less conscious will, but of a true alteration of bodily processes under the impact of unconscious conflicts, and that, for all that they were psychological conflicts, they nonetheless affected the body in a real way.

However, it is as if the old dualism of body and mind were preserved in some fashion at the very heart of psychosomatic theory itself – as if, at the very moment when the action of the psychic on the somatic had been recognized, we had set about assigning new limits to it. Indeed, as long as we remain within the framework of the voluntary system, we are, in a certain sense, still within the realm of the mind. It is simply a question of a distortion of the normal functioning of the central nervous system. *The body is not materially affected.* Conversely, when the organic dimension really does come into play, the psychosomatic theorists affirm that there is, strictly speaking, no representation. For reasons which, in the writer's opinion, arise from a veritable "epistemological block," the possibility that a purely mental phenomenon might act *directly* upon the most fundamentally organic processes is thus avoided in every case. In the same way, the specialists in psychosomatics continue to contrast the functional and the organic, when it is evident that the difference between them is only quantitative. In most cases, a lesion forms in response to a disturbance of a functional kind.

Let there be no misunderstanding. It is not claimed that all psychosomatic phenomena are the result of conversion. The circuits which govern relations between the psychic and the somatic are most certainly multiple and situated at different levels of the personality. Let us simply say that it seems undesirable to establish such clear-cut distinctions in an area that is still so little understood. By doing so, we run the risk of neglecting an extremely important dimension, and closing the door on experimentation.[12] Over the

----

[12] It is questionable, for example, whether the scarcity of experiments on blistering by suggestion is due exclusively to the fact that it is difficult to find subjects capable of producing this type of phenomenon. Such subjects are quite rare, it is true. But has there really been a systematic attempt to perform this experiment?

last half century, our knowledge of the nervous system has been greatly enriched. It is being increasingly recognized that the central nervous system and the autonomic system are not nearly so distinct as was formerly thought, but that there exists a whole series of relays between them, neurophysiological, neurochemical, neuroendocrinological, etc., of which only an infinitesimal part is known. A vast field of research thus stands open to be explored in all its aspects.

PART II

THEORETICAL
QUESTIONS

Admittedly, the author's experiments might seem a mere news item, or at best "a freak of nature" appealing to those who are attracted by the marvellous. However that may be, they leave us confronted with certain fundamental questions about the human psyche.

What is the result? It would seem to be two-fold – or rather, mixed!

In the first place, it is seen to be reassuring. To one who has engaged in psychotherapeutic, or indeed psychosomatic research, these experiments provide irrefutable proof of the influence of the mind on physiological processes, an influence which is not yet fully acknowledged in spite of the accumulation of data. A state of affairs which extends even to the researcher himself, who could sometimes end by no longer "believing in it," so arduous is this research on the methodological plane. Such obvious facts on a "macroscopic," massive scale are of a nature that could shake the resistance of the most sceptical.

While this is a source of reassurance on the one hand, it is also a source of frustration as well when one realizes that no theory can account for these phenomena (at least on the basis of existing concepts).

The author makes no claim to unravel this enigma. He merely seeks to formulate hypotheses and intuitive ideas which range from some degree of plausibility to pure speculation, or even science fiction. He could be charged with having raised more questions than answers, but can any more be done for the moment in a field where there are still so many unknowns?

On the one hand, it is clear that we do not understand the mechanisms by which a verbal stimulus at the cortical level can influence the perception of pain or produce *localized* vaso-motor changes. In spite of advances in our knowledge, the processes activated in the experiments presented here remain unexplained.

At the relational level, the mechanism is relatively better understood. Independent of the unconscious meaning which the hypnotized subject may attach to such or such a "performance," it is clear that the wish to conform to the hypnotist's injunction plays an essential role here.

But these considerations do not take into account the psychophysiological dimension of hypnosis. The question as to whether the latter represents a specific state on the physiological plane is, as ever, the object of a great deal of controversy. In spite of much research, it has not so far been possible to discover any physiological indicator offering a means of determining whether or not a subject is hypnotized. Nevertheless, if we cannot speak of a hypnotic state, in the strict physiological sense, it does seem undeniable that hypnosis constitutes an *altered state of consciousness, involving a certain modification of the psychophysiological reactivity of the organism.* While it is still not clearly outlined on the heuristic plane, this notion nonetheless represents the best hypothesis. The author has called this state the "fourth organismic state" (Chertok, 1969a, p. 3) following on the states of waking, sleeping and dreaming.

3

A Modified Psychophysiological Reactivity

Already at the induction stage, the body is subject to the action. The induction is always a simultaneous action, in which psychic factors are intimately interwoven with physiological factors. Kubie and Margolin (1942) showed that it was possible to induce hypnosis (or a state approaching hypnosis) by essentially physical means, by submitting the subject to a kind of sensory deprivation.[1] Even classical induction constitutes in certain respects a reduction in the subject's sensorimotor field (reduction of external stimuli, concentration on the hypnotist's voice, suggestions concerning muscular relaxation, attention concentrated on the body, etc.).

Induction can, therefore, be viewed as a process consisting of the

[1] Experiments on sensory deprivation have shown that, when the subject is cut off from sensory input, regressive phenomena are produced, sometimes accompanied by serious mental disturbances (hallucinations and dream states). This happens, for example, when the subject is enclosed in a cubic cage (Bexton, Heron and Scott, 1954) or when he is left immersed in a tank of water with an oxygen mask for breathing (Lilly, 1958). Such work dates, in fact, from 1954 (the Hebb School). But from 1944 onwards, Kubie and Margolin (1944) referred to similar experiments in an attempt to throw light on the process of hypnotic induction. Thus, it became possible to integrate the sensorimotor, corporal dimension into theorization about hypnosis. This aspect had been known to Freud and his immediate followers. Although Freud affirmed that the ego was first and foremost a body ego, he concentrated principally on the instinctual forces. The first writer to attempt a synthesis of the psychological and physiological aspects of hypnosis was Schilder (Schilder, 1922; Schilder and Kauders, 1926), who emphasized the changes which hypnosis introduced into bodily experience. The perspective introduced by Kubie and Margolin posed the problem of the relative importance of the psychic and physical factors in the induction process. There was a controversy over this between Kubie and Gill and Brenman. In Kubie's view (1961), even if psychological elements play a part in the process of induction, the triggering factor lies at the sensorimotor level. Transference, for example, is the consequence rather than the cause of the hypnotic state. Gill and Brenman (1959), on the other hand, emphasized that the two factors were simultaneous (for further details, *see* Chertok, 1966b, pp. 29–39).

progressive destructionalization of the regulatory mechanisms which control the subject's relationship to the environment. The subject is gradually cut off from all sources of excitation, except for the stimuli transmitted through the person of the hypnotist. In the hypnotic state proper, the link with the environment is re-established. The subject is once more able to talk, move, and perceive external stimuli (which actions, if they occurred during the process of induction, would immediately interrupt it). At the same time, there is a distortion of information as a function of the hypnotist's suggestions. Thus, in the case of hypnotic analgesia, the information about pain transmitted by the receptors is transformed.

Usually, processing of the information proceeds as a function of adaptation to the outside world. A selective process takes place, eliminating information which is not necessary for such adaptation or which contradicts the external impulses. The "de-afferentiation" (another term for sensory deprivation) produced by hypnotic induction leads to the lifting of these control mechanisms. A whole series of sensations and representations, which are ordinarily repressed or kept in the background, invade consciousness. It is thus that, from the induction onwards, there come into play modifications of the body image and intense affective reactions, corresponding to the reactivation of conflicts, forgotten memories, etc. Generally speaking, there is no longer any means by which the subject can distinguish between the reality of the external world and his own representations. Any stimulus beyond a certain intensity is accorded an index of reality.

This explains the subject's suggestibility in relation to hypnotic suggestions, insofar as his attention has, from the beginning of the process, been focused upon the hypnotist. As Kubie and Margolin (1944) stressed, it is again necessary to distinguish here between the induction phase and the hypnotic state. During the induction, the suggestions are especially intended to produce de-afferentiation. The more the subject is cut off from external stimuli, the more these suggestions assume for him the value of reality, and the greater is the degree of de-afferentiation, producing in its turn a further increase in suggestibility. The hypnotist's suggestions are no longer perceived as coming from an external person, but as emanating from the subject himself. Once this stage is reached, the hypnotic state becomes sufficiently stable for the relationship to the environment to be reestablished without bringing about its disintegration. External stimuli reach consciousness, but they are filtered and remodeled according to the suggestions received.

The experiment in blistering shows that the effect of suggestion is not confined to motor and sensory functioning, but also affects somatic (autonomic) processes, over which the central nervous system normally exercises only a limited influence. For example, the suggestion of a burn induces changes in tissue which are ordinarily produced only in response to stimuli transmitted by the receptors. The hypnotic state is thus characterized by a generalized plasticity at every level of the organism.

4

Hypnosis and Suggestibility

The characteristic of plasticity is not specific to hypnosis. All the phenomena which can be produced under hypnosis (amnesia, modifications of psychomotor behavior, hallucinations, somatic symptoms, etc.) can appear spontaneously in hysterical or psychotic subjects. It is also known that certain techniques, such as yoga, for example, render the subject capable of influencing physiological functions which are ordinarily outside voluntary control.[1]

Like hypnosis, hysteria and psychosis also entail a modification of the subject's state of consciousness. The same is true of yoga, presupposing as it does an apprenticeship in the psychic and psychophysiological domain. But phenomena similar to those obtained under hypnosis can be produced equally well in the apparent absence of this dimension (i.e. any transformation of the state of consciousness). Experiments have shown that most of the results obtained under hypnosis could equally well be produced by suggestion with subjects in the waking state. For example, warts have been successfully removed in this way when they have proved resistant to all other forms of treatment. Another example, all the more interesting here because it

[1] In a recent publication, Elmer and Alice Green (1973) report experiments conducted at the Menninger Clinic with an Indian Yogi, who showed himself capable of influencing, at will, his respiration, pulse, cardiac rhythm, the electrical activity of his brain, his skin temperature, etc. In particular, he succeeded in producing a difference in temperature of 10°F between the fingers of the same hand. A second series of experiments was carried out with another subject, Schwarz. Having sunk a needle into his arm, piercing the skin, the biceps and a vein, he stopped the bleeding occasioned by the wound on command (within 3 seconds). The writers also report that on another occasion, in front of a group of doctors, Schwarz plunged his hands into a brazier and handled the hot coals without any identifiable trace of burning on his hands ("negative blistering"). It will be noted that Elmer and Alice Green saw this phenomenon as possibly relating to parapsychology.

involves analgesia, is that of acupuncture. Analgesia produced by this method can indeed be as complete as that obtained under hypnosis. But it does not appear to involve any psychophysiological manipulation. The subject neither feels nor gives the impression of being in an altered state of consciousness. In a very different field, sorcerers sometimes succeed in inducing or suppressing somatic symptoms simply by reciting a formula. It is not by chance, moreover, that negative blistering (action designed to prevent or reduce tissue alteration following a real burn) is a traditional practice of sorcery.

It is known today that, generally speaking, there is practically no physiological function which cannot be influenced by psychic processes. In many cases, it is not understood how this influence is exercised, nor why certain subjects are more liable to produce one type of symptom rather than another. It may be wondered whether this is not a question of innate capacities, inscribed in the genetic code. Whatever the case, it can therefore be said that hypnosis itself creates nothing; it merely reactivates existing potentialities.

However, that does not mean to say there is no difference between suggestion under hypnosis and suggestion in the waking state. Experiments in suggestion conducted by Orne with simulators (subjects trained to behave like hypnotized subjects) and subjects really hypnotized have revealed, for example, that the former stopped carrying out the suggestions as soon as they were no longer in the experimental situation. The hypnotized subjects, on the other hand, continued to carry out the orders they had received, even when the experiment was officially over (Orne, 1972).

It would therefore seem that, in the first case, obedience to suggestions was essentially due to voluntary control and that it ceased as soon as the subject's attention and his will were no longer mobilized; the second case would involve a much more involuntary act, deriving from genuine automatism. Similarly, Orne reached the conclusion that there existed a "trance logic" and that hypnosis produced modifications in mental functioning which were not to be found in non-hypnotized subjects (Orne, 1959).

Experiments on hypnotic analgesia with groups of simulators have also been conducted by Shor (1959), one of Orne's colleagues. They showed that simulators could effectively control their pain reactions in such a way that it was impossible, from outside observation, to distinguish them from the truly hypnotized subjects. However, when the subjects were questioned after the experiment was over, it was established that the painful sensation was nonetheless experienced much more intensely by the simulators than by the hypnotized subjects. Greene and Rehyer (1972) have observed, moreover, that the threshold of pain tolerance was higher in hypnotized subjects than in those who received a suggestion of analgesia in the waking state.

The experiments of Hilgard and Hilgard (1975) are particularly interesting. They compared the pain reactions of the same subjects in three different situations: without suggestion; with suggestion in the waking state; and with hypnotic suggestion. The subjects were submitted to an increasingly painful stimulus which they were asked to evaluate on a numerical scale ranging from 0 to 10. On the one hand, it was established that the reduction in the sensation of pain was greater when the subjects were hypnotized than when they were under a suggestion of analgesia in the waking state. These data therefore confirm the results obtained by Greene and Rehyer. But most importantly they have demonstrated that under hypnosis *the painful sensation was perceived, even though it did not reach the subject's consciousness* (or only in an attenuated form). This observation was made possible through the use of a technique of automatic writing, which the Hilgards had already employed in previous experiments.

The method was as follows: asked to indicate the intensity of the pain verbally, the subject received, at the same time, the suggestion that his right hand would record the same intensity in writing (still based on the same numerical scale) *but without his being aware of it.* Thus each experiment gave rise to a double evaluation. It then became apparent that, generally speaking, the written evaluation was higher than the verbal one. The Hilgards quote the case of a subject who consciously felt no pain, even whilst his hand set down higher and higher numbers as the painful stimulus increased.

It is, therefore, as if part of the subject continued to perceive the painful sensation, but as if this perception was in some way cut off, or "outside consciousness," because of the suggested analgesia. This hypothesis is, furthermore, confirmed by the fact that this "covert pain," to use the Hilgards' own term, can also be made conscious by means of suggestion. The Hilgards indeed showed that if, once the experiment was over, it was suggested to the subject that he recall the intensity of the painful sensation, insisting on the fact that part of him had remained conscious of everything that had happened during the experiment, the subject's responses were identical with those obtained by means of automatic writing.

In the Hilgards' words, "The heart of the problem is explaining how sensory information can be registered and processed even though it is not overtly available, and even though its conscious processing has been distorted by hypnotic suggestion" (1975, p. 178). What is involved here, they stress, is a mode of functioning close to that of amnesia. The fact that the covert pain can be made conscious by means of suggestion strengthens the analogy still further. The Hilgards draw attention to an important difference, however. In the classical model of amnesia, the forgotten element was in the first place conscious, and was then for one reason or another obliterated. In the case in question, we are faced with the paradox of a perception which is in some way subject to amnesia, even before reaching consciousness, which does not prevent the possibility of its being subsequently remembered.

The author's experiments fully confirm the Hilgards' observations. In the case of Mrs. D., as well as that of Mrs. T., it is clear that the pain information was perceived through a series of distortions. The process here is more complex than in the examples quoted by the Hilgards insofar as the painful stimulus was much more intense at the outset. There is, however, a certain amount of agreement between them.

The distinction between manifest pain and covert pain appears in the contrast to be found between the responses given at the beginning of the recall, in which the presence of painful sensations is hardly mentioned, and the responses evoked by suggestions 2 and 3 (cf. pp. 15–18 above). It will, however, be noted that, even when it is finally acknowledged, the pain is presented in a very attenuated form, associated with another sensation (heat or sunburn) and described as if perceived by someone else and as if no element of suffering were really involved.

This observation tends to confirm the Hilgards' hypothesis that covert pain is essentially sensory pain. We know that, as a result of the work of Melzack and Casey (1968), neurophysiology today distinguishes two components of pain: sensory pain which plays a purely informative role (transmitting the locality and intensity of the stimulus) and suffering, which represents the subjective aspect of pain. This distinction was established more particularly after it had been observed that subjects who had undergone a prefrontal lobotomy continued to perceive the noxious stimuli, but that this perception was devoid of any feeling of suffering.

Similarly, it would appear that, in hypnotic analgesia, the suffering reaction is almost entirely abolished. That is fairly easily explained, inasmuch as this reaction is the product of the affective-relational system. It is a kind of signal arising in response to a stimulus perceived as a threat to the organism. And the effect of hypnotic suggestion is precisely that this stimulus is no longer experienced as such. The message bearing the information remains, but its stressful dimension has disappeared. The part played by these mechanisms in damping down the emotions is clearly apparent in the author's observations.

On the basis of what has been said, it therefore seems that hypnotic analgesia is characterized by a dissociated mode of functioning: on the one hand, the information is registered normally at the cortical level; on the other hand, it undergoes a distortion due to the hypnotist's verbal intervention. This state of dissociation is not solely specific to analgesia, but applies to the hypnotic situation as a whole. This splitting of consciousness appears clearly in the phenomenon of spontaneous post-hypnotic amnesia. It is not by chance, moreover, that amnesia and the question of multiple personalities have long been at the centre of thinking about hypnosis. It is an aspect which emerges clearly from the statements of hypnotized subjects. They frequently report having felt a sense of depersonalization, of splitting of the self: "It is as if it had happened to someone else," "I had the impression that it was someone else doing it," are expressions which crop up frequently in one form or another.

It may be noted that here is involved a profound change in the reactivity of the organism, going far beyond any more or less voluntary control. A highly motivated subject could be induced to control his behavior up to a certain point and, for example, to overcome his reactions to a perception of pain. But the sensation of pain would still be consciously perceived for all that. Beyond a certain threshold, the subject would no longer be in a state to continue to control his reactions. In the case of hypnotic suggestion, it is the perception itself which is transformed. This explains why hypnotic suggestion can affect functions which are normally beyond voluntary control, such as the autonomic functions (e.g. blistering).

Once again, dissociation phenomena of the same order as those observed under hypnosis also occur in the waking state. Such is the case, for example, with the partial amnesia represented by gaps in memory, lapses, etc. The fact that data can be registered at the cortical level without being accessible to consciousness is a basic principle of mental functioning. Independently of all that psychoanalysis has taught us on this subject, research into subliminal perception has provided experimental proof of the inscription of unconscious processes in the functioning of the nervous system. This type of dissociation is similarly at the root of many conversion symptoms, which, as we have seen, can sometimes occur as a result of a simple suggestion in the waking state.

But all these examples concern partial, circumscribed phenomena, which do not entail any overall modification of the subject's relationship to the environment. Hypnosis, on the other hand, involves the total organism. Not all functions are equally "plastic." Certain subjects will react far more strongly to one suggestion than to another. Nonetheless, a transformation takes place which affects the whole of the subject's functioning. It might be said that aptitudes which normally make their appearance in a limited and fluctuating way are here mobilized in a massive and, at the same time, more stable way. The fact that the observer, as well as the subject, senses a genuine change of state provides evidence of the truth of this statement.[2]

[2] A comparison between the waking state and hypnosis is rendered particularly difficult by the fact that the first term is hardly more clearly defined than the second. When the experimenter confines himself to suggestion in the waking state, he submits the subject nonetheless to a whole series of manipulations. He frequently asks him to relax and to concentrate, and speaks to him persuasively and with emphasis, so as to arouse in him sufficiently strong motivation. There are grounds for wondering whether these procedures produce some degree of sensory deprivation and, in some cases, represent the equivalent of a rapid hypnotic induction. Where does hypnosis begin and suggestion end? The question is all the more relevant in that, with highly hypnotizable subjects, hypnotic induction can be very brief.

5

Therapeutic Applications

Hypnosis is not only an object for the laboratory. It is also a therapeutic tool. Before dealing with the theoretical problems raised in the field of hypnotic research, it would seem desirable that the reader should have access at least to some basic information about the medical applications of hypnosis. No attempt has been made here to provide a comprehensive review of all that is being done in hypnotherapy. It is merely proposed to draw attention to some of the general trends in this field.[1]

In 1918 Freud wrote: "It is very probable, too, that the large-scale application of our therapy will compel us to alloy the pure gold of analysis freely with the copper of direct suggestion; and hypnotic influence, too, might find a place in it again, as it has in the treatment of war neuroses" (Freud, 1918, *S.E. XVII*, pp. 167–168).

This passage has often been quoted. Very early on, Freud's disciples wondered whether psychoanalytic treatment might not be shortened (and it was far shorter at that time than it is today). Thus were conceived Ferenczi's attempts, followed by those of Alexander, to introduce an "active method," i.e. a technique characterized by surrendering in some degree the absolute neutrality of the analyst, an attitude at once more gratifying and more directive. In more general terms, as psychoanalysis became increasingly available to larger numbers of patients, the analytic procedure was made less unwieldy. This is what was called POP (Held, 1968), Psychoanalytically Oriented Psychotherapy. In the last few years there has been an increasing trend, based on Balint's work (Balint *et al.*, 1972), towards short-term psychotherapies (Malan, 1963; Sifneos, 1972).

---

[1] For more detailed information, see Chertok (1963).

In the 1930s, the validity of this kind of approach was questioned by such eminent authors as Jones and Glover, who, referring to this passage of Freud's, spoke of a "metallurgical" metaphor (Glover, 1972, p. 71). They considered that such forms of treatment deviated from the standard model of therapy and were, in fact, based on simple suggestion. But, of course, the proponents of these methods claim to remain true to the psychoanalytic orientation. This point is still the object today of widespread controversy.

To return to Freud, the use of the term "suggestion" might lead one to suppose that, in this passage, he was thinking more especially of the employment of hypnosis in the suppression of symptoms. This aspect is indeed by no means negligible. The question of ascertaining whether the aim of psychotherapy should be to cause the disappearance of the symptom has been, and still is, the subject of numerous debates.[2] Clinical experience shows that the so frequently invoked argument that a direct attack on the symptom would entail the risk of inducing substitute phenomena, or even an aggravation of the pathological state, is far from proved. Substitute symptoms do not always appear. Some authors even consider that the suppression of symptoms can, in certain cases, constitute the indispensable starting point for the subject's entry into the analytical process. Thus in 1972 Kubie stated: ". . . many analysts lost sight of the fact that, although lasting therapy requires this basic personality emancipation, it must start with the resolution of symptomatic blocks. . . . In fact, this symptomatic breakthrough is vital for the therapeutic efficacy of all psychotherapies, including analytic therapy and the somato-therapies as well. The emancipation of the personality as a whole from neurotic imprisonment is indispensable for enduring change" (p. 219).[3]

---

[2] This dilemma sometimes places the psychoanalyst in awkward situations. The author once referred a patient suffering from ejaculatory failure, a complaint resistant to therapy, to a particularly gifted colleague. After six sessions, the analyst was in a highly distressed state: the patient's symptom had disappeared. (It was possible to ascertain, 6 months later, that it had still not reappeared, but the patient had left her.) What technical mistake could she have made? The author congratulated her. But it required a group session to alleviate the anxiety aroused in her by this incident. The idea that the symptom should have disappeared without her knowing why was unbearable to her in the light of the training she was receiving.

[3] The suppression of symptoms is sometimes an imperative. The author has in mind the cases of amnesia which he has had occasion to treat. As amnesiacs are in general good hypnotic subjects, is the psychoanalyst committing sacrilege by stepping out of his sacrosanct position as listener in order to suppress a symptom? Or is he supposed to resort to a specialized hypnotist to get his "dirty work" done?

But Freud's allusion to war neuroses shows that he was not, in this passage, considering hypnosis only under the aspect of suggestion. The method used in the treatment of these neuroses was, in fact, that of catharsis, i.e. the use of the hypnotic state as an altered state of consciousness with a view to inducing the recall of the traumata which caused the onset of the neurosis. It can be seen that this is no mere instance of "suppressive" therapy.

Attempts to ally psychoanalysis and hypnosis have indeed been made, mainly in the United States. It was wondered whether this would not allow the curative process to be speeded up, in dynamic therapies as in standard forms of treatment. To the extent that it entails a particularly intense emotional involvement, the hypnotic relationship could contribute to a faster removal of defenses and an acceleration of transference processes. Moreover, the performance of subjects under hypnosis is generally closer to the primary processes. Gill and Brenman, for instance, have observed that a patient under hypnosis is able, through the hypnotic investigation of dreams, to reach a deeper insight into his unconscious conflicts than when this investigation takes place in the waking state (1959, pp. 348 seqq.).

This integration of hypnosis into psychotherapy has taken various forms. In some cases, hypnotic sessions have simply been introduced from time to time, with no other modification of the psychotherapeutic technique; in others, procedures usually employed in hypnoanalysis have been used: induced dreaming, age regression, automatic writing, etc. Gill and Brenman (1959), Wolberg (1964), Kline (1975 a, b), Schneck (1954, 1965), Erika Fromm (1977, 1979), Edith Klemperer (1969), Watkins (1949), etc., have in this way allotted to hypnosis an important place on the clinical level. Reference may also be made to Milton Erickson who, after having worked with Kubie, elaborated some original therapeutic methods based on psychoanalytic concepts as well as on conditioning and learning therapies, combining with great imagination the most varied approaches (Haley, 1973; Bandler and Grinder, 1975; Erickson, Rossi and Rossi, 1976).

There remains one considerable objection: the positive transference would seem to be so strong in hypnosis that it inhibits the expression of the resistances, whose analysis plays a basic part in the development of the treatment. This is a real problem, but, as we shall see later, one that may be stated in less absolute terms than at first appears.

Apart from its use in a psychodynamic perspective, hypnosis is most often employed for making direct suggestions. These applications are important in psychosomatic medicine (warts, eczema, psoriasis, psychogenic obesity, enuresis and psychogenic retention of urine, headaches, amenorrhea, asthma, counteracting pain, etc.). Hypnosis is also employed to modify certain forms of behavior (alcoholism, excessive smoking, phobias). In these latter cases, the hypnotic technique is sometimes combined with behavior therapy (Kroger, 1977).

However, the patient can also simply be placed in an hypnotic state, without being given suggestions of any kind. This is called prolonged hypnotic sleep.[4] Sessions may last from 1 to 24 hours, or even several weeks. This technique was especially used at the beginning of this century (Wetterstrand in Sweden,[5] Van Renterghem in Holland, Janet in France).[6] The Russians have used it to treat hypertension and cardiovascular disorders. They still resort to it in a certain number of cases, and the Americans are in the process of rediscovering it with the creation of what they call "hypnotic parlours" where patients are simply placed under hypnosis for varying lengths of time, with the exclusion of any other form of treatment.

The curative value of "pure" hypnosis has, in fact, been attested since ancient times. It can be explained in different ways. Soviet authors, for instance, consider that hypnosis is a partial sleep, a cortical inhibition which, in the same way as total sleep, has a restorative effect. This question is, at the present time, widely debated in the U.S.S.R.

The debate bears on the following question: Does hypnosis constitute a therapy that is "pathogenetic" (acting on the causes of the illness) or symptomatic (solely affecting the symptom)? Each of these two theories has its proponents, both sides claiming adherence to Pavlov. It is not proposed here to consider in detail the physiological metaphors employed by the respective authors. A few examples will suffice. Rozhnov and Burno (1976), who defend the first (pathogenetic) viewpoint, consider that hypnosis constitutes an artificially induced "defensive inhibition" which allows the subject to face difficult situations. Apter (1976), a proponent of the symptomatic

---

[4] This method is, as it were, the precursor of prolonged-sleep treatment. One of its disadvantages was that it could only be applied to subjects who were highly hypnotizable. It was the Russians' idea to use sleeping drugs as adjuvants. In France in the 1950's, when prolonged sleep treatment began to be known, it was exclusively of the drug-induced type. The results of this form of treatment are currently the object of considerable controversy.

[5] Freud's famous patient, Emmy von N., underwent prolonged sleep treatment at Wetterstrand's sanatorium in the winter of 1893-4. It was Forel who had referred this patient to Freud, and later to Wetterstrand.

[6] For further details, see Chertok (1954).

theory, believes on the other hand that the active agent in hypnosis is suggestion, which is a process of cortical excitation. In actual fact, the neurophysiological bases of hypnosis are completely unknown and Apter himself admits that Pavlov was very cautious with regard to our knowledge of the neurophysiology of the nervous system ("Here," he wrote, "the mountain of the unknown will long overtop by far the small parts which we have succeeded in knowing" (Pavlov, 1951, p. 413)).

The new feature in this debate is that authors are beginning to employ a psychological language. Rozhnov and Burno (1976), side by side with the use of physiological terms, thus define hypnosis as a defense of a psychological nature that is *unconscious* and beneficent, which constitutes a treatment in itself. Apter (1976) is opposed to this view: according to him, there is no treatment by hypnosis, only a psychotherapy by suggestion under hypnosis.

For those holding the second view, the action of hypnosis remains symptomatic and limited. Apter (1979) even draws attention to the dangers incurred by placing the patient frequently under deep hypnosis. (This warning constitutes a new departure, and perhaps corresponds with the appearance of resistances, by reason of the calling in question of physiological theorization which had been reassuring.) Hypnosis comes at the very most within the sphere of "minor psychotherapy," and does not bring about any restructuring of the personality. To effect the latter, a "major psychotherapy" is necessary. In this connection, Apter calls upon Platonov (1962), for whom major psychotherapy would comprise "psychoanalysis, Dubois' persuasion method, and the reeducation of the personality." (A strange association! In the case of psychoanalysis, this is in all probability a lapsus. The present author was unable to find this word in the work by Platonov which is cited. One encounters there the term analysis in depth, which covers intensive anamnestic interviews, and the term hypnoanalysis, which corresponds with the cathartic method, which Platonov recommends in exceptional cases. On the whole, Platonov is anti-Freudian.)

Sakun (1977) of Leningrad supports the views of Rozhnov and Burno. Hypnosis is for him a treatment in its own right. He emphasizes that it is employed to advantage in the treatment of hypertension, asthma, gastroduodenal ulcers, etc. For Apter (1979), however, this argument proves nothing, because the psychogenetic nature of these illnesses is far from being established.

Baranov and Naritsin (1979), for their part, consider that hypnotherapy is of great practical value, and they employ it in conjunction with rational psychotherapy, autogenic training, and group psychotherapy. Feldman and Leizerovich (1978) reject equally the theoretical considerations of Rozhnov and Burno, as well as those of Apter. In their opinion, hypnotherapy is effective when there is a concurrence of two factors: suggestion, and the ability of the patient's nervous system to receive it.

Finally, Prangishvili, Sherozia and Bassin (1978c, II, p. 35), who are researchers in philosophy and psychology, but are not therapists, admit quite clearly that the problem of hypnosis is still completely unknown, particularly as regards the question of the relationship between hypnosis and suggestion.

It should be noted that, in psychoanalytical theory, the problem of the opposition between etiological and symptomatic treatment in hypnosis is highly complex and has not yet been resolved.

In conclusion, it may be said that hypnosis has proved its therapeutic value in many fields. But the modes of its application are still ill-defined and poorly codified. It can, at all events, hardly be otherwise until such time as it is decided to make an intensive effort to research this subject.

6

Hypnosis and Hysteria

All the phenomena experimentally induced under hypnosis appear spontaneously in hysteria; conversely, all the spontaneous symptoms of hysteria can be reproduced under hypnosis. It is therefore relevant to ask ourselves what is the relationship between these two phenomena.

In the late nineteenth century, the heyday of hypnosis, many authors asserted the existence of a close relationship between hysteria and hypnosis. Charcot regarded hypnosis as an artificial hysteria. Only hysterical subjects could be hypnotized. This conceptualization was abandoned as a result of Bernheim's work which showed that many subjects could be hypnotized, without their being in any way hysterical. Modern research has to some extent confirmed this view. It has indeed been observed that so-called "normal" subjects are easier to hypnotize than neurotics. The debate, however, is not really closed. In fact, as Ferenczi (1909, p. 103) emphasized, quoting Jung, normal subjects also suffer from the complexes found in neurotics; in other words, the frontier between the normal and the pathological is often only a quantitative one. We are all, fortunately, in some degree hysterical. The example of post-traumatic neuroses provides a good illustration of this aspect of the problem. There has been much discussion as to which element plays the most important role in the etiology of these neuroses: acquired factors – stress, or constitutional factors – the background, a neurotic predisposition (Crocq, 1974). In cases where one is faced with a weak or medium stress, the constitutional factors seem to be the determining one. But in cases of major stress, even subjects with no neurotic predisposition can produce an hysterical reaction. The latter then represents a sort of safety valve.

Moreover, if it has been possible to establish that normal subjects are more widely hypnotizable than neurotics, it is among the latter that we find the hysterics who are the most highly susceptible to hypnosis (Gill and Brenman, 1959, pp. 78–79).[1]

Among somnambulists, there is a large proportion of hysterical subjects. Finally, from a phenomenological point of view, there are points in common between the trance and the states of fugue, dissociation and hysterical attacks.

Having established the interdependence of these two phenomena, we may try to ascertain more closely where they converge and where they differ. Let us take the case of hysterical paralysis. This symptom arises from a conflict in which censorship and represssion are involved. Paralysis is a compromise solution. The symptom has a meaning. It can represent, for instance, a defense against a repressed wish to murder someone. The conflict can be said to be expressed by a kind of partial amnesia which withholds from the subject the normal use of his reflexes and motor acquisitions. Janet had already stressed that hysterical paralysis is basically a sort of amnesia (Janet, 1887, p. 462).

But in order for the symptom to occur, there must exist a psycho- or neurophysiological structure, a mechanism of "amnesiation" whereby repression can operate. We are dealing with two processes: that of repression and that of the psychophysiological mechanism.

What takes place in hypnotic paralysis or analgesia? The symptoms are the same. The same psycho- or neurophysiological mechanism is involved. But at what level do meaning and repression come in? It can be thought that on the psychological level the hypnotized subject uses the process of repression, or more primary defense mechanisms such as denial, negation, etc., in his wish to conform to the utterances of the hypnotist, and that, through the physiological mechanism of amnesiation, he eliminates, for instance, the ·suffering associated with pain.

Certain authors, however, and particularly Hilgard (1978), believe it unnecessary to involve meaning in order to explain the production of hypnotic phenomena, and prefer to confine themselves to the descriptive aspect of the phenomenon by resorting to the concept of dissociation. This

---

[1] The non-hypnotizability of a large number of hysterics seems to the author to lend itself to the following explanation: the hysterical symptom being linked to libidinal cathexes with persons from their past, these patients refuse to establish new transference relationships with the hypnotist. Everything occurs as though they did not wish to reconsider the problem or renounce the secondary gains of their illness.

notion, inspired by Janet, is at present finding confirmation in modern experimental research on the simultaneous existence of several control systems.[2] These are obviously only hypotheses. So far as the present author is concerned, it does seem difficult to eliminate completely the dynamics of the wish in hypnosis.

Hilgard's arguments are founded on the fact that the hypnotist's suggestions are not generally of a kind to arouse conflicts, and that it is therefore useless to invoke the concept of repression to explain amnesia. True as this is at a first level, it implies forgetting that the simple fact of being hypnotized and carrying out the suggestions made takes place within the framework of a dynamic relationship. The fact remains that there exists an essential difference between hysteria and hypnosis. The phenomenon of hysteria is part of a neurotic structure, whereas in hypnosis it is more a matter of a game in which symptoms can be reversed at will.

However that may be, hypnosis and hysteria have in common the fact that they use the same psychophysiological mechanism. One cannot really tackle the problem of hysteria without facing that of hypnosis.

---

[2] It is interesting to note that Nemiah, observing that no psychological conflicts seem to be found in psychosomatic patients (contrary to what occurs in hysterical conversion), prefers to use the term dissociation rather than the dynamic concepts of conversion and defense. He even postulates the existence in these patients of a disconnection between two cerebral areas, the limbic system and the neo-cortex (Nemiah, 1975).

7

Hypnosis, Relation Transference

Experimental psychologists, even when, like Hilgard, they acknowledge the specificity of hypnosis, do not study the relational factor. They cannot be blamed for it, for this variable is difficult to measure. Nevertheless, it does play a very important part in the hypnotic process. As soon as animal magnetism appeared as a concept, hypnosis was considered as a specific relationship—what Mesmer called the "rapport." As we have seen, Mesmer conceived this rapport as a physical action exerted on one subject by another. At the same time, he stressed the role played by will in the circulation of the fluid. Mesmer's successors emphasized more particularly the importance of the therapist's intention.

In the second half of the nineteenth century, hypnotists attempted to achieve a maximum depersonalization of the hypnotic relationship. It is well known that for Charcot hypnosis was a somatic state produced by physical causes. As for Bernheim, with his concept of suggestion, he laid stress on the psychological character of hypnosis. But he remained within the framework of a psychology conceived in terms of cerebral physiology. Other authors perceived the important link binding the hypnotist to the subject. Thus Binet (1888, p. 249) wrote: "The magnetized subject is like an exalted lover, for whom there exists nothing in the world but the loved one." Similarly, Janet spoke of "somnambulistic passion," declaring that this was "a very special form of love" (Janet, 1898, pp. 465-466). But it was with Freud that the dynamics underlying the hypnotic relationship first became intelligible, thanks to the discovery of transference. It is well known that Freud at first thought he could eliminate the transference by relinquishing hypnosis, and that he later rediscovered it within the analytical relationship.

Psychoanalysts were thus led to consider hypnosis as a particular form of transference relationship. Ferenczi (1909), for instance, made a distinction between a paternal hypnosis, based on fear, and a maternal hypnosis, based on love. Stress has often been laid on the passive, masochistic character of the hypnotic relationship.

Indeed, it cannot be denied that transference factors play an important role in this relationship. Thus, when it is asserted that the induction process constitutes a sort of sensory deprivation, it is clear that the term should be understood in its psychological as well as its physiological sense. Kubie did, of course, stress that hypnoid states could be brought about by purely sensorimotor manipulations. But in hypnosis as it is usually practiced, sensory deprivation is far from being so complete. The subject remains in partial contact with external stimuli. It is simply that his attention becomes focused on the person of the hypnotist. It is obvious that at this level the transference factor is involved. The fixation on the hypnotist will be all the more easily achieved as he represents for the subject a person endowed with affective significance (unless, on the contrary, this should turn out to be an obstacle). It is well known, for instance, that soldiers have a hypnotizability rate higher than the average, especially when the hypnotist holds a higher rank.

Moreover, hypnosis presupposes that the subject is willing to renounce certain controls in favor of the hypnotist. As Kubie wrote: "During the process of induction, with varying ease and in varying degrees, the subject temporarily abdicates the use of his own native, self-protecting and alerting mechanisms, placing himself and his sense of 'security' in the hands of another" (1961, p. 40).

The more the hypnotist is felt to be a protective figure, the more the subject will be inclined to accept hypnosis. Conversely, if the relationship to the hypnotist reactivates distressing conflicts, the subject can refuse to allow himself to be hypnotized. Thus Brenman, Gill and Knight (1952) have shown that fluctuations intervening in the transference have repercussions on the depth of the trance.

The transference can also influence the way the subject carries out hypnotic suggestions. Whether it be to accept them or to refuse them, his reaction is not indifferent. The simple fact that he is in a position of having to respond to the hypnotist's demands brings into play psychodynamic factors. His response is produced in relation to someone (the hypnotist) and it is obvious that something of the relationship which binds him to the latter becomes symbolized in it. Transference exists at this level as in every human relationship. This is no doubt the reason why hysterics, when they are hypnotizable, are often very good subjects. For them, the hypnotist's demand is charged with particularly intense significance and they respond to it all the better.

But, precisely because it applies to every relationship, one can wonder whether the concept of transference makes it possible to account for the specific nature of the hypnotic relationship.

It is true that the notion of transference has grown considerably richer as the history of psychoanalysis has progressively developed. At the beginning, transference was essentially conceived in relation to the Oedipal stage. The earliest stages of development have come to be increasingly studied, particularly under the influence of the English School and some American psychoanalysts (Melanie Klein, Winnicot, Greenacre, Jacobson, etc.). Stress has been laid on the relationship to the mother and on narcissism, that is to say on forms of communication which imply a certain undifferentiation of the individual and the environment (see below, p. 171).

Will this research bring some new knowledge to our understanding of hypnosis? It may perhaps shed light on certain of its aspects,[1] but the author does not believe that it will thus become possible to put forward a definition of its specific nature.

Transference, in fact, implies the intervention of a third figure. This already presupposes a certain subjective experience, as well as the elaboration of the beginnings of an organization at the level of fantasy and symbolism. We may ask ourselves whether the hypnotic relationship does not refer us back to a much more archaic dimension, a strictly dual, pre-objectal one – that of basic biological behavior, rooted in the animal world, where communication is situated at a purely affective level, preceding any representative content. This crude relational capacity would correspond with what ethologists have studied as the concept of imprint.[2] At this stage of man's development, the differentiation between psychic and somatic disappears; psychic contents become physiological realities.

It is all as though, at a given moment, there were a triggering which sets off

---

[1] One may in fact be surprised that authors studying such archaic relationships should take no interest in the hypnotic relationship.

[2] In an article entitled "Préliminaires d'une théorie ethologique de l'hypnose" ("Preliminaries to an ethological theory of hypnosis"), A. Demaret (1974) gives certain indications which lend support to this hypothesis.

the subject's automatic behavior and regression to an extremely primary stage of development. Which elements in the hypnotic situation are at the origin of this reorganization? As we have seen, there is the cutting off of relationships with the environment, and also – particularly at the relational level – the breaking of the structures that usually govern interhuman communication. In the course of the induction process, the subject, being placed in a position where he is unable to answer, loses, as it were, his place in the symbolic exchange. Thus, hypnotic behavior can be defined as an adjustment response to an unusual situation.

In this case, the subject would find himself returning to more primitive forms of communication, to a "purely affective" register, corresponding to the oldest structures of the nervous system, the paleocortex. This would be an *inborn, original, relational potentiality, constituting the matrix, the crucible where all future relationships will be inscribed.*

In actual fact, this original relationship is never produced in its pure form in man. As the individual progressively develops, more and more complex object relationships start to make their appearance. Thus, it can be said that relationship exists at two different levels, an inborn one and an acquired one. It is at the latter level that transference comes into play to reinforce – or counter – inborn hypnotizability. In other words, transference does not explain hypnotizability; rather it would account for non-hypnotizability.

The specific character of the hypnotic relationship was stressed by Freud in one of his last works concerning hypnosis, *Group Psychology and the Analysis of the Ego* (Freud, 1921). He emphasized the fact that this relationship constituted a largely enigmatic phenomenon,[3] whose main features lay in what he called a "purity of the attitudes of the libido" (p. 116, *Reinheit der Libidoeinstellungen*), and the existence of a "state of being in love, with the directly sexual trends excluded" (*ibid.,* p. 115). It is quite clear from the ensuing lines of the above-mentioned work that it is an inborn aptitude which is concerned here, preceding any object cathexis. In fact, Freud there advanced the hypothesis that hypnosis is the reappearance of a state which was once really experienced and has entered into the phylogenetic heritage – that it reproduces the relationship with the primal Father, as it was constituted at the beginning of the human family. The historic and scientific

---

[3] Amongst the elements which seemed to him to constitute the puzzle (p. 115) of hypnosis, Freud mentioned the variability of hypnotic susceptibility according to the individual.

postulates on which this hypothesis rests are more than questionable. But it shows that Freud was conscious of the specific character of the hypnotic relationship. In the same work, he also emphasized the relationship between human hypnosis and animal hypnosis. Schilder (1922), Schilder and Kauders (1926), and Pavlov (1921) similarly stressed this point.

A careful perusal of this work shows that these statements apply not only to hypnosis, but to the phenomenon of suggestion as a whole. Indeed, in this work Freud endeavored to define the "collective mind," that is, the nature of the psychological bond on which the cohesion of human societies is based. He found a privileged model in what he called "the crowd," which he described as a gathering of individuals linked together by means of the identical relationship they maintain with the figure of the "chief" – in other words, with the father figure. The fact that this is a somewhat summary and schematic definition of social life does not concern us here. It will simply be noted that this question led Freud to a lengthy reflection on the nature of identification, love, and hypnosis. He defined the latter as a "group of two," a formation halfway between love and the group since, like the former, it functions within the framework of a dual relationship; on the other hand, the hypnotized subject finds himself linked to the hypnotist by a relationship of identification similar to that which binds the members of the group to the figure of the chief. That, wrote Freud, is why: "Hypnosis would solve the riddle of the libidinal constitution of groups for us straight away, if it were not that it itself exhibits some features which are not met by the rational explanation . . ." (1921, p. 115). Thus, the enigma of hypnosis is clearly indicated as that which surrounds the very principle of all suggestibility, as that "primary identification" which is the prerequisite of all relational life and all psychotherapy.

8

Brief Historical Comments

What exactly is psychotherapy? An individual in a given state of distress decides to call upon the help of someone else. He will appeal to a specific person because, in view of the social consensus, he *believes* that this person is endowed with knowledge and a gift for healing. Belief is the prerequisite which will allow changes to take place.

This belief is sometimes sufficient in itself. Such is the case in what is called the placebo effect in which the administration of an inert substance which the patient believes to be endowed with therapeutic powers may act to suppress the symptom. In fact, the placebo always implies the intervention of another person, who actually prescribes it. Even when this other person is not physically present, he is always there in a kind of symbolic way: science, the medical institution, etc. The placebo is an indirect suggestion.

Sometimes, the therapeutic process takes the form of direct suggestion: "Rise up and walk." For example, warts can sometimes be caused to disappear by a simple verbal suggestion assuring the subject that at a given date they will have vanished.

The term "suggestion," as used here, is rather unprecise and often covers a number of meanings. Bernheim, the first to have used it so extensively, defined it thus: "the influence exerted by a suggested idea that is accepted by the brain" (Bernheim, 1884, p. 73). Since then, the meaning has widened to include more or less every form of influence. When a patient is said to have been cured by means of suggestion, this implies that his recovery rests on the influence exercised on the patient by the therapist, not on any real change that might have occurred at the organic or psychological level.

On the other hand, therapies such as psychoanalysis bring into play such elements as taking past experiences into consideration, revealing conflicts and unconscious fantasies, etc., with the aim of attaining an actual alteration of the subject's personality. By virtue of this, they require a complex procedure involving a length of time and successive stages.

Finally, one may on occasion resort to techniques involving the manipulation of the subject's state of consciousness: relaxation, hypnosis, prolonged sleep treatment, or chemical agents; or else one may seek to operate at the level of learning and conditioning.

These different approaches always interfere with one another to a greater or lesser degree. Nevertheless, they represent modes of access to the symptom which can be used more or less distinctly. Whatever method is used, the passage from a state of ill-being to a state of well-being consists basically in an affective rearrangement, which is essentially brought about through a relational process.

Some of these modes of intervention have been known to us since time immemorial. For centuries they were the essence of the art of healing as practiced by sorcerers, shamans, medicine-men, etc., and they still are today in so-called primitive societies. We can define this "traditional" medicine as a mixture of direct suggestion (the belief in the sorcerer's power and will to help the patient is the mainspring of his therapeutic action) and indirect suggestion (for the most part, he operates through a ritual: incantations, magic objects, and gestures, etc.). Diverse forms of manipulation of states of consciousness often play an important role here: the taking of drugs, fasting techniques, bodily manipulation designed to produce the effects of sensory deprivation, etc. In fact, these three elements are often intermingled.

In certain cases, this therapeutic action can assume very elaborate forms, reminiscent of present-day psychotherapeutic techniques. In a famous article, Lévi-Strauss analysed in this way the mechanisms of what he calls the shamanic cure (1958, pp. 187–205). He started from a ritual used by a South American tribe for difficult childbirth. In this ritual the shaman mimes for the parturient the process of childbirth in the form of a struggle with the spirits, the different stages of which correspond to those of her labor. Lévi-Strauss shows how this scenario provides the patient with a kind of guideline allowing her to regulate the chaos of her bodily sensations and to produce the physiological responses required by the situation. Thus, the cure functions due to the correspondence between two series – on the one hand, the bodily procedures; on the other, the intellectual activities around which the myth is structured, this homology allowing the shaman to manipulate the former through the latter. This is what Lévi-Strauss terms symbolic efficiency. The shaman, as he states, "provides the sick woman with a *language*, by means of which unexpressed, and otherwise inexpressible, psychic states can be immediately expressed. And it is the transition to this verbal expression – at the same time making it possible to undergo in an ordered and intelligible form a real experience that would otherwise be chaotic and inexpressible – which induces the release of the physiological process, that is, the reorganization, in a favorable direction, of the process to which the sick woman is subjected" (1958, p. 188).

It will be observed that the cure is effective only because it is experienced at the affective level. "The shaman," as Lévi-Strauss further states, "is a professional abreactor" (*ibid.*, p. 181). He literally puts himself in the place of the parturient. An important part of his song is devoted to the description of her sufferings, which in turn allows her to identify with him and obey his suggestions. This is a process that psychoanalysts would term transferential. Lévi-Strauss actually establishes the comparison with psychoanalysis: "it is true that in the shamanistic cure the sorcerer speaks and abreacts *for* the silent patient, while in psychoanalysis it is the patient who talks and abreacts *against* the listening therapist" (*ibid.*, p. 183).

In his analysis, Lévi-Strauss totally eschews the alterations which take place at the level of the state of consciousness. This aspect does, however, play a role in the curative process. To be convinced of this, it suffices to reread the account. One cannot but be struck by the repetitive character of the incantations, by the way that everything is conceived in order that attention will be increasingly centered on the person of the shaman. These are the very elements that characterize hypnotic induction. And, as we have already seen, hypnosis is sometimes used today for difficult deliveries.

This aspect does not contradict the explanation put forward by Lévi-Strauss. In fact, it appears to be complementary. One can, indeed, say that the induction process consists in establishing this correspondence between words and bodily sensations, which is, according to him, the mainspring of the cure. This occurs partly because in induction language serves directly to suggest sensations (your eyes are closing, your body is becoming heavier, etc.), but above all because it is used at a purely sensory level, as a physiological stimulus designed to reinforce the process of "de-afferentiation" (through rhythm, use of the voice, etc.). With induction, the difference between language and body tends to disappear. Thus, hypnosis appears particularly apt to promote the mechanism of symbolization.

A difference can, however, be noted. In the case of hypnosis, the process does not entail the setting up of a mythical universe. The hypnotist does not call upon the spirit world. Moreover, Lévi-Strauss shows that in the shamanic cure the presence of the group is very important. In hypnosis, it is not indispensable.

But these differences may perhaps be more superficial than real. What is expressed by means of the myth used in the shamanic cure (the struggle with the spirits) is a representation of the bodily functions, a way of naming the organs. Of course, the sorcerer is supposed to receive his power from the spirits. But can it not be said that the hypnotist, as any other doctor, is always regarded as something of a sorcerer? In this respect, even if the group is not physically present, the belief of the group is essential.

This passage of Lévi-Strauss is interesting in many ways, especially in that it makes it easier to understand the mechanism of the psychosomatic inter-action, the manner in which bodily functions can be manipulated by a procedure of a psychological nature. But one is rather left with the impression that for Lévi-Strauss the curative process is reduced to a series of logical operations. In actual fact, these operations are only effective provided there exists an affective participation on the part of the subject. Lévi-Strauss seems to take this participation for granted.

It is the social consensus which renders the subject receptive to the shaman's action. In the author's opinion, this is not sufficient. Symbolic effectiveness implies a specific "affective circulation" between healer and healed. This link remains very largely unknown, and constitutes the essential mystery of psychotherapy.

It is with Mesmer that the problem of psychotherapy entered an experi-mental phase. The mesmeric cure consisted, through a series of bodily mani-pulations (or passes), in inducing "somatic discharges," "salutary crises" which relieved the patient, and sometimes brought about the disappearance of the symptom. There was no talking during the treatment, so there were no direct verbal injunctions. However, these were implicit in the therapist's attitude. The passes, the music, the setting, the atmosphere round the tub ("baquet") were factors which were indirectly to increase the effect of the suggestion, but also contributed in producing a kind of "sensory deprivation" which induced an alteration of the state of consciousness, gradually ending in the "crisis."

Mesmer's patients did not all have attacks. Some showed, rather, a sort of lethargy, while still being able to walk, talk, etc. In other words, they were hypnotized. A disciple of Mesmer's, the Marquis de Puységur, centered his research on this phenomenon, which he named magnetic somnambulism. He observed that, in this state, symptoms could be acted upon by speech. The perspective was completely altered. The model of the crisis was abandoned in favor of action largely based on a verbal dialogue.

The treatment practiced by Puységur and his disciples was, in fact, fairly complex. Like Mesmer, they made "passes" over the subject designed to induce somnambulism while exerting a curative action by giving their patients "magnetized" water, amulets, etc. But the most important innovation introduced by Puységur and his disciples was to intensify the mechanism of suggestion by manipulating the relational factor in a more complex manner. They made no explicit mention of this aspect, except to point out that the doctor's "moral and physical sympathy" toward his patients was an indispensable condition of treatment. Through their works one can see a theory of the magnetic cure (de Saussure, 1968, and in Chertok and de Saussure, 1979, pp. 30–35) emerging, which shows that they had implicitly perceived relational dynamics.

Puységur (1811) and Deleuze (1825) were thus the first to understand that magnetic treatment was a process implying a certain duration, submitted to precise rules and comprising well-defined stages. Their observations on this subject were very close to those expressed by Freud on the psychoanalytical treatment. They pointed out that sessions must be regular, both in frequency and in duration. Like the psychoanalyst, the magnetist must remain neutral and patient when faced with the manifestations of his subject; he should not worry when the latter's symptoms show a temporary recurrence. Without understanding why, they had felt that, since the development of the treatment proceeded entirely at a "somatic" level, the subject had to go through a series of successive abreactions (in this case the reactivation of painful feelings) if the therapeutic action were to produce any results.

Finally, and this is the most important point, Puységur and Deleuze well and truly turned the tables by placing the magnetists in the position of listener with regard to the patient. One of the most original aspects of this method is that the latter was urged to verbalize his symptom. While he was in deep magnetic sleep, he was asked to establish his own diagnosis (the seat and nature of his ailment) and the form of his treatment, with regard to the remedies involved as well as to the magnetist's manipulations. He was also asked to predict the development of his treatment: when he would recover, when the attacks would occur, etc. Thus was produced a kind of psychodrama in which the patient caused the magnetist to play a part in a series of successive catharses. The body became the basis of a relational exchange, of a triggering and expression of fantasies (vomiting, diarrhea, fainting fits and other psychosomatic symptoms).

This treatment was possible, of course, only with true somnambulists, whereas with slightly hypnotizable persons its action was necessarily superficial. On the whole, the magnetic treatment was much more complex than simple suggestion. From this point of view, subsequent developments show a sort of regression. The second half of the nineteenth century, in fact, is characterized by two factors. On the one hand, there is an observable evolution of induction techniques. Faria (1819), followed by Braid (1843), showed that passes are not necessary for the induction of the hypnotic state, but that the latter can be produced by fixation of a bright object, accompanied by a verbal injunction.[1] At the same time, hypnotism became medicalized. This was the period of the triumph of medicine during which it acquired anatomo-physiological bases and turned to the study of cerebral localization. Thus was elaborated a physiological theory of hypnosis as "sleep," a special state of the nervous system produced by the concentration of attention (Braid, 1843; Liébeault, 1866).

Simultaneously, there was an awareness of the role played by verbal suggestion in induction and hypnotic manifestations. Indeed, experiments showed that it is possible to produce all sorts of psychophysiological phenomena by the power of words alone. The appearance of a concept of suggestion, through the works of Braid (1843), Liébeault (1866), and Bernheim (1884), corresponds, in a way, to the recognition of the psychological character of hypnosis. But suggestion is then defined on the basis of current neurophysiological theories, in a purely mechanistic manner. The relational dynamics foreshadowed by the magnetists thus came to be eliminated in favor of a less elaborate conception of the therapeutic process, conceived on the model of direct suggestion.

On the other hand, this growing number of experiments opened the way to spheres of psychic life which had remained hitherto unexplored. Charcot, by producing through hypnotic suggestion paralyses and other hysterical symptoms, brought to light the influence of psychic action on physiological

---

[1] The theory of animal magnetism, according to which hypnosis is the result of a fluid passing between the hypnotist and the hypnotized subject, was thus definitely abandoned.

processes. Bernheim's (1884, pp. 18 seqq.) and Richet's (1887, p. 193) experiments on post-hypnotic suggestion provided experimental proof that acts could be carried out which depended on representations unknown to the subject himself. In other words, there existed an unconscious memory.

The study of multiple personalities and the experiments on age-regression (Azam, 1860; Bourru and Burot, 1888; Binet, 1892) showed that there existed in the human mind a whole body of unconscious material made of fantasies, memories, etc., to which intense affectivity was often attached. Thus the concept of a psychological unconscious gradually evolved. The importance of the past experiences of the subject in the formation of neurotic symptoms was realized. It was noticed that the reactivation of these experiences sometimes brought about the disappearance of the symptoms. Suggestion came to be used in an entirely new way, in order to make possible the re-emergence of forgotten memories (Chertok, 1960).

Freud built up the psychoanalytical edifice on the basis of these data. He gave a scientific meaning to the word "suggestion" by showing that the effects of suggestibility originated in the subject's libidinal cathexes. In analytic treatment, however, suggestion is mobilized for work on the unconscious which is the true motivating force in therapeutic work. Ideally, it should disappear once this work has been done. But if one takes, for instance, the case of a "successful" analysis, how is one to know whether this success is truly the sign of a resolution of the unconscious conflicts or if it is not due to a simple effect of suggestion? And, whether or not the analysis is largely the equivalent of a placebo? This problem has often preoccupied psychoanalysts. Suffice it to recall the controversies which arose about the resolution of the transference. On the subject of hypnosis we have seen, in the preceding chapter, that beyond transference there remains an archaic primary level of the relation. It is the author's view that this aspect exists in all forms of therapy and that our ignorance in this sphere is responsible for a great many uncertainties.

9

The Psychotherapeutic Process

It is apparent that we do not have the methodological tools which would allow us to ascertain with certainty that a given therapeutic action will produce a given effect. Even when the treatment produces a positive result, it is practically impossible to tell which causes were really effective or even whether this result should be ascribed to the therapy or to a spontaneous process.

The great psychoanalytical idea which inspired the entire development of modern psychotherapy was that since neurosis was the product of psychological factors, it could be treated by these same factors. It is well known that Freud conceived this idea during his stay in Paris, when he saw Charcot producing – and removing – experimental paralyses through suggestion; "What one has done, one can undo" (Charcot, 1889, p. 259). Unfortunately, the results did not correspond with what might have been hoped for. There lies between the theory and the practice of psychoanalysis a serious discrepancy, indeed an abyss. We may perfectly well understand the origins of a symptom without in any way thereby having the means to suppress it. Paradoxically, the more clearly the psychological evolution of the illness appears, as for example in the case of delusions, the more difficult it is to intervene. Even classical transference neuroses – conversion hysteria, phobia, obsessional neurosis – which are the privileged realm of psychoanalytical investigation have proved extremely resistant to treatment,[1]

[1] Is this the reason why, in the United States, some psychoanalysts are turning increasingly to the treatment of "narcissistic" pathology (Kernberg, 1975; Kohut, 1971), an entity covering cases between neurosis and psychosis which more or less correspond to those termed "borderline"?

An American psychoanalyst to whom the author mentioned this idea suggested another explanation. In his opinion, it is not the psychoanalysts who are no longer interested in the neuroses, but those patients who prefer to try out other, easier and more rapid, forms of treatment. More and more today, the patients of psychoanalysts comprise difficult cases, for despite the lengthening of standard cures. Therapeutic results bear no relation to the vast fund of theoretical knowledge which has been accumulated.

A team of research workers at Paris VII University (Brès *et al.*, 1977) has devoted an article to the question of the length of analysis, in which are reproduced, in particular, the statistics published in 1922 by Eitingon covering 2 years' activities at the Berlin Institute of Psychoanalysis (Eitingon, 1922). Looking at these figures, one cannot but be struck by the number of recoveries obtained within an extremely short time by present standards: In 1921, 8 months for an obsessional neurosis, 6 months for an anxiety hysteria; in 1922, 4 months for an obsessional neurosis, and so on. Were these exceptionally favorable cases, or were therapists at the time less exacting in their criteria of recovery than they are today? Must we believe that the curative power of psychoanalysis was greater then than now? Did the factor of suggestion not play an essential role?

In the same article, the authors emphasize the progressive lengthening of the training analysis. In Berlin in 1922, the latter lasted from 6 months to 1 year. In 1935 the Vienna Institute of Psychoanalysis recommended 2 years. In London in 1947 it was estimated that at least 4 years were required. In France at the present time, the authors advise a period of 9 or 10 years for analyses undergone by "all this crowd of teachers, psychologists, psychoanalysts, and those aspiring to the psychoanalytic profession, who constitute today a large part of the analysts' patients, at least in Paris" (Brès *et al.*, 1977, p. 153).[2] Analyses which are strictly therapeutic are generally shorter, but they too have considerably lengthened since the beginning of psychoanalysis. It is true that, while analyses are becoming longer, some psychoanalysts, especially in France, are tending to shorten the sessions.[3]

which other types of therapy have proved ineffective. However that may be, present research on narcissistic pathology is interesting from a theoretical point of view. But it is still too recent for its therapeutic effectiveness to be assessed, and it may be predicted that it will come up against the thorny problem of the validation of results.

[2] In France, these patients are becoming increasingly numerous. In a recent article, André Green (1978b, p. 23) has concerned himself with this phenomenon. He considers that "involvement in the psy profession" (*psy*, not *psi*, in France means psychology, psychiatry, psychoanalysis) has become a mode of social regulation, the equivalent of what, for a certain number of people, was formerly represented by the entry into institutions such as the army, the convent, or the colonial service: "modes of cure no worse than any others." The only difference is that today "the psychoanalytic institutions provide the institutional framework in which this cure can be obtained with a label and diploma." Added to that is the prospect of later having a comfortable income and the assurance of maintaining the psychic equilibrium so dearly acquired, thanks to a continuous supply of such patient-therapists.

[3] Five to thirty minutes for the Lacanians. The analyst senses that a knot has been touched on, that the session has to be interrupted, and that it is then up to the analysand to go and do his homework. This shortening of sessions was one of the reasons for Lacan's expulsion from the International Psycho-analytical Association.

Psychoanalysis Challenged

This therapeutic disappointment has aroused the latent hostility of non-analysts, towards whom Freudian psychoanalysts have always shown an élitist and condescending attitude. In the United States, a frontal attack has been launched against psychodynamics as a whole. An example of this can be found in a recent volume, *What Makes Behavior Change Possible?* (Burton, 1976). The Editor, Burton, questions the usefulness of all psychoanalytic concepts in the understanding of curative processes. In his view, it was wrong to stress the existence of an unconscious memory and the role of childhood experiences. The only important things are the conscious and present reality, and the encounter with the therapist, inasmuch as he represents for the subject a model and a source of love. Burton is influenced by the scepticism towards science prevailing at the present time in the United States, and he emphasizes what he calls the S-Factor (from the word "soul"), which, he explains, is "the non-organic part of the psyche" (Burton, 1976, p. 147), "a factor non-describable in scientific terms, but which is manifested through its effects" (*ibid.*).[4] Communication with the therapist corresponds to a transcendent communication, a "cosmic feeling of oneness" (*ibid.*). In other terms: It is faith which saves. (See p. 164.)

Some authors even go so far as to say that psychoanalysis is anti-therapeutic. Thus Fix and Haffke write, in a study of the comparative effectiveness of psychotherapies: "Psychoanalytical techniques maintain communication models which are exactly the reverse of those factors which make it possible for a psychotherapy to be beneficent" (1976, p. 102).

Today, we seem to be witnessing a reaction similar to that which occurred with regard to hypnosis after Charcot's death. In order to explain the disaffection of the medical profession toward hypnosis, Janet wrote: "The enthusiastic exaggerations of the hypnotists had brought about the random applications of hypnotism in all sorts of disease, without any indication of its fitness, and that the usual results were meaningless or absurd" (Janet, 1924, p. 30). Hypnosis had indeed become a panacea, a miracle remedy for all ailments. The disillusion was in proportion to the expectations. In the case of psychoanalysis, too much hope may have been placed in it, making disappointment inevitable.

---

[4]This is Mesmer's definition of the fluid. But the fluid did, all the same, refer to a very elaborate conceptual system, which is not the case here.

But on a deeper plane, we may wonder whether this is not a new manifestation of the resistances which appear each time progress is made in the knowledge of the unconscious. Whether it was made by Mesmer, Charcot or Freud, each step forward in the exploration of this mysterious and disquieting realm has provoked violent reactions. In the United States, psychoanalysis was widely accepted. But from the first, this acceptance was accompanied by certain reservations. By emphasizing the autonomy of the ego, its independence in relation to instinctual drives, American psychoanalysis has "tamed" the unconscious, has deprived it of its disquieting aspect. The plague Freud boasted he was bringing to America has become a simple case of measles. We can only believe that this was not enough. Taking advantage of the fact that psychoanalysis is, as it were, marking time, there are some today who are seeking to evacuate the entire Freudian edifice. Of course, this "resistential" trend represents but one part of American psychiatry. As we shall see later, other research workers advocate a more thorough study of psychoanalytical theory, starting from those elements specific to the analytical situation.

The Multiplication of Psychotherapies

Simultaneously with this new calling into question of psychoanalysis, we are today witnessing a veritable profusion of all kinds of therapies, collective as well as individual.[5] Parloff (1975) counted as many as 140.

Karasu (1977) attempted to classify psychotherapies into three main groups: psychodynamic, behavioral, and "experiential." The first group comprises all the therapies inspired by Freudian or neo-Freudian theories. In contrast, behavior therapy is based on learning and conditioning. Finally, the third group brings together, somewhat artificially (and improperly), such different therapies as Binswanger's existential analysis, Boss's Daseinanalyse, Frankl's Logotherapy, Rogers' Therapy, Gestalt Therapy, the Primal Scream, bio-energetic analysis, Autogenic training, Transcendental

[5] Stephen Appelbaum, an orthodox psychoanalyst from the Menninger clinic, gives a pessimistic description of the state of analytical therapy in the U.S.A. "A tiger growls at the gates of psychoanalysis . . . psychoanalytic patients are harder to find. . . . In the last decade a host of other psychotherapeutic theories and techniques, loosely referred to as the human potential movement, have had a phenomenal growth. . . . In short, two decades ago when one was dissatisfied with his life, he had a limited choice as to what to do about it. Now he can turn in many directions, only one of which is psychoanalytic therapy" (1977, p. 675).

Meditation, Nirvana Therapy, Zen Psychedelic Therapy, etc. In a recent work entitled *Le Corps et le Groupe (Body and Group)* Schutzenberger and Sauret (1977) have listed a large number of these treatments and added others such as ideotherapy, groups naked or in bathing shorts, and many more. Most of these techniques are now appearing in France. They are practiced not always by professional therapists, psychiatrists, doctors, psychologists, etc., but also by individuals with no particular qualification, when they are not, as is often the case, former patients initiated to psychotherapy through their own treatment.[6] To quote a quip often heard in the United States: Soon one half of the population will be treating the other half.

In such conditions, it is to be feared that the limits of psychotherapy will become less and less clearly defined. How, indeed, is one to establish the difference between a session of psychotherapy and a friendly conversation or a week's group relaxation at the Club Méditerranée?[7]

Behavior Therapy

This technique first appeared in the 1950s and was at first applied especially in the treatment of phobias. However, its indications have become increasingly wide and now extend to alcoholism, sexual disorders, psychosomatic syndromes, depressions, marital problems, etc. It is progressively

---

[6] This tradition, in fact, comes to us from Mesmer. He was in favor of laymen practicing psychotherapy, considering that personal experience of the "magnetic rapport" was more important for the knowledge of animal magnetism than medical studies. It thus happened that several of his patients became magnetists. From the start, Mesmer's position on these questions provoked many reactions on the part of the medical profession (Chertok, 1966 b; Rausky, 1977). It is interesting to note that the same polemic took place one century later, over psychoanalysis, Freud being, like Mesmer, in favor of the practice of analysis by laymen. The debate is still going on today.

[7] I do not underestimate the possibilities of spontaneous group psychotherapy, in clubs or similar places; I have, indeed, known a patient suffering from serious communication problems who could only succeed in being happy and establishing relationships with others during his regular stays at the Club Méditerranée. Nor should one underestimate the help that can be contributed by non-professionals to the treatment of patients. Indeed, some turn out to be excellent therapists. I have in mind one of my patients, a suicidal depressive, who, asked to give foreign language lessons to schizophrenics in a day hospital for therapeutic purposes, was much appreciated by her pupils and was able to establish a very good contact with them which proved to be beneficial.

tending to invade the whole field of psychiatry. Meichenbaum (1977), for instance, treats schizophrenics by combining behavior therapy with what he calls the inner dialogue, not to mention pedagogy, the social sciences, etc. J. Cottraux (1978a) has just published in French a well-documented work on the different aspects of behavior therapy.

The author does not question the effectiveness of these behavioral techniques in a certain number of cases.[8] On the other hand, the theoretic postulates of behavior therapy seem to him extremely precarious. The way Cottraux approaches the question of hypnosis and suggestion is a significant example. Among the forerunners of behavior therapy, he mentions "the French psychologist, Coué" (who was in fact a pharmacist), the inventor of the famous method of autosuggestion. Indeed, in his view, Coué would have been "the first to have proposed methods of thought-control and emphasized the role of positive thought in the modification of behavior" (Cottraux, 1978, p. 11). The least one can say is that this is a somewhat reductionist conception of the mode of action of suggestion. The same observation applies to the idea according to which hypnosis is another forerunner of behavioral techniques, insofar as it acts as a "reciprocal inhibition" (*ibid.*, p. 11) and makes possible the systematic desensitizing of phobics.

It is not proposed to consider here in detail all the controversies which have surrounded behavior therapy. It does, however, seem of interest to report the criticism of Soviet authors, which are little known in the West.

Although it claims to derive from Pavlovian reflexology, this therapy is virtually not used in the Soviet Union. On the contrary, Soviet psychotherapy is tending to become increasingly "dynamic." In 1978, Lichko, a representative of the psychotherapeutically oriented School of Leningrad, while asserting that Pavlov's teaching should form the basis of medical psychology, believed that behavior therapists were using this theory in a "primitive-simplistic" manner.

For his part, Shternberg (1978), of the more organicist and pharmacodynamically oriented Muscovite School of Snezhnievski, in a review of the collective work, *Progress in Behaviour Therapy* (Breugelmann, 1975), comprising 36 papers presented at a meeting of the European Association of Behavior Therapy, shows a more than guarded attitude toward this form of treatment. According to him, this work has no interest whatever for the Soviet reader. It could, at most, serve to inform

---

[8] In fact we have introduced in our Center (where most of the psychotherapists are psychoanalytically oriented) a behavior therapist. Without yet being able to assess the results obtained, it can be said that she has shown an ability to take into care cases which are usually resistant to all forms of treatment (serious phobias, obsessional neuroses, etc., against which analytical treatment is for the most part powerless).

specialized therapists about Western fashions. He does, however, advise a "cautious and critical" appraisal. He particularly attacks Skinnerian conditioning (reward and punishment) and regards as naive the technique of electric shock aversion therapy, such as it is used, for instance, in the treatment of sexual perversions, including homosexuality. (It may be noted that Shternberg and Skinner are both in agreement as to the classification of homosexuality among the perversions.)

Another representative of the Leningrad School, Zachepitski, expressed the greatest reservations with regard to behavior therapy. He stressed that Pavlov was very critical of Watson, the creator of behaviorism, and that he criticized the explanation of human learning through conditioned reflexes. Bekhterev did, however, attempt to create a therapy based on the concept of the conditioned reflex. In the 1920s these forms of therapy did indeed have a certain vogue in the Soviet Union, but the results proved disappointing and their practice was abandoned. These therapies are still used occasionally, but in a psychotherapeutic context where the subject's personality, his history and his inter- and intrasubjective conflicts are taken into consideration – in other words, within the framework of a "pathogenetic" therapy, i.e. one based on a conscious elucidation of the psychological origins of the illness. Soviet psychotherapists always lay great stress on this aspect. It may be said that like Monsieur Jourdain, although they do not refer to the concepts of transference and counter-transference, they use them without knowing it. They practice the empathy so dear to the psychoanalysts of the British school. "They do care," Masud Khan would say, unlike French psychoanalysts, whom he reproaches for placing themselves on too intellectual a plane, to the prejudice of affective interaction (Green, 1976, p. 11).

I recall in this connection the account of a Franco-American child psychoanalyst of a visit she had made to the Soviet Union years ago to see how autistic children were treated there. She spoke of her admiration for what was being done in that country and expressed her regret that we did not have, in our institutions, those warm-hearted *babouchkas,* so much more effective than so many of our analyzed nurses who face the problem of their counter-transference every time they wipe a child's bottom.

Generally speaking, the psychological conceptions of the Soviets are less rigid than one would tend to think in the West. In 1934 Pavlov himself could write that in certain cases ("blocked affects") it might be necessary to resort to the "posivite art of Freud" (Pavlov, 1934, p. 296). From 1956 on, psychology was freed from the ascendancy of physiology, and interest in the unconscious became increasingly marked. Ten years ago Bassin (1968) and Sherozia (1969, 1973) published works on this subject. In another work, Sherozia asserts that Freud's discoveries (1978, I, p. 38) rank amongst the "Copernican" discoveries. How far removed we are from "psychoanalysis, a reactionary ideology" (Levocivi *et al.,* 1949, pp. 57–72). However, Sherozia and Bassin reproach Freud with emphasizing more the antagonism between the unconscious and the conscious than their synergy. (It may be noted that James T. McLaughlin (1978), an American psychoanalyst, has also attempted to call in question the antagonism between primary and secondary processes, in the light of the available data on the specialization of the cerebral hemispheres.) But for all that, they make use of concepts of conflict (Bassin, Rozhnov and Rozhnova, 1974) and psychological defense (Bassin, 1971), repression being only one of the several modes of the latter.[9] Finally, over the last few years, the Soviets have shown particular interest in the efforts of French Marxists to bridge the gap between psychoanalysis and Marxism, through the approach of structuralist theories. Structuralism is, in fact, opposed to Freud's biologism, and makes it possible to establish a link between the unconscious and Society, insofar as it grants a privileged position to language. The book by Clement, Bruno, and Sève (1973), which represents one of the most far-reaching attempts in this direction, was translated into Russian with a positive preface by Bassin and Rozhnov (1976).

A young Muscovite philosopher, Avtonomova, has devoted a whole book to structuralism in France (Avtonomova, 1977a), and has translated and written a preface to Michel Foucault's book, *Les Mots et les Choses* (*Words and Things*) (Avtonomova, 1977b). It is interesting, moreover, to recall that, as early as 1927, a Soviet author, Voloshinov, had written a book entitled *A Marxist Critique of Freudism* (Voloshinov, 1927), in which he stressed the relationship between the unconscious and language. The editors who produced an English version of this book considered Voloshinov as a forerunner of Lacan.

It is interesting to note that, while the behavior therapists claim affinity with Pavlov, other American psychologists are today discovering a far less "mechanistic" Pavlov. Toulmin (1978) emphasizes that the interpretation which gave rise to Pavlovian theories in the West rests on an error in translation. In actual fact, Pavlov did not speak of "conditioned," but of "conditional" reflexes. For him, it was a question of studying the differences between the reflexes which appear "unconditionally" (the automatic reflexes) and those which appear only "under certain conditions." In other words, one must understand how an active organism reacts to a total environment. But he never claimed to reduce all modes of behavior to a passive response to external stimuli. Inasmuch as man is not subjected to the same conditions as animals (and Pavlov always placed great emphasis on the importance of language), the mechanisms applicable to the latter cannot explain human psychic activity as a whole. Western researchers, in Toulmin's

---

[9] Bassin defines psychological defense as "a normal mechanism, which can easily be discovered, directed towards the prevention of behavior disorders and biological processes, not only in conflicts between the conscious and the 'unconscious,' but also in entirely conscious conflicts between affectively loaded attitudes" (1971, p. 279).

Rozhnov and Burno (1978) believe that Bassin borrowed this term from psychoanalysis, but gave it a new meaning by integrating it in "dialectico-materialist psychophysiology" (p. 346).

opinion, committed this error in interpretation because it agreed with their own behaviorist premises.

In the United States there exists today an "ecumenical" trend which seeks to combine the behaviorist and psychodynamic orientations (Wachtel, 1977; Marmor and Woods, 1980a). But generally speaking, the struggle between these two trends is very intense and the behaviorists' hostility surpasses that of the psychoanalysts. While some of the latter accept the existence, in analysis, of a part of conditioning or learning (Alexander, 1963), the behavior therapists want no part of transference, unconscious, or repression. The polemic sometimes assumes an acid tone: thus Cottraux writes that "hermetism, listenism and metaphysical gongorism all too often turn psychoanalysts into an *aboli bibelot d'inanité sonore*,[10] the kitsch form of which would not be out of place in the drawing-rooms of *A la Recherche du Temps Perdu* (Cottraux, 1978a, p. 174).

Validation Attempts

There has never been such a vast choice of psychotherapies as there is today; nor has there ever been such uncertainty as to their relative effectiveness.[11] Attempts have been made, since the 1950s, to make an objective, "quantitative" evaluation of the results obtained and the curative factors involved in different psychotherapies. In 1952, Eysenck, an English psychologist from London's Maudsley Hospital, issued a real challenge when he asserted, on the basis of existing studies, that psychotherapy had no effect on neuroses and that recoveries were due to spontaneous remission (Eysenck, 1952). In order to refute these pessimistic conclusions, many authors have

---

[10] A quotation from Mallarmé – the "sonorous inanity" or an "aboli bibelot," the latter being indeed, phonetically at least, an "abolished bauble," i.e. a worthless trinket (Translator's note).

[11] In a study published in 1975, Marmor stressed the fact that psychoanalysts with very different orientations (Freudian, Jungian, Adlerian, etc.), and even therapists practicing non-dynamic therapies such as behavior therapy, seem to obtain similar results. He concluded that these results depend not so much on the method used as on the therapist's degree of experience and his personality. He also believes that in all psychotherapies the same factors, in varying proportions, are always involved. He lists eight such factors, comprising a good relationship with the therapist, the lessening of emotional tension, the patient's insight into his difficulties, reconditioning, learning, suggestion, identification with the therapist, etc. (Marmor, 1975).

sought to demonstrate the effectiveness of psychotherapy through the application of statistical data. These researchers have been supported, especially in the last few years, by government organizations and insurance companies concerned with the ever-increasing importance of the place which psychotherapy occupies in the national budget. According to a recent survey by a commission appointed by President Carter (President's Commission on Mental Health, 1978), 20 to 30 million Americans are in need of psychological aid at some time or another. Indeed this figure is considered as too low by some, who consider that 40 million Americans suffer from emotional disorders requiring specialized treatment. The American epidemiologist, Dohrenwend, came to a similar conclusion (1979) after analyzing sixteen surveys concerning the population of Europe and North America: in his view, 15% of these subjects are suffering from psychic disorders demanding appropriate treatment.

There are, of course, other forms of treatment than psychotherapy. Yet the latter still remains one of the most commonly used methods and it is understandable that attempts are being made to determine more precisely its degree of effectiveness.

It took many years for this research to acquire a relatively strict methodology. In 1955 Meehl analysed 200 articles, published between May 1953 and May 1954, all concerning questions of psychotherapy.[12] He observed that, as far as the evaluation of results was concerned, none of these articles was based on truly scientific criteria (control groups, precise case studies before and after psychotherapy, follow-ups), and that none helped to explain which were the operative factors in the cure (Meehl, 1955). Since the 1950s there have been more surveys, and the methods have been improved. Conscious of the fact that one cannot really apply a quantitative evaluation to the experience and the feelings of patients, these authors' main purpose was to study the impact of various therapies by basing their work on behavioral evidence, in the widest sense of the word: the disappearance or persistence of symptoms, social adaptation, anxiety level, the subject's relationships with his environment, his psychophysiological responses, etc. Tests and interviews were carried out before and after treatment. In order to be able to establish

---

[12] Meehl referred in particular to the work of Wolpe, the founder of behavior therapy in the United States, stating that, in his opinion, this method was not destined to develop, for it was contrary to the Zeitgeist. It may be said that, for a psychologist, Meehl showed on this occasion a lack of perspicacity.

comparisons with the percentage of recoveries and spontaneous remissions, the same type of procedure was for the most part applied to groups of subjects with identical diagnoses, but undergoing no treatment (control groups).

It is not possible to summarize here the considerable body of literature which exists on this subject. Amongst the most important authors mention may be made of J. Frank (1978, 1979), L. Luborsky (1975, 1979), H. Strupp (1978), and A. Bergin (1971). For a more detailed analysis, the reader is referred to two articles by Strupp (1973, 1978),[13] which constitute a review of everything that has been done in this field. Suffice it to state that the results achieved by one and another author are not always in agreement. Indeed, according to Eysenck, 60% of neurotics recover or improve spontaneously after 2 years, and 90% after 4 years (Eysenck, 1975).[14] Smith and Glass (1977), on the other hand, after analyzing works published on different types of psychotherapy, consider that the chances of improvement of treated patients are 75% greater than those of control groups (non-treated patients).

Some psychoanalysts have also realized the need for quantitative research. Let us recall that from the start Freud had greeted with sympathy the initiative of the Berlin Institute of Psychoanalysis, which had published statistics covering 2 years' activities.[15] He was later to return to this point (Freud, 1933b), declaring that this kind of survey was not very instructive and that psychoanalysis could only find a verification of its hypotheses and its practice in its clinical experience. This position has, in fact, been that of the psychoanalytical profession for a long time. But in the last few years, some research workers, believing this to be an antiscientific attitude, have undertaken statistical research. In order to ascertain whether analytically oriented therapies had different results from those which could be obtained with other techniques, Malan (1976) compared two groups of subjects, the first having undergone a treatment comprising the recall of childhood experiences, the analysis of fantasies, etc., while in the second group only the

---

[13] The second has been published in the *Handbook of Psychotherapy* (Bergin and Garfield, 1978, 2nd edition). Reference may also be made to an article in French by Cottraux (1978b), which is a summary review of studies published in the United States.

[14] Authors who are not, as Eysenck, adversaries of psychotherapy, nonetheless recognize the occurrence of a relatively high percentage of spontaneous cures. According to Bergin (1971), they amount to 30%, while Malan (1975), on the basis of a survey of forty-five non-treated patients from the Tavistock Clinic, considers that in 51% of cases there is spontaneous improvement after 8 months.

[15] See above, p. 96 (Eitingon, 1922).

present aspects of the illness were dealt with. He observed that the results obtained were better in the first group than in the second. Gill's project[16] is even more ambitious. For more than 10 years he has been carrying out research with the object of studying scientifically the development of the cure by submitting recordings of the sessions to experienced psychoanalysts. The latter are asked to evaluate the effect of a given interpretation according to a pre-established system of scoring. Gill's purpose being to show in what consists the specificity of psychoanalysis as compared to other therapies, he has chosen to center his research on the role played by the transference and its interpretation.

It is also relevant to mention a study undertaken in 1954 by a team of research workers at the Menninger Clinic, a first account of which was published by Kernberg and his colleagues (1972). In the framework of this same study, Appelbaum (1977) has published a book entitled *The Anatomy of Change*, which attempts more precisely to identify the transformations which take place in the course of a treatment and their mode of operation.

In the same way as Malan, Appelbaum ascertained that those patients who had acquired the greatest insight were also those who obtained the best results. This confirmed the original hypothesis, according to which structural change is encouraged by the acquisition of insight and the resolution of conflicts. But he also observed the existence of a second group of subjects who underwent important changes without these factors seeming to have played any appreciable role. This led him to questions about the nature of the processes at work in therapy.

Simultaneously with this study, Appelbaum (1978) has departed from the traditional contempt of psychoanalysts for everything which is not psychoanalytical and made an excursion into the realm of the "new therapies." While holding the view that they are based on questionable technical and theoretical principles, he does not believe that they should be rejected as a whole, inasmuch as no one has yet been able to demonstrate their ineffectiveness. It seems to him, unfortunately by no means obvious that psychoanalytical treatment is in every case the shortest and most effective method of bringing about changes in the subject's personality.

His research led him to pose a number of questions about the curative

---

[16] Personal communication.

factors. He wonders whether these therapies do not reveal the existence of parameters unknown to psychoanalysts, but no less important for that, and whether it would not be in the interest of analysts to take them into consideration rather than ignoring them under the pretext that they are not specific to the analytical situation. Thus, he considers that the roles of suggestion and of the altered states of consciousness deserve to be studied more seriously than has hitherto been the case. He even goes so far as to say that Janov's primal cry technique has led him to believe that the question of affective discharge in psychoanalysis should be studied anew. His concluding idea is that each patient operates changes on a different level, according to his personality, and he stresses the need for surveys to be effected in sufficiently long perspective. But, he adds, psychotherapy, like artistic creation, no doubt comprises a part that eludes all measure. [17]

What are we to think of these studies? They certainly represent a courageous, if not indeed a bold, undertaking. The wish to base psychotherapy on verifiable data is, *a priori*, a legitimate one. But these attempts raise many problems, for psychotherapy brings many variables into play, some of which are difficult to apprehend and even harder to measure. To take but one example, the notion of similar diagnosis is particularly difficult to establish. On what can one base the assertion that two cases are truly comparable? There are also the questions which arise as soon as one seeks to define the objective criteria of recovery. These vary, in effect, according to the therapist's reference system. We may add that there is the risk that the research worker's own subjectivity, his preference for such and such a technique, will weigh heavily in the evaluation of results. The fanaticism of the psychotherapists and the conflicts that exist between different

---

[17] One of the great mysteries of psychotherapy is the role played by the therapist's personality. All psychoanalysts are aware of this, even if they never mention it officially. Independently of knowledge and clinical experience, some personalities are more "therapeutic" than others.

Watkins (1978) thought he was able to study the characteristics of what he calls the "therapeutic self." The effective therapist is, in his opinion, one whose "self" is "resonant" with that of his patient. There are two ways available to know another person. On the one hand, it becomes possible through objective observation to apprehend another as a separate entity. Such observation allows the construction of an internal model capable of being cathected by the libido and introjected. This brings us to the second way: the subjective experience of another. What characterizes a "good" therapist is the fact that he is able to place himself at both points of view simultaneously – thus avoiding the external failure to understand objectivity alone, as well as the *folie à deux* of pure subjectivity.

schools are hardly likely to induce the serenity and detachment required by scientific investigation.

It can be said that, so far, the findings have been anything but decisive. Taking, for instance, two books with promising titles, *What Makes Behavior Change Possible?* (Burton, 1976) and *Successful Psychotherapy* (Claghorn, 1976), one cannot but help feel disappointed by the tenuous answers which they put forward. In this field, we are in a stage of clearing the ground. We have no truly operational tools for measurement.

As a result, the findings of one research team will often be questioned by another. To give but one instance, a commission of the American Psychiatric Association spent 2 years on the elaboration of a survey of behavior therapy. Its conclusion was that the effectiveness of this technique was demonstrated (Task Force Report, 1973). But hardly had this report been published than it was criticized on methodological grounds in an article entitled "The behavior therapies: therapeutic breakthrough or latest fad?" (Shapiro, 1976).

We are far from the wish expressed by Strupp when he wrote: "It is not entirely utopian to envisage the creation of an analogue to the Food and Drug Administration to protect the public from worthless or potentially damaging therapies" (Strupp, 1978, p. 42).

Is Psychoanalysis a Therapy?

This sort of investigation has not yet appeared in France. Is this because the responsible authorities, and particularly the Social Insurance, do not pay enough interest to psychotherapy? Is it because of the lack of funds to support such investigations, which are necessarily costly? Or the traditional condescendence, in certain circles, towards Anglo-Saxon pragmatism? No doubt all these factors are involved, but it is perhaps also due to the fact that in France psychoanalysis plays a particularly important role. During the last 20 years it has indeed undergone a remarkable development which is shown by a very strong influence on all cultural circles.[18] While some physicians and psychiatrists still persist in the defence of an essentially organicist medicine, which takes no account of psychodynamic factors, psychiatry is on the whole

---

[18] As Darnton (1968) and Rausky (1977) have shown, Mesmerism, in its time, exercised a similar influence in France on the entire intellectual and political life of the nation. In this connection, Darnton cites Lafayette, Marat, Sieyes, Madame Roland, Condorcet, Desmoulins, and others.

dominated by psychoanalytical discourse. Psychoanalysis sometimes comes under attack, but this especially from a political and ideological point of view: because it is the main tool in the psychiatrization of life, as an instrument for internment, for the retrieval from social revolutions, etc. Moreover, these critics are a very small minority, and psychoanalytical knowledge continues to function as a model of reference which allows one to avoid questioning the results really obtained by psychotherapy. It may indeed be supposed that the idea of applying statistical methods to psychotherapy would meet with the opposition of most psychoanalysts. For some, the very principle of an evaluation of the therapeutic effectiveness of psychoanalysis could not have any meaning, for psychoanalysis is not, in essence, a therapy. This is a widely controversial question, but in the author's opinion, one which relates to pure scholasticism. Reference is often made to Freud, who did in fact on several occasions show his lack of enthusiasm toward therapy. First at the level of his personal vocation. The famous sentence from a letter written to Fliess is well known: "I have become a therapist against my will" (Freud, 1954, p. 162). In his letters, or in the course of friendly conversations, Freud returned several times to this point. But other statements show that the "will to cure" was not absent from his motivation, witness these lines written to his fiancée on the eve of his departure for Paris: ". . . become a great scholar and then come back to Vienna with a huge, enormous halo, and then we will soon get married, and I will cure all the incurable nervous cases" (Freud, 1960, p. 166). Similarly, in 1896, he wrote to Fliess that he felt sure that "granted certain conditions in the person and the case, I can definitely cure hysteria and obsessional neurosis" (Freud, 1954, p. 162). In the whole course of his work, quotations can be found which show that he never ceased to consider psychoanalysis as a method which should make possible the treatment of neurotic disorders. Let us simply say that, at different periods, he showed a greater or lesser degree of optimism. At the outset, he was indeed convinced that the subject's insight into his history and his conflicts in itself had a therapeutic action. With the introduction of transference, and as he gradually progressed in the knowledge of unconscious processes, his belief in the effectiveness of therapeutic action became somewhat attenuated, as is apparent from the pessimistic views he expressed in 1937 in "Analysis terminable and interminable" (Freud, 1937). Indeed, Freud had already wrily remarked to Pfister: "the optimum conditions for (psychoanalysis) exist where it is not needed, i.e. among the healthy" (Freud, [1963], p. 15).

It is not proposed to give more quotations here.[19] They show that, on this question as on many others, Freud's positions were always contradictory. Psychoanalysis was certainly for him far more than a simple therapy, but he was not indifferent to its results, be it only because of the validation they could bring to his theoretical hypotheses.

In a recent article, Castoriadis, a philosopher and psychoanalyst, adopts the following position in this respect: "In France, people have been chattering for years about the 'wish of the analyst'. But who cares about the wish of the analyst? What counts – and what this chatter is trying to conceal – is the analyst's aim, his will and his project. It is false and mystifying to say that the analyst 'wants' nothing for his patient: if he is unable to want anything with regard to his job, and therefore to his patients, if he has still remained purely and simply at the level of a desire, it is urgent that he should return to the couch or take another job" (Castoriadis, 1977, p. 59).

Be that as it may, whether one calls the subject under analysis "a patient" or "analysand," whether or not one calls the analyst a therapist, a relationship is always established between one who "helps" and one who is "helped." One may ponder the question of knowing whether the therapist's "wish to cure" is useful or not to the development of the treatment. Some authors believe that this element can but trouble the pure waters of the analytical situation. It remains that the patient counts on a recovery, and that the latter is for him the most important thing. However it may come about, there is still the problem of knowing whether it can be obtained by one technique or another.[20]

In this chapter, we have only dealt with the United States and France because these are two countries where, for different reasons, psychoanalysis has assumed considerable importance, both from the medical and the cultural aspect. In other countries, such as Argentina and Great Britain, some authors have brought to psychoanalytical thought original and important contributions; but psychoanalysis does not have the same impact there.

[19] In Roazen's latest work, *Freud and his Followers* (1975), one can find all Freud's statements on this subject, as expressed in his works or in the course of various conversations. In order to shed light on the life and thought of Freud, Roazen in fact undertook a systematic investigation among his immediate pupils and intimates.

[20] Let us admit that the profession of psychotherapist is a very special one, since it is submitted to virtually no control. Freud compared the psychoanalyst's action on the human psyche with a surgical operation. But if a surgeon forgets his scissors in a patient's abdomen, it can be detected. No X-ray can reveal the untoward action of a psychotherapist. However, American research workers are now starting to study the negative effects of psychotherapy (Hadley and Strupp, 1976).

10

Affect

All that has been said so far shows that psychotherapy is still very poorly known. We know some of the factors which condition the process of treatment but an essential element eludes us.

This is indeed what emerges from the statistical studies mentioned above. One of the main difficulties in comparing the different forms of psychotherapy arises from the fact that, apart from those factors which are specific to one or another particular technique, there are what are termed in the literature non-specific factors to be found in all forms of therapy: human warmth, empathy, the degree of availability of the therapist, the patient's confidence in the treatment, etc. It seems to the author that, in the midst of the very vagueness of these terms, the problem in question arises from the difficulty in defining certain fundamental aspects of the therapeutic relationship.

Every form of psychotherapy comprises two dimensions, one intellectual (insight, language, representation), the other emotional (the affective experience). Words without affect are, as we know, ineffective in the dynamics of treatment.[1] It is said that words carry the affect - when they do

[1] We are all familiar with cases of interminable analysis, where the patients are veritable walking textbooks of psychoanalysis, having gained full insight into all the causes of their illness but without anything ever having "moved" on the affective plane. In this context, we may mention the extreme case of a patient who spent 17 years in analysis with two reputable analysts without ever having experienced a single emotion of even the slightest intensity. His wish to experience one day a real catharsis led him to try all sorts of therapy, one of which was a technique at the same time employing bio-energy and Gestalt therapy, the "rêve éveillé" (day dreaming technique). As acting out was allowed, the patient was able one day to engage in a real fight with his therapist, after which he felt liberated. According to available information 3 years later, it would seem that this treatment had a favorable outcome. What was the curative factor here?

111

so. An understanding of affective life is therefore essential if we wish to understand the therapeutic process.

Freud was faced with this problem as soon as he began to practice the cathartic method. He became aware that the recall of forgotten memories was effective as a cure, only if accompanied by emotional abreaction.[2] Later, with the technique of free association, the emphasis was placed on the role of interpretation: the gaining of insight on the subject's part as to the meaning of his symptom was supposed to bring about the disappearance of the latter.

Freud, however, very soon perceived that the effectiveness of the interpretative work depended on the way in which the relationship to the analyst was experienced at the affective level. That is why he introduced the concept of transference.

But it is no mere chance that this term remains one of the most obscure in analytic theory. Whether in treatment or in psychic life generally, everything that involves the question of affect is, in fact, very poorly understood.

The Energy Metaphor

The uncertainties which persisted in this area, as much on Freud's part as on that of his successors, have been summarized by André Green in his book *Le Discours Vivant* (*The Living Discourse*) (1973), as well as at the 30th International Congress of Psychoanalysis held in Jerusalem (Green, 1977, pp. 129–156). For his part, the American psychoanalyst, Rangell, similarly stated, during a symposium devoted to the question of affect, "We still do not have a complete psychoanalytic formulation regarding affects and, moreover, that any comprehensive theory of affects needs to include the physiologic segment as well as the psychoanalytic." (In: Pietro Castelnuovo-Tedesco, 1974, p. 612.)

The term *affect* was taken by Freud from German psychiatry. It covered

---

[2]Famous cases such as those of Anna O. and Janet's patient, Marie, are well-known examples of how the recall of the traumatic experience effectively led to the disappearance of the symptom. It will be remembered that Marie was suffering from blindness in her left eye, which disappeared when she recalled the incident which preceded its onset. As a child she had been extremely frightened one day when she had been obliged to sleep next to a child who had impetigo on the left side of the face (Janet, 1889, pp. 439–440). But one may wonder whether the recall of this event was the decisive factor, or whether the cure ought not rather be attributed to transference. Historical reconstruction in psychoanalysis is increasingly being questioned today. There is a tendency to speak rather of the construction of an "analytic space" (Vidermann, 1970).

the whole realm of feeling, emotion, passion, etc., as traditionally opposed to representational activity. This concept involves a quantitative and a qualitative dimension. This emerges from the immediate experience. One can experience different sorts of affect (anger, rage, sorrow, joy, etc.); on the other hand, these feelings can be more or less intense. The idea of quantity relates directly to the problem of psychic energy which is at the base of the economic concepts of Freudian metapsychology. This concept has very often been challenged. A good example is the debate which took place in 1962 at the American Psychoanalytic Society (Modell, 1963). This discussion revealed a considerable divergence of views amongst the participants, particularly on the question of whether this energy could be assimilated to physical energy. Opponents and advocates of such an assimilation could both claim Freud as their authority, insofar as he oscillated between different positions in the course of his life. In his closing address, David Beres emphasized the considerable confusion that still reigned on this subject, concluding with the consoling observation that the "hallmark of the person with a mature mind is the ability to live in uncertainty" (*ibid.,* p. 617).

Beres likewise drew attention to the danger of attributing a metaphysical meaning to the word energy. Indeed, certain interpretations of economic concepts do appear to be associated with presuppositions of this kind. Thus Pasche, while understanding that Freud could not do without metaphors "borrowed from hydrostatics," could state during a discussion at the Paris Psycho-Analytical Society: "Psychic energy can be displaced, concentrated, sublimated, diluted . . . but remains irreducible . . . We are doomed to make use of it; *in this it is an aspect of our finiteness and of our destiny*" (Pasche, 1967, p. 232) (italics added).

Interestingly, this controversy recalls the debates about the magnetic fluid which took place at the beginning of the nineteenth century among Mesmer's followers. Mesmer considered that the fluid was a "physical energy" which could be "accumulated, concentrated and transported" (Mesmer, [1971], p. 77). But to some of his followers, particularly members of the Lyons School (Chevalier de Barberin, St. Martin, etc.), the fluid was a mystical element, a means of communication between man and God. An anonymous author wrote: "This inexplicable spirit (the fluid) is neither the magnet nor electricity, nor elemental fire, nor phlogiston, nor the chemists' *acidum pingue,* but, to call metaphysics to our aid for its definition, it is the first impulse imparted to matter by the Supreme Being" (*Recueil Général,* 1787). A writer such as

Villers, on the other hand, saw the fluid more as a purely metaphorical concept, the essential element being the therapist's desire to cure (Villers, 1787).[3a]

Two centuries after Mesmer, the interaction between the quantitative and qualitative processes remains so obscure in the absence of any scientific verification that our knowledge in this area has hardly progressed at all.

Is this term energy destined to remain for ever a metaphorical one? In 1975 another symposium on this question was held in the United States. The debates which took place on this occasion were published in a number of the *Journal of the American Psychoanalytic Association* (1977, No. 3). As Gill observes in his paper, these discussions are likely to appear to many people as "a futile exercise, if not downright boring" (Gill, 1977, p. 581). He compares this type of controversy to political or religious debates in which everyone presents his own point of view ardently, without anyone ever changing his opinion. It is not possible here to summarize all the points mentioned in the course of this meeting, but a few can be singled out as particularly significant.

In the course of a very long contribution, Swanson (1977) showed that the Freudian idea of the circulation of energy in the neurones is in contradiction with the laws of conservation of energy in physics.

Rosenblatt and Thickstun (1977) tried to combine cybernetics with dynamic psychology by replacing the energic model (*power engineering*) with the information model (*information engineering*). From this point of view, affective phenomena correspond not to modifications of energy, but to the transmission of informational data released by the emission of signals. Needless to say, the transmission of information necessarily implies movement and consequently a "force," but the quantities of energy involved are so small that they can be considered negligible.[3b] Applegarth, (1977)

[3a] In a recent book (Popper and Eccles, 1977) the philosopher Popper and the neurophysiologist Eccles (Nobel prizewinner for medicine) express views reminiscent of the "spiritualist" theories of Pasche and our anonymous eighteenth-century author. They rehabilitate the Cartesian distinction between soul and body, postulating the existence of a kind of metaphysical "third force", neither psychological nor physiological.

[3b] It should be noted that in physics a signal of weak intensity can trigger an appreciable movement of energy. Kubie, who adopted an "anti-economic" position, namely against what he called the "muscular" model of the psyche, proposed the following metaphor borrowed from Lord Adrian, the famous neurophysiologist. The latter, as he wrote, "likens neurones to an unruly mob, a milling mass of men, until a command is given which imposes discipline and order and triggers them all off in the same direction at the same pace towards the same goal. The energy of the triggering command is small and has no relation to the energy of the ordered ranks. It is this which renders invalid such concepts as libido, cathexes or the energies of instincts" (Kubie, 1975, p. 18).

pointed out that Freud had already attempted to make use of the signal concept, but had never abandoned the energetic model as an explanation of pleasure and unpleasure. In his view, the informational alternative is more difficult to use to account for the conflictual aspect, the interaction between the drive, the wish and the defense. Gill, for his part, considers that this hypothesis merely replaces a model derived from the natural sciences by an outline from the same source. Understanding the relational interaction, he asserts, is a psychological phenomenon and not a biological one.

It is difficult to reach a conclusion in the present state of our knowledge. Suffice it to observe that the informational plan can be used from a descriptive point of view to give an account of our experiences. It can be said that, in the case of analgesia, the information transmitted by the receptors is modified, while in blistering, the representation replaces the real stimulus in setting in motion an informational system. But this does not explain why the informational process is triggered, or why, at *a given moment, a meeting between two individuals provokes such an action.* We lack the concepts which would enable us to understand this phenomenon. The "thermodynamic" model,[4] which dominates the Freudian model, has no scientific basis. When we speak of the psychophysiological dimension of the affect, we are not *a priori* postulating that this dimension comprises processes of a quantitative nature. It may be discovered some day that the mechanisms brought into play are purely qualitative, that they have nothing to do with the increase or decrease of a sum of energy, that this notion of energy has no foundation. Nevertheless, while awaiting a scientific revolution[5] which would open up as yet unsuspected perspectives, we are in practice obliged, for want of a better approach, to preserve the idea of "affective energy" capable of producing profound psychic and physiological changes.

[4] Cohen (1966) observed that the hydrostatic model, in one form or another, lies at the root of our neurophysiological concepts since Greek Antiquity (particularly since Galen). He mentioned Haller, Galvani, Mesmer, Freud, and Lorenz by way of examples. The word *libido* might come from the Latin *libare*, meaning to pour, energy thus being compared to a liquid. The present author is well aware of the pitfalls concealed by the use of metaphors such as psychic energy, libido, and cathexis to describe psychic processes. A metaphor is not a theory, nor even a hypothetical explanation, since it can neither be validated nor disproved.

[5] Perhaps molecular biology will succeed in opening up new perspectives in so far as it conceives biological functioning as a system in which information circulates through the intermediary of a molecular substance. Perhaps this research will enable us to understand the biological processes governing the psychophysiological functioning of the human being. We can but hope so. But here we are entering the realms of science fiction.

The Primary Relationship

The existence of hypnotic phenomena appears to support this thesis. What happens in hypnosis? On the basis of a prior break in the subject's relationship with the environment, a regression takes place, which is manifested in a massive production of affect, an intense "affective current" between hypnotist and hypnotized (an exclusive concentration by the subject on the person of the hypnotist).

What is significant about this process is that the production of the relational bond follows a manipulation of the bodily field.[6] At a given moment, for little known reasons, a process is triggered producing this particular relationship with another, along with a change in the psychophysiological reactivity.

These are the factors which have led the author to postulate that at the root of our exchanges with the environment there exists *an innate automatic relational function manifested in the release of a certain "quantum of affect."* The choice of this term is a provisional one insofar as the concept of energy is, as we have seen, devoid of any precise scientific content. *All that is meant is that the activation of this relational potential sets off a certain number of biological processes, of which we know nothing except that they are fundamental to the equilibrium of the organism.*

It involves, as stated, an innate mechanism which exists before any cathexis of the object, comprising a basic undifferentiated "affective energy" with no representational correlate, which constitutes, as it were, the substratum of relational activities. With the maturation of the nervous system, this "energy" comes to be placed at the service of the functions of symbolization. It is interesting to note that Fisher (1965), who attempted to interconnect the psychological and the physiological aspects of dreams within a psychoanalytic perspective, arrived at the formulation of relatively similar hypotheses.

---

[6] The induction of affect by manipulation of the bodily field raises very subtle problems which cannot be dealt with in detail here. The reader is referred to a panel of the American Psychoanalytic Association in 1973 (Schmale, 1974), entitled *Sensory Deprivation, An Approach to the Study of the Induction of Affects.* It contains some extremely interesting observations on data acquired from groups of subjects who had been in natural conditions of deprivation (people who had spent a year in the Antarctic, children who were deaf or blind or who were isolated from the outside world in a plastic bubble as a result of some immunological abnormality).

Modern neurophysiological research has indeed shown that, in man as in animals, dreams have a physiological substratum. The paradoxical phase of sleep is characterized by a specific kind of electrical activity (REM sleep). Dreaming would have a "purifying" function in the nervous system, ridding it of "metabolites" accumulated in the course of dreamless sleep; this is a necessary function for the equilibrium of the living organism. Some authors have, on the basis of this discovery, minimized the role of the dream as a psychological event, considering it an epiphenomenon of little importance. In Fisher's view, this biological dimension is not in opposition to the psychological function of dreaming, which is that of hallucinatory wish-fulfillment. Referring to research by Jacobson (1954), Schur (1958), and Peter Wolff (1959), he postulates that, in the neonatal period, there exists a "psycho-economic" state and a basic undifferentiated "physiological" drive energy. At a certain stage of development, as the psychic structures are progressively established and mnemonic traces laid down, the discharge of "physiological" energy would be partly replaced by the "psychological" discharge of the dream.

Research carried out in recent years has demonstrated the importance for personality formation of the interpersonal interactions which take place in the first few months of life. To mention but one author,[7] Spitz (1945, 1965) showed that, with babies subjected to long periods in hospital, the absence of affective exchanges had serious consequences on both the infant's psychic and somatic development. Little is known of the nature of interpersonal relationships in the very first stages of development. All that we know is that they begin very early (some authors even believe that the fetus is receptive to the mother's reactions). How is the communication transmitted? What channels are used? Must we speak in terms of excitation and discharge? Are the infant's sensations at first organized, as Freud tended to believe, around the opposition of pleasure and unpleasure? Or does man have at his disposal from the very beginning a battery of affective reactions which are biologically registered? It can only be observed that a certain number of stimuli originating from another person set in motion processes which are necessary for the maturation of the organism.

The author considers that, at the start, these processes are very largely

[7] Of course, particular mention should also be made of the work of Bowlby (1963, 1973) and Margaret Mahler (1968).

quantitative in nature. They constitute, as it were, the "economic basis" of affective life and determine the "quantity of libido" available to the subject in his subsequent relationships. They play a fundamental role in the establishment of narcissism, which is increasingly recognized as of crucial importance in the child's development. Another person is not, at this stage, perceived as an object. He forms an integral part of the child's sensorimotor field. Of course, the first modes of recognition very soon take place – recognition of the mother's smile, for example, the early appearance of which was shown by Dolto (1971, p. 30); identification, and the play of the mother's presence and absence, which heralds the beginnings of the child's transition to symbolization. As this development progresses, the child differentiates himself from the environment. Object relations appear with the whole series of identifications, projections, introjections, etc. But the fusional, symbiotic dimension never entirely disappears from human interactions.[8]

The Primary Relationship and Psychotherapy

Psychotherapy operates at different levels. It can be said that all psychotherapy effects a mobilization and transformation of affect, even where conditioning is the technique employed. How is the affect mobilized? Knowledge of transference mechanisms allows us to understand it to a certain extent. But whatever the technique employed, in every therapeutic encounter there is always that unknown element, that *primary "libidinal tie,"* which, as Freud already stated, eludes our understanding. And it may be asked whether the reactivation of this attachment is not one of the factors essential to the effectiveness of the therapy, insofar as it represents a kind of "influx of energy," which in itself exercises a positive influence.

Hypnosis enables us to come a little closer to this aspect of the

---

[8] It is interesting to note that, even in 1953, Kubie postulated specifically in relation to Spitz's work the existence of a pre-symbolic phase corresponding to a stage where *cerebral myelination is incomplete* (present author's italics) and the unconscious and conscious are not yet differentiated. At this stage, what he calls the "central emotional position" is established, which plays a major role in the subsequent evolution to the stage of symbolization (Kubie, 1953a). It may be mentioned in passing that, in the same text, Kubie calls once more in question Melanie Klein's theory of child psychology, which he calls the "adultomorphization of the infant" and regards as pertaining to the realm of science fiction.

therapeutic process, for it favors a regression to this primary stage of the relationship. A few examples follow.

The first concerns a young student, aged 22 years, treated by the author in 1969. Antoine was suffering from sexual dysfunction and a character disorder. He had been in analysis for a year when he came to see the author, and throughout this whole period he had never once spoken to his analyst. He lay on the couch completely silent. Dissatisfied with the lack of apparent results from the treatment, he approached another analyst who sent him to the author in the hope that hypnosis would help free the situation. After two sessions spent in a medium trance, the patient literally exploded with an expression of intense aggression toward his former analyst and the author. It was then possible to begin a classical analysis with him, which lasted for 4 years and proved successful, since the patient now leads a normal sex life and no longer presents any major disorder.

The second treatment took place in 1970 and concerned a young woman, Maryse, a 25-year-old dancer, who had been an alcoholic since the age of 17. She had reached the stage of polyneuritis with loss of the patellar and ankle reflexes and had just undergone a course of disintoxication in a sanatorium. The psychiatrist treating her predicted a relapse within 6 weeks and it was to be feared that she would develop progressive blindness and become bedridden. The patient showed great indifference to all this and came to see the author only on the insistence of her family and her fiancé.

After an initial interview, it was decided to use hypnosis. From the very first session she seemed to be deeply hypnotized. There was no attempt to establish a verbal dialogue with her (out of laziness or intuition? It must, however, be said that the patient had previously undergone verbal psychotherapy which had failed, and that she did not seem keen on establishing communication.) The author, therefore, contented himself with conducting hypnotic sessions in silence, without formulating any suggestion whatever (although the latter was clearly implicit), nor inciting the patient to verbalize in any way. Several weeks passed and Maryse had still not started drinking again. After 6 months without a relapse, she stopped treatment. Nine years have passed during which the author has received regular news of her. The cure has lasted; her reflexes have returned; she is married and the mother of two children, and seems satisfied with her present life. There is an important detail to be added. Her alcoholism had started after the death of her stepfather as a result of a heart attack. On the day of his death, she should normally have been at school, but she hid in the barn and played truant. She had, therefore, heard her stepfather call for help, but had not dared to come to his assistance. Following this incident, she had felt intensely guilty and it was then that she began drinking.

The third case which the author had occasion to treat in October, 1978, is particularly interesting in that it establishes with considerable probability the relationship of cause and effect between the therapeutic activity and the disappearance of the symptom. Ahmed is a 28-year-old Libyan who worked as a mechanic before his illness. He developed a hysterical hemiplegia (paralysis of the left arm and leg following a surgical operation on his clavicle) which confined him to bed. The atrophy of his left arm was pronounced. Before being sent to France, he had been hospitalized for 5 months in Libya, 5 months in Italy, and 1 month in Stockholm where a very thorough investigation led to the conclusion that the symptom was non-organic in origin. Some slight question remained, however, regarding the possibility of a lesion of the brachial plexus caused by the operation. The first interview, conducted in rudimentary English, revealed several factors indicating the presence of unresolved psychic conflicts (which it was possible to examine later in more detail with the help of an assistant who spoke Arabic).

It was recognized that the patient felt a very strong need for affective relationships. From the very first sessions of hypnosis, he showed himself capable of a medium trance (without amnesia, but with modification of body sensations) accompanied by a great degree of suggestibility. After the second session, he began to move his toe, then his foot, and 12 days later he was able to walk with a stick. The paralysis of the arm was resistant and, at one point, a neurologist concluded that the symptom was organic. A subsequent consultation with a second neurologist, however, proved this hypothesis wrong; a few days later, the patient began to move his arm. On December 19th he left the hospital, having completely recovered.

These, then, are three cases in which the action of hypnosis seems to have played an important part. This does not mean that other methods would not have achieved results. That question can be posed about any form of treatment and obviously cannot be answered definitively. But if it is attempted to describe how the influence of the hypnotic relationship was manifested, the most obvious factor is the immediate result obtained in response to the treatment. This aspect appears less clearly in the second case. But, taking into account the fact that psychotherapy had previously failed and that the patient seemed altogether entrenched in her alcoholic behavior pattern, the results were indeed extremely rapid – all the more so when it is recalled that cases of alcoholism are generally resistant to psychotherapy, especially when they reach such a degree.

In the first case, the process appears fairly easy to follow, from a descriptive point of view. The silence maintained by the patient during his 12 months of analysis was manifestly linked to the anxiety aroused by his aggressive fantasies. Hypnosis enabled this aggression to be expressed.

It is also possible that the change of analyst created a favorable situation. All therapists know such periods when, after analytic work has seemed to stagnate entirely, suddenly all that had remained silent for months finds expression. A similar process may have taken place, culminating in the revelation of all the material hitherto accumulated in silence. The fact that he rejected his analyst was in itself an aggressive act on the subject's part which may have exercised a liberating influence. Whatever the case, in this situation the introduction of hypnosis represented a trigger or acted as a catalyst. It may be that, at the same time, it both facilitated an intensification of aggressive affect, and a lifting of the anxiety which opposed its expression.

The second case is perhaps the most interesting. Inasmuch as the treatment was almost entirely silent, there are few data to help us understand how the curative process operated. The little information supplied by the patient and her mother during the preliminary interviews gave a picture of a disturbed family background, which will not be given in detail here. It seems that the death of the stepfather acted as a real trauma. Moreover, the patient had been subject to spontaneous somnambulism for 6 months and it was then that she began to drink. It may be that this death, for which she felt partly responsible, plunged her into strong Oedipal guilt, and that a positive transference to the hypnotist was established, enabling her to resolve this conflict. There would have occurred, as it were, a spontaneous working through.

The whole question is obviously to ascertain what stimulated this process of working through. It is all the more relevant because this is not a case of temporary relief from a symptom under the impact of suggestion. The fact that for 9 years there has been no relapse suggests that, through the hypnotic relationship, a profound reorganization of the personality took place. (It may be noted that this case contradicts the widespread idea that hypnosis is always a symptomatic treatment, suppressing the symptoms.) It is, let us repeat, very difficult to guess what happened.

It is known that alcoholism causes a reversion to an intense affective frustration, a fundamental lack associated with very archaic phases of the object relationship, particularly the oral stage. The author's hypothesis is that hypnosis, by enabling the patient to experience a fusional relationship, played a restorative role, filling, as it were, this lack, and that it was the affective input which made the working through possible.

The third case is more recent. It is, therefore, impossible to say whether or not the symptom will reappear or be replaced by a substitute symptom. It is an example of the intensive use of suggestion, in which the role of hypnotic action is apparent. The improvement began after the second session even though it was a particularly difficult case. (It is paradoxical that conversion hysteria in its most extreme forms – amnesia and paralysis – should not be curable by classical psychoanalytic treatment, when it was the point of departure, the basic model, for the elaboration of Freudian theory. But it is a fact. No analyst would contemplate undertaking the analysis of such a case (Widlöcher, 1979).)

Again, the symptom was set in a psychological context (conflict with his father, separation from his wife, professional difficulties). However, on the basis of these few data, it seems clear that it is a case of conversion hysteria in the most classical sense of the term: the expression through a somatic symptom of repressed unconscious representations. The meaning of the symptom is less important here than its mechanism. We are confronted with a phenomenon of dissociation, a kind of motor amnesia.

Hypnosis is often effective in the treatment of hysterical amnesia. It constitutes a treatment of choice. For the therapist, it is one of the most disturbing experiences there is. The mechanism is at the same time very simple and completely mysterious. Generally, it is sufficient to hypnotize the subject (patients suffering from amnesia are for the most part good somnambulists) and suggest to him that on waking he will remember. It really does seem like a magic trick.

The author has twice had occasion to treat a case of amnesia. The first of these cases was referred to in the Prologue (Montassut, Chertok and Gachkel, 1953) – a patient who had "forgotten" the last 12 years of her life. The amnesia was associated with an event which had affected her profoundly a few months earlier; she had assisted in an abortion and had been reported, convicted and, finally, pardoned. This had awakened in her a sort of latent depression. The amnesia clearly corresponded to her wish to erase this episode from her mind. At a deeper level, there was the wish to obliterate her life as a married woman, which was a source of continuing conflict.

The second case (Chertok, 1975) was a young man aged 19, who, for more than 2 weeks, had forgotten his identity. He could not remember his name, nor anything about himself. It was not possible to determine the factors which lay at the root of the amnesia, the patient having interrupted the treatment as soon as he had recovered his identity.

In both cases, all that was required to lift the amnesia was one hypnotic session, during which the patient was asked to give an account of the "forgotten" data and the suggestion given him that he would be able to remember these upon waking.

To explain amnesia, Freud implicated repression. The forgotten representations would be charged with some fantasied meaning which was intolerable to the subject, who therefore expelled them from consciousness. It is a coherent explanation, and it is true that in every case of amnesia, if it is indeed possible to conduct a minimal psychotherapeutic investigation, one or more conflicts are always found which have a very definite link with the "forgotten" representations. But why does repression adopt this route in certain (rare) subjects? Above all, what factors effect the lifting of the amnesia with the help of hypnotic suggestion?

Since Freud, it has become customary, in order to explain the effectiveness of hypnotic suggestion, to repeat the famous sentence: Hypnosis short-circuits the resistances. But what is the cause of this lifting of resistances? Psychoanalysts do not ask themselves this question. For them, in any case, it is a phenomenon of suggestion and is therefore, by definition, something impure, unworthy of psychoanalytic research. Did not Freud explain suggestion once and for all as the effect of a positive transference?

In fact, as we have seen, for Freud the problem was far from resolved. And the explanation by transference in no way enables us to resolve the question of the specificity of hypnotic suggestion. It does not explain, for example, why the establishment of the hypnotic relationship constitutes a particularly favorable situation for the lifting of amnesia.

The author's hypothesis is that *by enabling the subject to experience a fusional relationship, with affective symbiosis, hypnosis effects a sort of "bodily reunification"* which is manifested in the lifting of repression (in this case, the restructuring of memory) and the relaxing of the barriers separating primary and secondary processes. The process is located at a directly psycho-physiological level.

Of course, the process is not independent of the psychodynamic context in which it takes place. The hypnotic relationship creates favorable conditions for the lifting of repression. That does not mean that it magically resolves all the conflicts. It represents a catalyst which may facilitate shifts and working through processes. In no respect is it a shortcut as far as these processes are concerned.

The author is at present treating a young woman aged 20, Suzanne, suffering from a disability in walking. She was referred after having unsuccessfully undergone an amphetamine shock and treatment based on conditioning techniques. Hypnosis seemed all the more indicated in that 7 years previously, following her parents' divorce, she had shown attacks of somnambulism (which are generally the sign of good hypnotizability). Her disorder is quite clearly psychological. She is perfectly aware of this, but firmly refused any psychotherapeutic approach when she came for her consultation. In fact she had no intention of abandoning her symptom. Treatment by suggestion, carried out under these conditions, obviously proved unsuccessful. She showed herself a good hypnotic subject, but the disorder continues unabated (good hypnotizability does not always include hypersuggestibility). The author has the impression, moreover, that while allowing herself to be hypnotized, she refuses to let herself go too far, so as not to be led into abandoning her defenses.

The establishment of the hypnotic relationship has had a certain beneficial effect, however, where it has been possible to establish a transference relationship, with the patient accepting the idea of psychological treatment.

It must be emphasized, nevertheless, that in the present state of our knowledge it is very difficult to describe with any certainty the processes at work in these different cases. We may have intuitions and formulate hypotheses, but we are unable to assert anything definitively. All that can be said is that the hypnotic relationship facilitated a mobilization of affect capable of generating change at the psychic and physiological levels.

Affect and Language

We are witnessing today in France a sort of "linguistic" [9] imperialism which tends to make language the exclusive basis of the therapeutic process. It seems to the author that to do so minimizes the problem of the body and affect. It is true that the Lacanian School has again called in question the opposition between affect and representation, energy and meaning. For Lacan, this opposition has no significance, because all communications between human beings are symbolic in nature. The famous phrase that "the Unconscious is structured like a language" is well known. [10] For his part, André Green (1978a), who recently published an article synthesizing the question of affect, sums up his position in epigrammatic form: "Language without affect is a dead language; an affect without language cannot be communicated" (Green, 1978a, p. 404).

While the first half of this sentence may be correct, the second, in the author's opinion, is arguable. Of course, the concept of language is not restricted to linguistic signals. Gestures, mimicry, the tone of voice, silences, and all non-verbal manifestations function as signs as long as they can be broken down into a number of distinctive units; they enable certain messages to pass between the subjects.

It is true that psychoanalysis began by showing that apparently the most insignificant factors possessed an unconscious meaning. It showed that emotions, instincts, and even the most elementary bodily functions were not blind organic processes subject to purely mechanical laws, but that they carried a meaning unknown to the subject himself. From this point of view it is understandable that Lacan became interested in structural linguistics, and made the attainment of symbolization the fundamental element of psychic development. But by insisting solely upon this aspect, one leaves the psychophysiological dimension of the communication out of account. The function of words cannot be reduced to a transmission of signals. It is also an

[9] *Langagier* in the French text, meaning *language-centered* (the adjective *langagier* is difficult to translate into English, owing to the fact that French has two separate words: *langue*, which refers to spoken language, and *langage*, which refers to abstract systems of properties common to all languages spoken or formal).

[10] It is not proposed here to enter the labyrinth of Lacan's own writings. The latter are, in fact, subject to various ambiguous interpretations, if not indeed to contradictory commentaries. For this reason, the author will confine himself to a discussion of a so-called "Lacanian" position, which has gained considerable attention.

activity which mobilizes the body directly at the level of the drive. Language itself has an economic dimension. In addition to signals, rhythms and intensities are exchanged. There is often a tendency to forget that the acquisition of the symbolic ability is of a progressive nature. It seems exaggerated to reduce the mother–child relationship in the first months after birth to a mere exchange of signals. Even if this process is established very early, long before the acquisition of language, as Lacan and his pupils have shown, it is based on a pre-existing relationship; affective language is older than speech. We may even say that the capacity for affect is nurse to the symbol.

In fact, there are several levels of language. The question is precisely to understand how, in the different modes of exchange, the "representational" structures interact with elements relating to drive and affect. As long as the psychobiological bases of the relationship are unknown, it appears better to maintain the distinction between affect and representation.

Freud, for his part, had more imagination than many of his disciples. He was interested in telepathy. In a recent article, François Roustang (1978), an analyst of the "Ecole Freudienne" (headed by Lacan), attempted to analyze the reasons which induced Freud to return several times to this phenomenon.[11] He shows that Freud's position varied. Analyzing examples of fortune-telling, Freud gave them at first a purely psychological interpretation. The fortune-teller had simply guessed the secret thoughts of his client concerning an event which in some way had been unconsciously foreseen by him. The similarity between the position of the fortune-teller and that of the analyst is evident. Even if the latter relies on the associations contributed by the patient, interpretation presupposes a particular receptiveness, a "communication from one unconscious to another." Commenting on a few lines written by Freud in 1925 on a case of telepathy, Helene Deutsch emphasizes this connection: "One may therefore suspect that the condition for this transfer of 'emotionally colored recollections' consists in a certain unconscious readiness to receive them. Only if this condition is fulfilled can the recipient function as a 'receiving station.' These emotionally cathected ideas must mobilize in the unconscious of the second person analogous ideas of similar content, which then manifest themselves in for the conscious as 'internal experiences'" (in: Devereaux, 1953, p. 135).

[11] Roustang refers to the book by Christian Moreau (1976), which is an excellent exposition of Freud's writings on this subject.

But how is this transmission accomplished? Returning to the question in "Dreams and Occultism" (Freud, 1933a), Freud ended by acknowledging the existence of telepathy, in which he saw the survival of an archaic form of communication which was maintained in early infancy. But he avoided facing the problem which, for Roustang, is the most essential one: the fact that this dimension is present in the analytic experience itself.

Roustang remarks that by introducing the concept of transference, Freud enabled the analyst not to feel personally involved in the relationship, since his patients' fantasies and wishes were not really directed to himself, but toward a third person.[12] If it is required that the analyst himself be analyzed, it is precisely so that he will be capable of denouncing this illusion and remain a pure recording apparatus, maintaining between himself and his patient the distance which would gradually permit the latter to recognize that his identifications are rooted in fantasy.

But the whole construction is in danger of collapse if the analyst can be suspected of exercising an occult influence on his patient and if the latter's fantasies are in fact those of the analyst. The analysis then threatens to be no more than a disguised exercise in suggestion, or, as Roustang puts it, "a long-term suggestion."

It is in this respect that the idea of thought transference is worrying for the analyst. It returns to a pre-verbal mode of communication in which subjects are no longer distinguished from each other, but are caught in an archaic fusional relationship, nothing of which guarantees that it is analyzable. The danger is all the greater in that analysis, by inducing a regression, favors this type of relationship: "What is set up in analytic treatment, and reinforced whether we like it or not by the analyst's words or his silence, is therefore an immediate relationship of the archaic, infantile, erotic type, whose aim is the negation of all separateness . . . an immediate transference, on the principle that there will never be any separation, that the protagonists will remain stuck together as one, or better still be inside one another" (Roustang, 1978, p. 187).

Archaic relationship, immediate transference, and communication beyond language. The similarity between these terms and those used by the author will not go unnoticed. Roustang speaks neither of hypnosis nor of affect. He is not concerned about the energic and psychobiological aspects of

---

[12] The author has drawn attention to this point in an article: "The discovery of transference" (Chertok, 1969c).

the relationship. But this paper is important, for it shows that some analysts are beginning to recognize that the frontier between suggestion and analysis of the transference is not a precise one, and that at the very heart of the transference experience there is an unanalyzable residue, in that it is of a nature which cannot be reduced to that of verbal experience.[13]

For his part, the present author considers it unnecessary to invoke telepathy as an example in order to postulate the existence of "*pre-language*" communication. But Roustang's thesis will give renewed courage to a few "enfants terribles" of psychoanalysis, who have persisted in extending the ideas of Freud and Helene Deutsch on telepathy. The attitude of psychoanalysts on this question is an ambiguous, not to say embarrassed, one. It is above all members of the Hungarian School, Ferenczi, Hollos (who succeeded to the presidency of the Hungarian Psychoanalytic Society upon Ferenczi's death), Fodor, Roheim, and Balint, who have pursued this line of research. At the present time, the best-known researchers are Ian Ehrenwald in New York, Jules Eisenbud in Denver, and Emilio Servadio in Rome.[14]

These psychoanalysts, far from thinking that telepathic phenomena are an obstacle to the psychoanalytic process, consider that they may constitute a catalyst. For example, Balint (1955) asserted that he had on several occasions seen cases in his practice which could not be explained by an implicit transmission of information by signals or words. He stated that he had noticed that telepathic communications always took place in situations where the patient was motivated by a strong positive transference to which the therapist could not respond because of some external preoccupation. In other words, the patient had recourse to this means in order to gain the analyst's attention. Hann-Kende, another Hungarian psychoanalyst, wrote: "The patient produces such 'insights' when he unconsciously senses a decrease in the analyst's libido" (1933, p. 166). Balint posed the following question without attempting to answer it: Is it better, as it were, to overprotect the patient, while undertaking in due course the necessary interpretations, in such a way that he does not need to turn to telepathy? Or "would it be a better technique in the sense of one producing more fundamental and lasting results, to

[13]See Note A, p. 132.
[14]In a fairly recent report entitled "Parapsychology in psychiatry and psychoanalysis," Moreau (1975) summarized research in this field. Devereux (1953), who is very critical in regard to telepathy, collected the most important psychoanalytic writings on this subject.

tolerate the patient's getting into this situation of very high tensions and to enable him to learn to cope with these high tensions also?" (Balint, 1955, p. 32).

Hypnosis has always been associated, in the mind of the general public, with paranormal phenomena.[15] (Dingwall, 1967, devoted four volumes to the study of all the cases in the nineteenth century where a hypnotic phenomenon appeared to be linked with a paranormal phenomenon.) This association, which still persists today, is very largely responsible for the disrepute in which hypnosis has always been held by the scientific world. Thus, on the grounds that it was impossible to prove the existence of true extra-retinal vision (reading a text without the aid of the eyes), in 1840 the Academy of Medicine definitively concluded that animal magnetism did not exist (Chertok, 1964).

That is why research workers who have taken an interest in hypnotic phenomena have always attempted to rescue hypnosis from this embarrassing association. Nowadays, if one talks about parapsychology to an experimental psychologist who is working on hypnosis, he will shrug his shoulders or become very angry, depending upon how emotional he is.

This does not prevent parapsychologists today (Honorton and Krippner, 1969) from using hypnosis for their research. Honorton and Stump (1969) and Moreau and Rogez (1977) have conducted experiments which tend to prove that hypnosis increases telepathic abilities.

It seems that psychiatric circles are at present showing some signs of opening up to parapsychological research. The American Psychiatric Association has held several symposia on the subject in the course of its annual meetings. In France, the periodical *Evolution Psychiatrique* has recently published the work of Moreau and Rogez mentioned above.

As far as the author is concerned, he has no particular experience in this

---

[15] In the 1880s, some very famous authors such as Richet, Bergson, Lombroso, Schrenck-Notzing, Janet, etc., were interested in paranormal phenomena. In 1882, the Society for Psychic Research was founded in London and Freud became an honorary member in 1911. On November 30th, 1885, and May 31st, 1886, Janet read two papers before the Society of Physiological Psychology, at meetings presided over by Charcot, on the subject of his experiments in mental suggestion at a distance with a famous somnambulist, Léonie (Janet, 1885, 1886). Some have wondered whether Freud might not have attended the first of these lectures during his stay in Paris and whether this may have contributed to arousing his interest in telepathy. It may be noted that, just as Freud's disciples have sought to minimize the significance of the master's statements about telepathy, so Janet's interpreters tend to avoid this aspect of his research. Janet, unlike Freud, later ceased all comment on this subject.

field. At the very most he has, like all analysts, sometimes been aware of a remarkable correspondence between what the analysand was saying and what he himself was thinking at that very moment. It has also happened that during hypnotic sessions the subject has wakened just at the moment when the author was intending to suggest it to him. But these experiences are too few for any conclusion to be drawn from them.

Supposing that telepathy exists, the author does not exclude *a priori* the existence of a link between it and hypnosis. It is a fact that mediums are often hypnotizable. It may be that hypnosis plays the role of a catalyst insofar as it creates a condition of increased psychic and physiological plasticity. Bassin and Platonov (1973) could write that hypnosis liberated what they called the "hidden reserves of the higher nervous system."

It may be asked what role the relational factor plays in the production of telepathic phenomena. Do these presuppose the establishment of a particular relationship between the subjects concerned, or is telepathy simply an innate instrumental capacity, which, for unknown reasons, is more developed in some subjects than in others? In experimental telepathy, the subjects between whom the information is transmitted have no particular link with each other. But if one is to rely on the observations by Balint and other psychoanalysts, it does seem that the relationship has an influence on these phenomena.

The same question applies to hypnosis. It is known that hypnosis, or closely related states, can be produced by purely physical means (sensory deprivation) which involve at the outset no relational factor. But in fact it is not as simple as that. If one takes the example of experiments on sensory deprivation, it has been observed that it was accompanied in most cases by a psychological regression, particularly in the form of depersonalization phenomena and the establishment of increased dependence upon an imaginary person, perceived as a protective or persecutory presence. In other words, sensory deprivation has the effect of a kind of opening up of affects, thus allowing the emergence of a potential for relating which is released in the absence of any real support. One might say that this is a case of adaptive reaction, a protective mechanism which is set off in response to the stress occasioned by the deprivation of all perceptual or environmental connections.

Kubie describes this aspect of the hypnotic process as follows: "There is a presence in another sense: a hovering if unseen and unacknowledged presence, sometimes consciously perceived but more often preconsciously and/or unconsciously . . . *this is transference in purest culture,* even when there is no present object, whether real or imagined, whether conscious or subliminal" (Kubie, 1961, p. 43 – italics added).

Here we touch upon the interconnection between the instrumental and relational aspects. That is what the author has attempted to express by introducing the concept of a primary relational function, biologically inbuilt.

One might say that in a situation of experimental hypnosis the relational exchange is for the most part restricted by the setting, which prevents the process from being deepened. In therapeutic hypnosis, on the other hand, the transference situation is such that this relationship is experienced far more intensely and involves the whole personality.

Energy, empathy, symbiosis, fusion, primary relationship, immediate transference, affective flow – we must needs recognize that all these are merely operative metaphors devoid of any scientific basis, to describe the *transfer* of affective influence from one individual to another.

It may be said that affect, in its relational aspects, entered the experimental stage with Mesmer and animal magnetism. Mesmer approached the problem essentially from the energetic point of view with his theory of a fluid. Only once in his writings does one find a reference to the role of feeling: "Animal magnetism must in the first place be transmitted by feeling. Feeling can alone render the theory understandable. For example, one of my patients, accustomed to experiencing the actions which I produce on him, has, in order to understand me, one more faculty than other men" (Mesmer, 1781, p. 25).

Mesmer's successors, while still remaining fluidists, began to employ such psychological terms as will, passion, the wish to cure, etc. The hypnotists of the second half of the nineteenth century clearly sensed that there was an affective link, a "selective affinity," between themselves and somnambulists; but they explained it by the subject's cerebral state.

Freud, in introducing transference, achieved an immense step forward, by clearly situating the question of affect in its relational context. But, as often happens in scientific activity, the revealing of one part of the field of the unknown only succeeded in enlarging the latter. In order to explain the affective trend, Freud had recourse to metaphors of energy – libido, cathexis, etc.[16] He was unable to formulate a truly scientific theory of affect.

Lacan, for his part, relinquishes in a certain way the problem of affect. His theory rests on the exclusion of the biological, bodily dimension of the unconscious and of the relationship. While it is extremely productive, it cannot on this account pretend to be complete. So long as there is no theory of affect, both psychological and physiological, psychotherapy and psychoanalysis cannot aspire to scientific status. There are those, it is true, who will think that this is perhaps not desirable.

[16]Some authors believe (Rausky, personal communication) that Fechner, who inspired Freud with his constancy principle, had in turn been inspired by Mesmer, whose theories were well known to him.

Note A (see page 128, footnote 13)

It will be seen that the pessimism already shown by Roustang in a book entitled *Un Destin si Funeste (So Fateful a Destiny)* (Roustang, 1976) persists in that author's more recent article quoted above, in which he raises the crucial question of the termination of analysis, and of the further production of analysts which is but its corollary.

To attempt to obliterate the power of the "immediate" transference is to risk returning to the repressed in the form of an "infinite" transference, never to be resolved. It involves the risk that the theory may be transmitted by osmosis from the analyst to the analysand, and that analysis would thus become but a mere method of producing analysts.

The same author rejects the solution of the didactic process instituted by the Lacanian school, as that most likely to engender such interminable analyses.

Nor is it a question that "Mr. Nobody" should suddenly become "Mr. Everyone" with the intention of putting a full stop to analysis by abandoning his anonymity in order to establish with the analysand a "normal" relationship, between one individual and another. This is one way of purely and simply denying the immediate transference, which does not abolish it but allows it to subsist in a place which is all the more inaccessible in that it can no longer be traced anywhere. This amounts to placing the analyst definitively on a pedestal.

Roustang puts forward a solution which is certainly not easy. He considers that the analyst should be able to both have a "hold on" and be "held in" what has happened. Thus he is able to ascertain, and especially to allow the patient to ascertain, how, in the course of treatment, the latter has let himself be caught in the snare of suggestion and the analyst's wish. This recalling in question of the analyst by himself would require the never-ending renewal of a task of humility, but it is no doubt the only means through which the analysand can demystify the analyst.

This implies a radical questioning of psychoanalysis. It may be noted, in this connection, that while in the United States the attacks directed at psychoanalysis always come from outside, in France the criticism comes from within, arising in the very places where, in principle, it is supposed to be transmitted.

Subsequent events, since these lines were written, have not borne out the author's optimism here. Lacan, the "père sévère" ("père sévère": a Lacanian pun on persevere and stern father), decided to tidy up his School by dissolving it, in an effort to winkle out the unfaithful and the lukewarn. He then went on to form a new association, "la Cause freudienne" (the Freudian cause), with himself as director, as "keystone," and in which he has granted himself virtually limitless powers. This new grouping "points the way for those who wish, in the field opened up by Freud, to pursue (their road?) with Lacan." Of the remainder he says: "The emblem that I have handed down to you is now fallen into the hands of patent forgers" (*Le Monde,* Mar. 15th, 1980).

Yet another incident to mark the conflict-ridden history of psychoanalytical institutions. Freud's reactions to dissident disciples seem almost tame and innocuous in comparison. We would need to go all the way back to Mesmer to find a comparable reaction. When Deslon founded his "competing–opposing" School, Mesmer, jealous of his prerogatives, also called his adversary a forger: "Never have I revealed to him the very extensive and, I believe, fairly profound, theory that must be studied in order to be able to claim with some truth to possess my doctrine and my discovery" (Rausky, 1977, p. 106). Lacan condemns the "deviations and compromises which are holding up (the) progress (of his work) by degrading its application" (*Le Monde,* Jan. 11th, 1980). And when Mesmer declared: "It is empiricism and the unthinking application of procedures which have given rise to the hostility and indiscreet criticisms that have been levelled at this method" (Rausky, 1977, p. 101), one cannot help thinking back to those "patent forgers," who do nothing but "turn to dishwater a teaching in which everything is carefully weighed" (*Le Monde,* Jan. 11th, 1980).

Make no mistake, jealousies between the power brokers of the mind are far older than this latest flare-up (Chertok, 1966).

The latest news (January 1981) is that the newly formed "Cause freudienne" has splintered yet again into several fragments.

While this book was in page-proof stage, Roustang published a new book, ...*Elle ne le lâche plus* (*She Never Lets You Go*: the French are fond of elliptical titles that give nothing away as to the contents). The title refers to Binswanger's dictum, "Once psychoanalysis has you in her grip, she never lets you go." Roustang, who does not practice hypnosis himself, and who is not interested in the phenomenon *per se* (he belongs to a group of French analysts who believe that the best chance of rescuing analysis from its present crisis lies in scrutinizing its weak points), summarizes his argument (back cover) in the following terms: "Frued considered, not without misgivings, that the technique of free association, 'telling all,' would free psychoanalysis of whatever links it might have with hypnosis. His successors have banished all doubts on the subject. We, however, may well wonder whether the real wellspring of transference is not the same as that of hypnosis, namely the desire to merge with and absorb the other." Similarly, Ida MacAlpine (1950) remarked that "analytic transference manifestations are a slow motion picture of hypnotic transference manifestations." Roustang returns once more to this notion of fusional or symbiotic relationship which is currently exercising so many analysts. We attribute to the infant such "adultomorphic" fantasies as devouring, destruction, annihilation, etc. One wonders whether these verbal metaphors reflect the child's actual subjective experience. Are we not in fact here touching upon some pre-verbal, biological level of the relation on a "primary (*ur-*) relation" (see above, p. 116), which seems to be the common core of hypnosis and every other kind of psychotherapy?

According to Roustang, Freud's abandoning of hypnosis failed in its aim of rendering the psychoanalytic relationship more scientific than the hypnotic relationship. It is worth wondering whether the hypnotic origins of psychoanalysis may not, on the contrary, to some extent guarantee its scientific character. At a time when doubt is being cast upon the effectiveness of psychoanalysis, the hypnotic element contained in it ought to reassure analysts, if only by virtue of its experimentally proven ability to influence behavior.

11

An Embarrassing Legacy

The relationships between hypnosis and psychoanalysis have always been marked by an Oedipal ambivalence. It was by abandoning hypnosis that Freud discovered psychoanalysis. And since then, in approaching this subject, every analyst feels bound to prove that he also has achieved this primordial rupture and that he is not guilty of regression to a pre-analytical stage.

Fortunately, it is the same with hypnosis as with those shameful forebears who are kept out of sight, but always reappear on the most inopportune occasion. However much it is relegated to a part of analytical prehistory, it is reborn like the Phoenix from its ashes.

The attitude of psychoanalysts is all the more paradoxical as the analytical situation is not without its hypnogenic elements: concentration, silence, reclining position, the subdued atmosphere constitute the first stages of sensory deprivation. Silence can also act in two different ways: on the one hand, it encourages the activity of fantasies; on the other, it may induce alterations in the subject's state of consciousness, through which he is liable to fluctuate from one level of regression to another, and find himself brought back to that specific form of communication which characterizes hypnosis. Freud himself described, in 1891, a silent technique of hypnotic induction (1891, p. 108). It may be thought, moreover, that this primary, pretransferential relationship facilitates or reinforces the phenomena of transference. From this point of view, it would be interesting to investigate whether subjects with a strong hypnotic susceptibility are not the most suitable for analysis, insofar as they are the most accessible to an affective dialogue. It is also true that this deep regression may constitute an escapist attitude, a resistance to analytical work.

The resistances of psychoanalytical circle toward hypnosis assume different forms, depending on the country. In the United States, interest in hypnosis underwent a revival following the Second World War. Hypnosis is part of the therapeutic arsenal. Psychotherapists working in a psychodynamic perspective do not hesitate to resort to it in various forms. Psychoanalysts such as Kubie, Margolin, Gill, and Brenman have taken an active interest in it. It may be noted, however, that they are the only "card-carrying" analysts to have seriously studied this question, and even they have given up their work in this field.[1]

It cannot, therefore, be said that hypnosis is fully accepted by the psychoanalytical community. Some American analysts even consider it to be incompatible with the practice of psychoanalysis.[2] It is thus sometimes asserted that a therapist who has undergone a personal analysis is no longer capable of being a good hypnotist.[3] The wish to hypnotize, according to them, is linked with infantile fantasies of omnipotence, and disappears when these have been sufficiently analyzed.

Thus, Giovacchini (1972) explains that, since his analysis, he can no longer accept the "melodramatic" atmosphere that characterizes hypnosis. It may seem surprising that so eminent a psychoanalyst should still maintain a music-hall image of hypnosis. One could also mention the instance of therapists whose analysis has in no way impaired their hypnotizing power. The author, for his part, wonders whether psychoanalysts relinquish hypnosis because they have become aware of their infantile motivations or whether this relinquishment is not rather due, in the words of Gill and Brenman, to "his growing wish to cease being a deviant rebel and to join the respectable ranks of his analyst and his teachers" (Gill and Brenman, 1959, p. 172).

[1] As Karl Menninger told the author, "they researched themselves out of hypnosis." Kubie (1972, p. 206) nostalgically evoked the time when he was not a "drop-out."

[2] Kubie (1972, p. 217) spoke in this connection of "interest in the phenomenology of hypnosis to the occasional psychoanalytic bigot who regards such an interest as disloyalty to analysis." They are the same ones who assert that any dealings with hypnosis are proof of a resistance. In the article mentioned earlier, Castoriadis denounces the way this type of argument is used in the controversies that stir psychoanalytical circles, whenever one wishes to disqualify his adversary. He emphasizes "the essential identity of this defense mechanism with that used by totalitarian regimes for whom any questioning of the official dogma was excluded *a priori* from the discussion." He cites as an example the controversy "between traditional and Lacanian psychoanalysts who each let it be understood that the others are resisting analysis. . . . And what, then, are both of these groups resisting together?" (Castoriadis, 1977, p. 26).

[3] Reference is usually made, in this connection, to Ferenczi, who after his analysis would appear to have lost his ability to hypnotize. One is here forgetting that he can hardly be taken as a model of a well-analyzed subject.

The second interpretation would seem the more likely, for, in the author's opinion, awareness of the counter-transferential aspects of the hypnotic relationship should render the therapist capable of using it with greater freedom and understanding, rather than being expressed by an inhibition verging on phobia. It may be supposed that, if one day hypnotism is rehabilitated, many analysts will discover that they are gifted hypnotists. Of course, all therapists are not equally fitted to practice the hypnotic relationship. But that is another problem.

To return to the hypnotist's so-called omnipotence in the hypnotic relationship and to its supposed corollary, the dependence of the hypnotized subject, there is admittedly an important part of suggestion in this relationship, but the subject retains his freedom to accept hypnosis or not, and the treatment is generally shorter. The dependence of the analysand on the analyst is more subtle, but basically far deeper, since it goes so far as to make the patient spend years on the couch.

In France, although the country of Bernheim and Charcot, hypnotic research is in a particularly underdeveloped state. Within official research institutions (CRNS, INSERM, Ecole Pratique des Hautes Etudes) there is no laboratory working on this problem. When a research project was recently proposed to a commission of scientists, they asked which were the objective criteria by which one might recognize hypnosis. Insofar as these criteria are not at present known, it might be thought that it is precisely this lack of knowledge that justified the need for such investigation. This was not the opinion of the commission which considered that, since these criteria had not been discovered, hypnosis did not exist – at least as an object for scientific investigation. As research work is extremely centralized in France, such an attitude, coming from a central organization, effectively blocks any working possibilities on a large scale. Moreover, the Research and Study Units (UER) on psychology and psychophysiology in the universities are dominated either by experimental psychologists, who consider hypnosis too unscientific, or by psychoanalysts who reject it for ideological reasons.

At the therapeutic level, the taboo is so strong that hypnosis has been renamed sophrology.[4] As if one could change something by changing its

---

[4] Sophrologists use the same induction technique as hypnotists. But they consider themselves to be different from the latter in that they do not attempt to induce a deep trance. They forget that, in any case, a deep trance can be obtained in only 5% of the population. Thus we can say that they are making a virtue of necessity. It may be noted that the term "sophrology" exists

name! There is an even more total rejection on the part of psychoanalysts. Anyone dealing with hypnosis is exposed to anathema, not to say excommunication. Cases have thus been brought to the author's attention of young psychoanalysts occasionally practicing hypnosis in secret.

A few anecdotes may perhaps be cited here, which illustrate this situation. Having learnt that some dentists use hypnosis to alleviate the pain caused by the drill, a young trainee psychoanalyst was horrified at the consequences of this type of procedure, in view of the symbolic significance of this instrument. The author reminded him of a story. One day, someone drew Freud's attention to the symbolic meaning of the cigar. "You know," he replied, "a cigar can also be a cigar." The drill can also be a drill. If one is to believe his colleague, the author would have committed a real crime by using hypnosis in the dental extraction reported above.

Roudinesco declares without hesitation that hypnosis comprises a "fascist rite" (1978, p. 16). According to her, this is the reason the Nazis were so particularly interested in it. A young and brilliant philosopher-analyst of the Ecole Freudienne (Lacanian School) who visited the author's laboratory also leveled accusations of perversion and voyeurism against its psychologists. She asserted that psychological experimentation was contrary to the ethics of psychoanalysis. When it was suggested to her that she should let herself be hypnotized, she answered with an indignant, "Never!"

One can wonder what frightened her so. It is true that all the members of the Ecole do not seem to share her point of view, since, as we shall see later, one of them is carrying out research of an experimental nature.

Maud Mannoni, who has a reputation for "open-mindedness" and as a "liberal," even expresses, in a recent book, her indignation at the reappearance, in hospitals, of a "psychiatric practice one thought had been long abandoned." "Young analysts," she adds, "(in Paris) do not hesitate to

only in Latin countries. The Anglo-Saxons have not felt the need to resort to this device, perhaps because hypnosis is more widely accepted in their countries.

Analytical relaxation (Sapir, 1975), which stems from Schultz's Autogenic Training, an "auto-hypnotic" technique, is also unknown in the United States. It can be assimilated to what is termed hypnoanalysis in that country. Basically, both techniques bring the same elements into play: induction of a regression through bodily action, and working-through (free association, interpretations, etc.). The only difference is that, in the case of deeper hypnosis, hypnoanalysts bring more specialized techniques to bear (age regression, experimental conflict, induction, etc.). But here again, the depth of the trance depends more on the subject than on the experimenter. However that may be, analytical relaxation is now enjoying a widespread development. It is an original method of approach and has proved to be fruitful.

take part in pure experimentation, where the patient acts as guinea-pig"
(Mannoni, 1979, p. 80).

It would be interesting to know where she obtained this information. It is
extremely rare, nowadays, to find a young psychiatrist who knows how to use
hypnosis. Thus a young amnesiac recently mentioned in the newspapers
spent 6 months in a psychiatric hospital in the suburbs of Paris without
anyone resorting to hypnosis to remove the amnesia. It would seem that the
assistant had thought for a moment of bringing him to the author, but for
many reasons this turned out to be impossible.

Perhaps Mannoni and other critics consider that to allow a patient to
recover his identity by removing his amnesia through hypnosis is to violate
him.[5]

It is possible, moreover, that the young analysts to whom Mannoni refers
do use their patients as guinea-pigs. It is not possible to discuss this point, as we
do not know what she is speaking about. It is only regrettable that she should
imply that the use of hypnosis necessarily entails such an attitude, thus
demonstrating once again the ignorance that prevails on this subject.

These would be amusing facts if they did not show the existence of a form of
alienation of *Homo psychoanalyticus,* and if they had no bearing on the
development of research. One may wonder what factors motivate this
resistance on the part of psychoanalysts. Throughout the whole of the
nineteenth century, the rejection of hypnosis came mainly from medical
circles, largely because hypnosis disturbed the categories proper to the
medical discourse of that time, but also because doctors sensed that they
could not broach the subject of the hypnotic relationship without touching on
sexuality (Chertok and de Saussure, 1973).

It is hard to imagine that this motive should arise amongst psychoanalysts,
whose job it is, in principle, to confront this dimension. One can, however,

---

[5] With the usual anti-Americanism of some French psychoanalysts, Maud Mannoni likewise
expresses her indignation about the fact that American psychiatrists had collaborated with the
military, during the war, to assess the soldiers' mental state (*ibid.,* pp. 69–70). We will not be
betraying any secrets by pointing out that American psychiatrists have done things even more
"horrible" than that. They used hypnosis for the treatment of combat neuroses in order to
return soldiers to their units as fast as possible (which was generally considered to be the best
way to avoid more serious disorders). Maud Mannoni certainly knows that Simmel, a disciple of
Freud, had already used hypnosis for the same purpose in the German army during the First
World War, with Freud's entire approval. It was, in fact, in referring to the results obtained
in the treatment of war neuroses that, in 1918, at the Budapest Congress, he spoke the words
already quoted on the future of hypnosis as a therapeutic procedure (see p. 74).

wonder whether this fear does not persist to some extent. In fact, hypnosis presupposes a very high level of bodily involvement. It is a sort of clinch, a fusional relationship that conveys archaic fears which are often poorly mastered.

This, no doubt, is the aspect to which Freud referred in speaking of the "mystical" element contained in the hypnotic relationship. One is inclined to believe that this is one of the main reasons which led him to abandon hypnosis. As we know, he reached this decision after one of his patients, whom he had just hypnotized, threw her arms around him. This incident was also the basis of the discovery of transference (Chertok, 1969c). In order to explain the desire of which he had been the object, Freud interpreted it as the repetition of an earlier relationship. We may wonder if this was not a way to protect the therapist from the present dimension of the relationship, the establishment of an affective current perceived to be dangerous.

Freud's genius was to create a framework which allowed the relationship to continue over a very long period. With this aim, to enable the therapist to withstand the repetition of the relational confrontation, he imagined a comfortable situation for the latter, which allowed him to avoid the gaze of the analysand and, thanks to transference, to disinvolve himself, as it were, from the relationship. We may wonder whether excessive recourse to language and intellectual dialogue in some analyses does not partake of the same process.

It is true that the hypnotic situation can also be a means for the therapist to protect himself from relational involvement through the "technical" manipulation of the subject, whereas analysis forces the psychoanalyst to confront the fantasies of his patient and to live out his own counter-transference. *This objectivation is the permanent danger of hypnosis.* But as soon as the hypnotist renounces this defensive attitude, the hypnotic relationship is less "comfortable" than the analytical one. There is more contact between the unconscious of the patient and that of the hypnotist.

But more than anything else, hypnosis reminds us concretely of the limits of our knowledge. It causes us to perceive precisely that we are playing on only a small part of the relational spectrum and that psychotherapy rests on factors which are as yet largely unknown to us. This is a fact that few analysts are prepared to hear.

It seems, however, that one can discern in France today a renewed interest in hypnosis in psychoanalytical circles, especially on the part of Lacan's disciples. Thus, over several years, Gérard Miller has started to study hypnosis, first in an epistemological perspective, but also at an experimental level. In an article entitled "Sur le discours du Maître et l'hypnose" (On the discourse of the Master and hypnosis) (1977a), he gives us a first glimpse of his work.

He states that he is trying to practice hypnosis divested of all "ceremonial." This is what he calls "subway hypnotism." It is hard to understand precisely what he means by this term, since he gives no concrete example. But it would seem to consist in a maximal simplification of the induction process, so as to "let function what is at stake" (*ibid.*, p. 301). It will be noted that this approach amounts to the eschewal of whatever, at the psychophysiological level, is specific to hypnosis – the setting up of an apparatus, a framework, favorable to the emergence of an altered state of consciousness. Indeed, for Miller, only on the surface does environment play any determining role in the production of hypnotic phenomena. "I have performed experiments in hypnotism in the waking state," he writes, "because I wanted to make this perceptible: that one never knows when it begins. Or, again, that it always started earlier than you thought" (*ibid.*, p. 306). In other words, hypnotism only works because the subject is already hypnotized. Hypnosis presupposes, prior to any manipulation, the establishment of a symbolic pact, of a rule of play whereby the subject submits to the will of the hypnotist and takes the position of "slave" with regard to a "master" who wields the power.

The hypnotic relationship thus finds itself reduced to a simple phenomenon of suggestibility. In this sense, Miller's approach is somewhat similar to that of certain American authors who have attempted to show that hypnotic phenomena can also be obtained by suggestion in the waking state. There is a basic difference, however. These authors are, indeed, experimental psychologists who tend, generally speaking, to remain on a purely descriptive level. Miller, on the other hand, places himself in a psychoanalytical perspective. If hypnosis is a game, it is a game with an unconscious meaning.

We cannot enter into the details of this analysis which rests on the concepts and the mathematical formulae of Lacan. Let us simply say that, essentially, it takes up the theses elaborated by Freud in *Collective Psychology and Ego-Analysis* (1921) and commented on by Lacan (1964, pp. 244–245) according to which, in the hypnotic relationship, the object – the hypnotist – takes the place of the Ego ideal. Thus, the suggestibility shown by the hypnotized subject is only a means to realize a fantasy of omnipotence through identification with an imaginary "master." The hypnotist's power is, therefore, a sham. He is only serving in the capacity assigned to him by the hypnotized subject.

It will be noted that Stewart (1969, p. 201) had already put forward a similar idea, comparing the hypnotic situation to the British parliamentary system. The Queen only has the power delegated to her by the people.

While Miller only approaches hypnosis from the point of view of suggestibility, Nassif (1977) takes into consideration the hypnotic experience in its innermost specificity. But this is more in an historic perspective. In an outstanding book, he analyses the role of hypnosis in the elaboration of psychoanalysis. We shall not attempt to summarize here such a rich and vast text. We shall simply point out some of the elements that seem particularly important, because they bear witness to the removal of the taboo which has hitherto surrounded hypnosis in French psychoanalytical circles.

Basing his work on Freud's writings between 1886 and 1892 - that is from his return from Paris to the "Preliminary Communication," five major years in his evolution - Nassif covers the distance with Freud and declares, as in jest: While Freud did give up suggestion, he never, on the other hand, abandoned hypnosis. As hypnosis was, in his time, considered to be an abuse of power, it was simple strategy to say that he had given it up. In fact (as emphasized at the beginning of this chapter), what Nassif calls the "practicable"[6] in analysis - the couch, the reclining position, etc. - originated in hypnosis. Psychoanalytical discourse is inseparable from the practicable. It cannot be realized without this kind of trade where the objects exchanged are the gaze and the voice.

Hypnosis is crucial in that the subject relinquishes his gaze (many patients do, in fact, close their eyes) in order to rely on his voice. There is always something of hypnosis in the practicable: the hypnotic session was the origin of the analytical session and analytical discourse would never have seen the light of day if Freud had not practiced hypnosis. Yet analysts have all chosen the "medical repression" of hypnosis.[7]

---

[6] In the theatrical sense (i.e., a movable stage prop).

[7] Some while ago, a polemic, the contents of which remain at times obscure, opposed Jacques Nassif to Gérard Miller, the latter taking J. Nassif to task for speaking of hypnosis without full knowledge of the subject, since he does not practice it. This gave him an opportunity in this instance to describe in picturesque terms the attitude of those psychoanalysts who, "grimacing in disgust, at the very most, consent from time to time to turn a tired glance (towards the hypnotists), just to see whether they are to be found on the side of the quacks, rather than that of the fools." As for hypnosis, it is compared to "a poor demented ancestor, hitherto buried in a country asylum . . ." (Miller, 1977b, pp. 71-72).

The author agrees with Nassif as to the common ground that exists between the psychoanalytical and the hypnotic orientation. But on reading his works, one feels somewhat that with the discovery of psychoanalysis, Freud brought the hypnotic entity back to its basic truth by ridding it of what Nassif calls the "matrix" of suggestion.[8] This point of view could easily become a subtle way of eliminating hypnosis, while acknowledging its importance. If hypnosis and psychoanalysis are one and the same thing, there would no longer be any need to concern ourselves with the former, except for historical purposes, inasmuch as it brought about the psychoanalytical discourse. The author for his part believes that the problem has not yet been solved and that the study of hypnosis is indispensable if we wish to broaden our knowledge of relational phenomena. If psychoanalysts really wish *to know what they are about,* it is entirely in their interest to study the question of hypnosis. One is, in fact, always confronted with the same problem. Nassif, like Miller, is blind to the psychophysiological dimension of hypnosis. In order to explain such phenomena as anesthesia or hypnotic blistering, Lacanians resort to metaphore: the signifier, according to them, is inscribed in the body. But this is supposing the problem solved beforehand. In what, indeed, does this inscription consist? As long as there is no answer to such questions, terms such as signifier and inscription will remain obscure.

---

[8]It may be recalled that J. H. Schultz, practicing his Autogenic Training, also aspired to "pure hypnotism" (in the form of self-hypnosis), devoid of suggestion. Is this feasible?

12

A Psychobiological Dilemma

"... psycho-analysis must keep itself free from any hypothesis that is alien to it, whether of an anatomical, chemical or physiological kind, and must operate entirely with purely psychological auxiliary ideas" (Freud, 1916, p. 21).

"The phenomena with which we are dealing do not belong to psychology alone; they have an organic and biological side as well, and accordingly in the course of our efforts at building up psycho-analysis we have also made some important biological discoveries and have not been able to avoid framing new biological hypotheses" (Freud, 1938, p. 195).

We could lengthen the list of quotations which show that Freud, throughout his life, never ceased to oscillate between two positions. On the one hand, he always claimed that psychoanalysis was independent of any established knowledge and refused to base psychoanalytical discourse on anything but the experience of the psychoanalytical situation itself. On the other hand, he asserted at the same time that psychoanalysis would only become a true science when its main concepts were translated into the fields of biology and neurophysiology.

These fluctuations are also to be found in the works of his successors. In the United States, after the Second World War, the "physicalist" trend prevailed with the creation of Ego-psychology by the Hartmann, Kris, Loewenstein "troika," to whom one should add David Rapaport. Some voices, however, have been raised against Ego-psychology. This controversy is illustrated by two articles published in the same issue of the *International Journal of Psychoanalysis*, one by Holt (1965, p. 151), the other by Apfelbaum (1965, p. 169), each author defending radically opposed points of view.

Holt goes so far as to declare that the psychoanalytical model should be totally rebuilt in an anatomic-physiological perspective. His proposal is that

Freud's *Project for a Scientific Psychology* (1895) should be taken as a starting point; according to him, it still remains valid and can interact with the progress achieved in neurophysiology since the beginning of this century. Holt, a pupil of Rapaport, pursued his crusade for the liberation of the Ego from instinctual subjection. He opposed, sometimes lyrically, two types of nineteenth-century man: the one free, responsible for his choice of behavior, endowed with rational thought, and the other influenced by romanticism and a victim of irrational passions. The former embodies the world of the Encyclopedists, of Kant and Hegel; the latter is the world of Schopenhauer, Nietzsche and Kierkegaard, a world sung by Beethoven and Wagner. Influenced by both these trends, Freud would seem to have hesitated between them, that is, between the autonomy and the non-autonomy of the Ego. As for Holt, he clearly declared in favor of its autonomy. With Hartmann, he insisted on the Ego's independence in relation to the Id, and with Rapaport on its autonomy in relation to the environment. He emphasized that Rapaport arrived at his theory largely owing to his interest in sensory deprivation and hypnosis, two phenomena where the interactions between body and mind are particularly striking. The fact that by manipulation of the bodily sphere one can obtain regressive phenomena – and so, one might say, a loss of autonomy – is proof, for him, of the existence of an autonomous Ego. For such a loss to be possible, it would mean that this autonomy did exist in the first place. Holt considered experiments on sensory deprivation as physiological experiments bearing out a psychoanalytical concept. It is hardly necessary to say that for him, as for Hartmann, any parallel with neurophysiology is welcome.

At the very same time, however, other authors stressed that psychoanalytical concepts could not be expressed in terms of general psychology. This point of view is reflected in the article of Apfelbaum, who believed that Hartmann's formulations represented a retrograde tendency in that they used a non-analytical model for an analytical subject. In Apfelbaum's opinion, Hartmann only resorted to quantitative notions, without taking qualitative notions into account. He considered the quantitative conception to be dangerous, not only on the theoretical level, but also on the clinical level, even if only used metaphorically. For Apfelbaum, the dynamic theory, on the other hand, was exclusively psychoanalytical, and had nothing in common with physics, physiology, or general psychology.

Positions have not always been expressed in such categorical terms as are used by Holt and Apfelbaum. The former, in particular, would seem to have largely overstepped the theoretical hypotheses of Ego-psychology. In 1946 Hartmann, Kris, and Loewenstein formulated their concepts on this subject in the following manner: "In adopting the *functions* exercised in mental processes as the decisive criterium for defining the psychic systems, Freud used physiology as his model in concept formation. However, this does not imply any correlation of any one of the systems to any specific physiological organization or group of organs, though Freud considered such a correlation as the ultimate goal of psychological research. Psychological terminology, he assumed, has to be maintained as long as it cannot be adequately substituted by physiological terminology. It seems that the time for such substitution has not yet come" (Hartmann, Kris, and Loewenstein, 1946, p. 15). As can be seen, this is a far more flexible position.

In France the problem of the relationship between psychology and physiology had also been raised. In 1966 André Green protested any attempt to use an anatomic-physiological language in metapsychology, which cannot express the phenomena relating to meaning and wish. He acknowledged that it was impossible to exclude a certain structural[1] conception if one wished to organize and shape the different levels of psychic life: "If one wishes," he wrote, "to connect the interplay and the effects of meaning, it is indispensable, in the first place, to localize, so to say, those levels that have to be assembled in order to reestablish discourse, inasmuch as this is the mainstay and the relation of a mutilated truth" (Green, 1966, pp. 19-20). But he rejected all resort to "apparatus" which bore the risk of using "the language of substantialization" (*ibid.*, p. 19). However, no doubt in order to remain faithful to Freud's thought, he did not go so far as to break completely with physiology in general nor to challenge out of hand "the data of neuro-biology as being inapt in their principles to reveal anything essential about the unconscious" (*ibid.*, p. 24).

Similarly, in a work published in 1965, J. and E. Kestenberg wrote (p. 9) that "psychoanalysis begins where biology ends." The human phenomenon, they believed, could not be reduced to physical or biological reality, but should be considered as "a singular and irreductibly original object" (*ibid.*, p. 7).

[1]Not to be confused with the linguistic structuralism with which Lacan's theories are associated.

They were, however, cautious enough to add that this was the case "in the present state of our knowledge," recalling that Freud had always wished to see his ideas confirmed by other scientific disciplines.

While the attitude adopted by Green and the Kestenbergs was, in spite of everything, a flexible one, Ego-psychology has been radically criticized in France by Lacan and his pupils. Lacan takes Ego-psychology to task for wishing to reduce psychoanalysis to the level of general psychology, thus losing sight of its specific dimension: the discovery of the unconscious desire insofar as it is irreducible to any "instrumental" description ("Ego apparatus" or autonomous Ego). For Lacan, Freud's merit was that he drew attention to the meaning of human behavior. The wish is a language; rooted in instinct, it receives its human dimension from the submission of the subject to the symbolic order. Thus, it is in structural linguistics that psychoanalysis must look for a support. Such is the meaning of the "return to Freud."

Ego-psychologists have, of course, likewise referred to Freud, but to a Freud who, for Lacanians, had seemingly remained a prisoner of the scientist theories of the nineteenth century. A Marxist philosopher and follower of Lacan, Althusser, summed up this position, stating that one had to come back to "the maturity of Freudian theory, not to its childhood, but to its mature age, which is its true youth . . . beyond the theoretical infantilism, the reversion to childhood, where a good part of contemporary, and especially American, psychoanalysis is tasting the fruits of its relinquishments" (Althusser, 1964, p. 65).[2] In the same paper, all those who resort to the related disciplines were accused of "bio-psycho-sociological revisionism."

In the United States, a somewhat similar movement has started over the last few years. Pupils of Rapaport, including Klein, Gill, and Schafer, have criticized the use of concepts derived from the natural sciences in the interpretation of clinical reality. They believe that two theories can be distinguished in Freud's work: the one, which they call the *clinical theory*, is formulated in terms of motivation, meaning, and wish, and affords an understanding of the significance of symptoms; the other, which comprises the metapsychological writings, constitutes an attempt to provide clinical observation with a "scientific" basis in the light of the natural sciences. But

---

[2]Since these lines were written, Althusser's position has changed. He has roundly criticized Lacan's ideas and his antics, calling him a "pitiful clown" . . . "waffling his one-string patter, for his benefit alone" (*Le Matin*, Mar. 17th, 1980).

these two discourses are, in fact, entirely heterogeneous; far from affording a better understanding of clinical phenomena, metapsychology is seen as an obstacle insofar as it organizes phenomena in terms of pre-established concepts which do not take into account the specific nature of the inter-subjective relationship which is the object of psychoanalysis. It is thus thought necessary to create new instruments, stemming solely from what is experienced in the analytical relationship, from what is available to *hic et nunc* observation in the development of the cure. In this connection, Roy Schafer (1976b) speaks of a "new language," a "language of action" which would allow the interpretation of the subject's emotional responses. This is, as it were, a directly phenomenological approach, through which Schafer seems to wish to return to the beginnings of Freudian psychoanalysis, to the views of Brentano rather than of Brücke. He prefers the term "action" to that of "intentionality" used by Brentano; to the present author the meaning appears the same. On the whole, the formulation of the adherents of the clinical theory are not without similarity to the analyses developed in France after the war by certain phenomenologists, such as Merleau-Ponty, on the subject of Freudian theory.

Several authors, however, such as Mayman (1976), while declaring in favor of the clinical theory, believe that the metapsychological perspective should not be entirely rejected. Kaplan (1977), for his part, is reserved as to the validity of the clinical theory.[3]

Let us emphasize, in passing, the original attitude of Kubie, who retained, so to speak, a foothold in both camps. On the one hand, he was critical of metapsychology. In one of his later papers, he expressed his regret that "(Freud) turned from his earlier dynamic metaphors to the more static, structural metaphors of his later years. My conviction is that this change in emphasis had unfortunate effects on analysis and temporarily brought to a full stop the forward movement of analytic theory, techniques, and inquiry" (Kubie, 1972, p. 218). But, while he protested against the use of physicalist concepts which are actually only metaphors, with no precise scientific content, he nonetheless asserted the need for a link between analytical and psychophysiological research. For him, both approaches are complementary. Thus, referring to hypnosis, he wrote: ". . . what we can say with confidence

---

[3] It is interesting to observe Holt's change of opinion (1976). After being an enthusiastic follower of Ego-psychology, he became an adept of the clinical theory.

is that, in the induction of the hypnotic state and in the state itself, and also in its secondary manifestations and consequences, there is no conflict between the roles played by psychodynamic processes and those played by concurrent psychophysiological processes. Psychoanalytic and psychophysiological influences are not mutually exclusive, but are so clearly interdependent as to be synergistic" (Kubie, 1972, p. 212).

The evolution of an author such as Gill is particularly interesting. He used to set great store by a rapprochement between psychoanalysts and experimental psychologists. His work on hypnosis, written in collaboration with Brenman, represented an attempt to build a metapsychological theory of hypnotic phenomena, effecting a synthesis between Ego-psychology and experiments on sensory deprivation. In it, he defined hypnosis as a regression at the service of the Ego (Gill and Brenman, 1959).

In this same perspective, in collaboration with Pribram, he undertook a re-evaluation of the main hypotheses formulated by Freud in the "Project for a Scientific Psychology," in the light of modern physiological knowledge. For various reasons, this work was not published at the time and has only recently appeared (Pribram and Gill, 1976). Meanwhile, however, Gill had become one of the most fervent adherents of the clinical theory. Thus, while agreeing that present neurophysiological research work bears out some of the postulates put forward by Freud, the two authors diverge in the conclusions they draw from this fact: ". . . we are still in some disagreement as to whether the time is now ripe for rapprochement between psychoanalysis, experimental psychology, neurophysiology and neurochemistry. More accurately, we disagree as to whether the time will *ever* be right or whether these disciplines – as different levels of inquiry and explanation, one in the universe of human meaning and the other in the universe of natural science – must inevitably go their separate ways . . . Gill feels that psychoanalysis must go its own way, and that means purging it of its natural science metapsychology, while Pribram welcomes psychoanalysis back into the natural sciences. Pribram doubts that the differing views of the two authors are really, in the long run, incompatible, while Gill finds them irreconcilable" (*ibid.*, pp. 168–169). We will see in a later chapter that Gill's attitude is more subtle.

In concrete terms, this means that Pribram considers it possible to establish collaboration between researchers and practitioners whose field of work overlaps both disciplines, and that important progress can be achieved in this sphere. He asserts that neurophysiology has undergone a true revolution since the 1960s and that it would be possible to study the cerebral substratum of certain unconscious processes (Pribram, 1977).

In the same spirit, Shevrin, who is both psychoanalyst and neurophysiologist, believes that if psychoanalysis confines itself to the study of the analytical situation, excluding the concepts derived from classical physiology and the knowledge acquired in neurophysiology and biology, it will become "if not a ship of fools, a boat load of eccentrics lost in a limbo of their own making" (Shevrin, 1976, pp. 225–226). In the same paper, he reviews the work carried out in the field of neurophysiology, which according to him provides concrete data for the understanding of unconscious phenomena. In particular, he cites various studies on subliminal perception, attention, the stopped retinal image, binocular rivalry, etc.

What is to be thought of this controversy? It may well be understood that Gill, prisoner as he was of Ego-psychology, should have rebelled against a conceptual narrow-mindedness which was of no help to him in his daily practice, and that he should have sought other perspectives. It is obvious, for instance, that the knowledge that dreaming is linked with paradoxical sleep does not necessarily help the practitioner to understand the meaning of his patients' dreams at a psychological level. Fisher (1965) rightly stressed these problems in a controversy which opposed him to certain neurophysiologists who denied that there was any psychological dimension in dreaming. Dement (1964), for instance, assigns to dreaming sleep the fulfilment of an essentially biochemical function, which would purge the nervous system of the "endogenous metabolites" arising from its activity.

Fisher, however, objects that, "Granting the physiological and biochemical primacy of REM sleep, we are still left with the problem of the function of the concomitant psychic activity of dreaming, which cannot simply be reduced to the underlying somatic and physicochemical processes. What Ketty said about memory, that we may some time have a biochemistry of memory but never of memories, holds true for dreaming and dreams" (Fisher, 1965, p. 283). Similarly, the fact of knowing the organism needs to ingest a certain number of calories does not explain why some prefer caviar, and others foie gras.[4]

It remains, nonetheless, that the human wish has biological determinants

[4] Although here, too, purely physiological factors may come into play: a hypoglycemic subject will wish for sugar.

and limits, and that the evolution of the conceptual models used in psycho-physiology and biology cannot fail to influence our understanding of the psychological mechanisms of the unconscious. It would be artificial to draw an impassable line between the human and the natural sciences. One may wonder whether Freud would have been able to conceive the notion of free association if he had not had at his disposal an anatomical sketch of the nervous system seen as a set of interconnecting neurones. It is also likely that if important discoveries are made at a psychophysiological level in the field of memory, there will necessarily be repercussions on our knowledge of the unconscious, since the latter is primarily defined as a set of memory traces. It will, of course, never be possible to reduce the wish to physicochemical formulae, but the author believes that the *absolute* dichotomy that Gill introduces between the clinical theory and neurophysiology is too categorical. It seems to him, as it does to Pribram, that a constant dialogue between the two disciplines is necessary, and mutually enriching.[5]

Another question is raised – that of knowing whether we have today sufficient knowledge in physiology to account for the complexity of unconscious processes. On this point, Pribram seems to show a certain optimism. The risk in wishing at any price to establish a bridge between the two fields is that it is all too easy to fall back on mechanicist, reductionist conceptions of the psyche.[6]

It is interesting to see how this question of the relations between the psychological and biophysiological dimensions of the unconscious is viewed in the Soviet Union. A great deal of work was done on the physiology of the nervous system in the years prior to the revolution by Sechenov, Pavlov, and Bekhterev. The ideas of Freud also attracted a great deal of attention. It was in Russia that Freud's writings appeared for the first time in translation.[7] After the revolution, the Soviet authorities tended to look favorably upon the development of psychoanalysis. Pavlov himself kept in touch with analysis-inclined clinicians, some of whom attended his famous Wednesday clinics. Still, Pavlov's theories were themselves rooted in a narrowly physiological

---

[5] Pribram, in a personal communication, told the author that he considered hypnosis to be a privileged field for such collaboration in research. Such a collaboration would, so he stated, be first and foremost in his sphere of interests as soon as he proceeded from his present study of the Primates to that of human phenomena.

[6] See Note A, p. 163.

[7] For the history of psychoanalysis in Russia, see Marti (1976).

determinism. In the 1920s, however, a Georgian psychologist, Uznadze, came out in defense of a purely psychological notion of the unconscious, although from a standpoint far removed from that of Freud. For a full account of Uznadze's theories, the reader is referred to the volumes published on the occasion of the Tbilisi Symposium (Prangishvili *et al.*, 1978a–d). Uznadze was not a clinician but an experimental psychologist. He criticized Freud for his pansexualism and, more generally, his theory of drives, which he regarded as being based on biological determinism. The central notion in Uznadze's theory is what he calls the "Ustanovka" (attitude), which in English is translated as "set" (Uznadze, 1966a, b). This term refers to a sort of unconscious psychic configuration which governs the subject's relations with its environment. Ustanovkas are formed in the course of the individual's development, as and when the organism is called upon to react to a given situation. They therefore possess a certain historicity, are capable of changing and of clashing with each other.[8]

   The hardening of the cultural line in the Soviet Union in the 1930s led to a radical condemnation of psychoanalysis and, more generally, of all psychology that did not fit in with the framework of Pavlovian physiology. Psychic processes were described as the product of the activity of the higher

[8] Other authors played an important role in this period. In an article which I have already had occasion to cite (cf. p. 102), entitled "The Mozart of Psychology," Toulmin has drawn attention to the ideas of Vygotsky and his pupils. Born in 1898, Vygotsky began by studying literature before specializing in psychology and medicine. In his work on child psychology, he always sought to articulate data relating to the physiology of the nervous system with the perspectives opened up by social science. He showed that neither the growth of the nervous system nor the action of the environment were in themselves sufficient to account for the child's development, but that this resulted from the interaction of these different factors. His work was prematurely cut short by his death in 1934 at the age of 37, but his influence has persisted down to the present day in spite of the tight control exercised on Soviet psychology in Stalin's time. Certain authors (the most celebrated among them being Luria, recently deceased) have been trying for the last 20 years to work along the interdisciplinary lines indicated by Vygotsky (1971, 1978), comprising psychology, neurology, linguistics. Toulmin takes this occasion to criticize the overspecialization of American research, which has led to some partial and often oversimplified results. He cites in evidence the attitudes of Skinner and Chomsky, the former claiming to explain everything in terms of conditioning, while the latter sees language as a series of structures contained in the genetic code.

   In Toulmin's view, in the days when Stalinism had not yet succeeded in perverting historical materialism, the latter was of great help in supplying a framework for the articulation of society with nature. He compares the neglect of Soviet writers in the United States with early-nineteenth-century England's ostracism of all that came out of France, a nation of atheists and regicides.

nervous system (conditioned reflexes, excitation and cortical inhibition). In the wave of liberalization that followed destalinization, several authors began to criticize the reductionist and mechanical character of these conceptions. In particular, numerous Soviet philosophers and psychologists adhered to the theories of Uznadze, rehabilitating the notion of the psychological unconscious. Psychoanalysis is still widely attacked today and no one practices it, but it is no longer subject to absolute anathema. It is now possible to acknowledge the importance of certain Freudian discoveries. Freud's writings are still unavailable in the bookshops, but they can be consulted in libraries (there is even talk of republishing the works of Freud in a scientific series). In October, 1979, a symposium on the unconscious was held in Tbilisi, organized by the Georgian Academy of Sciences and the Uznadze Institute of Psychology. Western specialists from every branch of scientific inquiry were invited to attend. Even before the opening of the Congress three volumes were published containing the contributions of those taking part, who included psychoanalysts from all the present-day currents of psychoanalysis.

This trend may be ascribed to a certain easing of cultural life that has occurred in the U.S.S.R. over the last 20 years. Another factor undoubtedly plays an important part. With the development of Soviet society, its leaders are having to cope with the multitude of psychological problems that are the lot of an industrial society, for which Pavlovian psychology is of little help. There is a need for a better understanding of the unconscious mechanisms at play in the behavior of social groups and individuals. They realize their backwardness in this sphere and are concerned to gain fuller knowledge of the theoretical concepts and techniques developed in the West.

The best way of discovering the outlook of Soviet authors now investigating the question of the unconscious (as we shall see later, many of them continue to deny its existence) is to refer to the three volumes published on the occasion of the Tbilisi Congress. In a long concluding article (hereafter referred to as PBS) Prangishvili, Bassin and Sherozia, the chief organizers of the Congress and editors of the volumes, set out their views on psychoanalysis and state their position on the controversy between advocates of metapsychology and those of clinical theory in the United States. They take as their starting point an article by Wallerstein, a well-known American psychoanalyst, entitled "Psychoanalysis as a science" (1976).

This article by Wallerstein is mainly concerned with the scientific status of psychoanalysis. Wallerstein starts by setting forth what he takes to be the position of the advocates of clinical theory, basing his arguments on a paper by Home (1966). In his view, where psychoanalysis seeks to elucidate the meaning of a symptom it is a science of "why," a hermeneutic, as opposed to the nature sciences, which are sciences of "how." It leads to formulations in terms of reasons and understanding, not in terms of causes or explanations. This is why Home believes that psychoanalysis is not a science in the customary sense of the term; its logic is closer to that of artistic creation.

For Wallerstein, psychoanalysis can and must be a science. But this means that it cannot confine itself to elucidating the why, the meaning of symptoms. This dimension, he believes, is a matter of individual history. If we want psychoanalysis to be a science, then it must be capable of formulating general laws of the workings of the psyche. This is only possible if we have a structural model of the psychic apparatus, if we shift our ground from that of reasons and interpretation to that of causes, forces, and mechanisms. Therefore, Wallerstein thinks it necessary to preserve metapsychology.

However, Wallerstein disclaims any intention of elaborating a physicalist theory: "What I want to make clear (. . .) is that the general psychological theory (the metapsychology, if you will) that I am talking about is truly appropriate (i.e. is consonant with) the particular nature of our subjectivistic data and the introspective and empathic methods by which we derive those data" (pp. 223–224). He adds, in a note: "To me, metapsychology is not, as it is to some, equivalent to a biological or neuro-biological explanatory framework imposed upon the data and the phenomena of psychology" (p. 224). He thus declares himself willing to abandon the energy model which can, in his view, be thrown overboard without invalidating Freudian metapsychology in the process.

It will be observed, however, that Wallerstein's position is a little ambiguous. For, whatever he may say, his model of reference for assessing scientific method is that of the natural sciences for the most part. Thus, in support of his argument he cites a statement by Modell (in Abrams, 1971) according to which psychoanalytic theory corresponds to two modes of thought, the first of which considers man "as a part of nature and subject to the same regularities that influence all other natural phenomena" (Wallerstein, 1976, p. 216), the second studying man as the product of history, where it is impossible to formulate general laws. Here, generalization clearly seems to rhyme with physicalism. Similarly, he establishes a correspondence between his "why"/"how" opposition and that formulated by Sandler and Joffe (1969) between "the experiential," which can be apprehended through clinical experience, and the "non-experiential," which belongs to the domain of theory. Yet Sandler and Joffe describe the "non-experiential" as a system of "forces and energies, mechanisms and apparatuses of organized structures, *both biological and psychological* (my italics), of sense organs and means of discharge" (p. 82).

PBS broadly summarize Wallerstein's article, laying particular stress on the following points. Firstly, they believe that present-day psychoanalysts are right to emphasize that psychology's domain is that of meaning and intentionality, and that this domain cannot be reduced to any form of biological determinism. They consider that this represents a major step forward from the "biologism" of Freud and his successors.[9] Secondly, they echo Wallerstein's criticisms of the advocates of clinical theory. Recognizing the opposition between the "why" and the "how," they accuse the latter of having arrived at mistaken conclusions although their premises were correct. Just because in psychology one is dealing with the dimension of meaning does not imply that methods other than those employed in the natural sciences are called for: "It is absolutely impossible to bring the 'humanistic' approach to the point of creating a science of the unconscious, regardless of all its refinement, regardless of all its striving to undo subtle psychological 'knots' and nuances of an irreproducibly individual nature" (Prangishvili *et al.*, 1978d, III, p. 726). The big mistake of Freud and his successors was precisely the fact that they chose his "humanist" path, thereby preventing the integration of

---

[9] In their introduction to the three volumes, PBS point out that the dialogue with psychoanalysts was facilitated by "the structural-linguistic psychoanalysis of Lacan and by George Klein's conception which rejects metapsychology" (Prangishvili *et al.*, 1978b, I, p. 24). They make no further reference to Lacan's theories in their concluding article (Prangishvili *et al.*, 1978d), but Bassin and Sherozia (1980) have recently written an open letter to Serge Leclaire, "Can Jacques Lacan's ideas save psychoanalysis?" in reply to the latter's paper presented in Tbilisi, "The role of Jacques Lacan in the revival of the psychoanalytic movement" (Leclaire, 1980). Again at the Tbilisi Symposium, Avtonomova (1979) presented a paper entitled, "The Unconscious: epistemological aspects," which critically analyses Lacanism from a philosophico-historical standpoint.

psychoanalysis into general psychology. This did allow them some highly interesting insights into psychological life, but at the cost of a lack of scientific rigor.

Uznadze's great merit lies in having placed the psychology of the unconscious on the path of science by formulating his theory of "Ustanovkas," which are realities accessible to experiment.

PBS thus take the view that Wallerstein's position is more "progressive" than that of Klein or Gill. This does not mean, though, that they acknowledge Freudian metapsychology. The volumes taken as a whole are clear evidence that they do not.

In fact, the discussion of the problem of metapsychology suffers from an underlying ambiguity. For Wallerstein, as we have seen, metapsychology as he conceives it is a psychological theory (even if, as pointed out earlier, the concepts to which he refers contain a certain residue of physicalism). PBS do not adopt this standpoint. They have no quarrel with Freudian metapsychological conceptions from a psychological viewpoint. For them, metapsychology is clearly a physicalist theory. The problem they are concerned with is that of the interaction between psychology and neuro-psychology.

In this respect, PBS criticize Wallerstein's position, calling it idealist. For them, psychological concepts cannot be developed without reference to neurophysiology: "When Wallerstein rejects the neurologization of the explanatory categories of psychoanalysis, he commits an error which, in our view, greatly reduces the possibility of these categories" (Prangishvili *et al.*, 1978d, III, p. 727). PBS consider that, when Freud created metapsychology, he was obliged to make up for the shortcomings of neurophysiology at the time, which prevented contemporaries from understanding the cerebral bases of mental processes. Today, according to them, neurophysiology has progressed greatly, and it is indispensable in accounting for certain aspects of psychic functioning: "Attempting to elaborate a theory of psychoanalysis as to build a theory of the unconscious without having recourse to the working of the brain means taking a basically incorrect stand in regard to methodology" (p. 727).

PBS are careful, however, to stress that this does not mean that they think one can explain mental processes in terms of cerebral activity: "Their dynamic, their directionality, consequently their content are determined by factors that are distinguished qualitatively from their activity; these factors refer not to the realm of neurophysiological relations, but to the realm of social relations that connect man to the world in which he lives" (p. 725).[10]

PBS insist also on the fact that the relation with the environment should not be seen merely as the action of this environment upon the individual, in terms of stimulus and response. Responses to the environment depend on how this is perceived and interpreted. The great merit of Uznadze lies precisely in having shown that one cannot isolate human activity from the psychological sets that condition it. The development of these sets is rooted in cerebral activity. They are "connected" with it. However, they are not chiefly determined by this activity, but by interaction with the social environment.

Gill (1979) has written a paper dealing with both Wallerstein's and PBS's articles. He criticizes all of them for having misunderstood the positions of the advocates of clinical theory when they claim that to reject metapsychology implies a rejection of psychoanalysis as a science. This is, he says, Home's position, in effect, but it is not shared by Klein, Schafer, or himself. To say that psychoanalysis is a science of meaning, a hermeneutic science requiring an approach and methods of its own, is not to say that it is not scientific. It is

---

[10] It is interesting to note that, in the case of hypnosis, whence the discovery of the unconscious arose (psychoanalysts and Uznadzians agree on the role played by post-hypnotic suggestion in the discovery, Chertok, 1979), PBS hold that recourse to physiology is unavoidable. Hypnosis, they assure us, is today still an unknown quantity. Pavlov's physiological theory has proved unable to provide an explanation for it. Even so, purely psychological or clinico-psychological concepts are not going to shed much light on the relations between hypnosis and unconscious psychic activity. Both hypnosis and suggestion will remain a mystery as long as we remain ignorant of the physiological criteria of the hypnotic state. PBS do admit, however, that the hypnotic relation ("rapport") is connected with psychology (of meaning): the essential action for the hypnotized subject, they suppose, occurs at the level of what they call non-verbal thought (Prangishvili *et al.*, 1978a, II, p. 35). Apart from hypnosis, Bassin is particularly interested in pre-verbal thought. He devotes an article to this subject entitled "At the bounds of the cognized: the problem of the pre-speech form of thinking" (Bassin, 1978), and ventures onto the (slippery) ground of relations between the affect and unconscious thought. Starting with a tribute to Vygotsky's contribution to this field, he points out that he has by no means exhausted the subject. Bassin tries to settle the matter, at least for the time being, by minimizing, or even erasing, the frontier which separates these two agencies. If these two happened to be distinct entities, then we would, he confesses, be faced with insuperable difficulties. Uznadze opposed this distinction, which was commonplace in orthodox psychoanalytic doctrine in the 1920s. In order to preserve a rational method of analysis, it is therefore necessary, according to Bassin, to accept this amalgamation. (In our view, only progress in our knowledge of the affect, which is a psychobiological agency, can extract theory from the dead end in which it is still floundering to this day.)

true that psychoanalysts are all too often content to work empirically and purely intuitively, without bothering to formalize the data collected or seeking quantitative verification of the validity of their hypotheses. Such methods are needed if psychoanalysis is effectively to become a science. But this does not imply abandoning the clinical field, which is the chosen ground of analysis.

Gill contests Wallerstein's opposition between, on the one hand, the sciences of "why" = sciences of reasons = sciences of the individual, and on the other sciences of "how" = sciences of causes and general laws. The way Wallerstein uses these terms strikes him as imprecise. A cause is just as much a "why" as a "how" (p. 5). To be specific, the domain of meaning is just as much governed by laws as any other. Psychoanalysis is just like any science. On the one hand we have individual facts, on the other general laws. The main criticism to be leveled at Wallerstein is that he confuses generalization with metapsychology. To reject this does not necessarily entail no longer formulating laws or verifying their validity, merely that one rejects reference to concepts that do not originate in psychoanalytic observation. Gill takes the example given by Wallerstein, that of the opposition between the interpretation of this or that defense in a given situation and the psychological defense mechanism as a law of psychic functioning. In both cases we are equally in the domain of what Wallerstein calls the "why." The psychological defence, as formulated by psychoanalysis, can be understood only in terms of intentionality: the rejection of unpleasant representations. "What apparently he (Wallerstein) fails to realize is that they are all hermeneutic concepts employing reasons as explanations" (p. 10). The defense mechanism is a concept originating exclusively from psychoanalytical clinical practice.

In fact, Wallerstein confuses metapsychology with generalization. His position on neurophysiology is unclear. Gill stresses the ambiguity, which the present author has also noted, between his statement that psychoanalytic theory ought to be purely psychological and his physicalist vocabulary.

Similarly, Gill considers that the Soviets have no precise idea of the relations between psychology and neurology, since on the one hand they claim that the dynamics of psychological processes are extra-physiological, while on the other they attack Wallerstein and the other psychoanalysts for wanting to elaborate a pure psychology devoid of all reference to neurological categories. He interprets this position in the following way: "I believe that the

editors do believe that psychology can be studied as a self-contained discipline
. . ." but they mistakenly believe that "to come out flatfootedly for the
necessity to study psychology as a self-contained discipline commits them to
the idealistic position that there is no connection between brain and mind"
(p. 12). He claims that they have misconstrued the positions of clinical theory.
Advocates of this theory do not hold that there is no relation between the
brain and the unconscious: "The fact that psychoanalysis claims to be able to
study the unconscious psychologically does not mean that it does not recognize that the organic substrata of the unconscious also have to be studied"
(p. 6). "Complete understanding of both consciousness and unconsciousness
requires neurological as well as psychological knowledge" (p. 19). But the
psychoanalyst's position is that if one wishes to study the unconscious in its
specifically psychological aspects there is no point in borrowing concepts from
neurology. Of course, alterations in the nervous system do influence the
working of the mind. But if one wishes to describe how the working of the
mind is influenced, then one should use psychological, not neurological,
terms.

In fact, Gill's position is not all that far removed from that of the Soviets.
Although they refuse to establish a rigid boundary between psychology and
neurology, they too insist on the fact that the explanation of psychological
behavior implies recourse to concepts that can give an account of the meaning
such behavior has for the subject in his relation to the environment.

When reviewing this controversy, one sometimes has the impression that
everyone is really quarreling over words: what does it matter, after all, if
some people call metapsychology what Gill calls generalization, since they all
seem in agreement on two principles: (a) that psychoanalysis needs to be more
"scientific," i.e. ought to comply with the same criteria of validation and
formalization as prevail in the other sciences; (b) that psychoanalysis is a
science of meaning, irreducible to any form of cerebral determinism.

This impression is strengthened by the fact that the discussion remains very
general. When Wallerstein, for example, claims to favor a non-physicalist
metapsychology, what exactly does he mean by that? Which concepts of
Freudian theory does he plan to preserve and which reject? His text is silent on
the matter. Similarly, in their article, PBS do not discuss the validity of
psychoanalytical concepts. To find out their position on the subject it is
necessary to read right through these volumes.

In fact, closer scrutiny of the texts shows that the similarity of the terms used conceals wide divergences. PBS may claim that they want to elaborate a psychology of meaning, but that does not prevent what they understand by meaning from bearing very little relation to what psychoanalysts understand by the word. Meaning, in psychoanalysis, is what lies beyond what is manifest, what is apprehended through that rather special intersubjective relation, the psychoanalytical setting. Seen thus, the notion of the unconscious cannot be reduced to any kind of instrumental dimension. It exists on another level than that of the apparatuses or mechanisms governing the subject's relation to the environment. In this sense, we may say that psychoanalysis does not work on the totality of the unconscious, if by this we mean all those phenomena that are not consciously registered by the subject. For psychoanalysis, the unconscious is what the subject has repressed in his own history. Deciphering it is inseparable from the emergence of an individual speech. Not that psychoanalysis is incapable of formulating general laws; certain mechanisms recur in all analyses. But it is indissolubly bound up with the approach that consists in creating conditions for liberating what is repressed in what the subject says. It is this specific dimension which underpins the original character of psychoanalysis in relation to psychology in general.

PBS take a much more instrumental, functional, view of the unconscious, in which the dynamics of repression play only a secondary role. PBS criticize the assimilation of unconscious to repression in Freud, moreover. To be sure, they acknowledge the existence of what they call "the psychological defense" (see above, p. 78). But for them this is merely one mechanism among others; from this standpoint, there is no question of creating conditions for the emergence of any latent meaning, but merely of studying relations between conscious and unconscious phenomena from an essentially experimental point of view. Sets are a kind of pattern which condition behavior over and beyond what the subject consciously perceives. In this sense we may say that they are unconscious. But their analysis remains necessarily descriptive, superficial, inasmuch as the Uznadzians neglect the question of drives or fantasies. In so doing, they make it impossible to understand underlying conflicts since these are not revealed to observation pure and simple but require exploration of those "psychological knots" which PBS regard as irrelevant to a science of the unconscious.

It is no accident that there should be no such thing as an Uznadzian psychotherapy. Broaching this topic, Bassin and Sherozia (1979, p. 6) cited the psychotherapists of the Leningrad School, who, they claim, work from a standpoint akin to their own. These adopt a "pathogenetic" approach (see above, p. 101), which consists in revealing the "significant relations" at work in the symptom. A case history reported by Zachepitski and Karvasarsky (1978, p. 359) illustrates their approach; this involved a 33-year-old woman suffering from cancerophobia.

A series of interviews showed that this phobia appeared in connection with marital problems. Having discovered that her husband had a mistress, she found the situation hard to bear. Marital life deteriorated and her husband threatened divorce. The authors show that there was a conflict in this woman between her resentment toward her husband and her desire to keep the family together, which was heightened by her having been orphaned at a very early age. Her phobia was a means both of expressing the anxiety brought on by this conflict and of preventing the break-up of the family: if she had cancer, her husband could not abandon her. These interviews having given her an insight into the "pathogenetic mechanism" of the symptom, the patient began to recover, and the phobia ultimately disappeared.[11]

As we can see, this does represent an attempt at elucidating the meaning of the symptom, but the interpretation is confined to a quasi-manifest level. What is stressed, essentially, is the present conflict; the past is evoked, but only to explain certain present characteristics of the subject—her attachment to family life stems from the fact that she had been an orphan—not because it would enable us to trace the conflict back to its origins. Soviet psychotherapy rejects both the notion of infantile sexuality and that of transference.[12]

---

[11] It is striking to note that this observation tells us nothing either about the patient's psychosexual development or about her sexual relations with her husband. Not that Soviet psychotherapists are utterly averse to penetrating the intimate details of the sex lives of individuals, but they do so only when the symptoms are of an explicitly sexual nature (frigidity, impotence, etc.).

[12] One does, nevertheless, come across certain authors now attempting to investigate the relational phenomena described by psychoanalysis. A sociologist working in Tbilisi, Sardzhveladze (1978, p. 485), is currently studying, for example, the role of identification in empathy. He believes that empathy corresponds to an equilibrium between projection and introjection. Meanwhile, a Leningrad psychotherapist, Tašlykov (1979, p. 48), also speaks of the empathic relation and of the importance to the therapist of identification. Libikh (1979, p. 154) mentions the existence of phenomena that we would call countertransferential. Analysis of a certain number of psychotherapeutic interviews shows, he claims, that these often tend to reflect the preoccupations of the therapist rather than those of the patient. The fact that the Soviets deny transference does not mean that they deny the role of the relation

Zachepitski states this clearly, moreover: "the curative affect is not determined by transference onto the doctor (...) of the patient's infantile mystificatory relations with his parents, but by the modification of his real subjective experience *vis-à-vis* his interpersonal relations and his social position" (family, society, place of work).

One cannot help thinking that the success of this kind of therapy can be put down essentially to persuasion. This is not to say that this kind of therapy is ineffectual. Just as long as the therapist has a good capacity for empathy (see below, p. 171). But the author does not regard this as a sufficient basis for a psychotherapeutic theory.

To return to PBS, the study of the more instrumental, functional, aspects of the unconscious (I am thinking, for example, of the phenomena of synergy between the conscious and the unconscious, which PBS are at pains to stress) is not, on the face of it, without interest. But the difficulty comes when the Soviets claim that this level of analysis is sufficient to account for all the complexity of unconscious psychological life.

What strikes one most forcibly in this discussion between Soviet authors and American psychoanalysts is the extent to which the participants are just not speaking the same language, even though they employ similar terms, such as psychology, meaning, unconscious. I would cite one last, particularly significant, example: PBS congratulate Wallerstein, and more generally all those modern psychoanalysts who have, according to them, rid psychoanalysis of its pan-sexualism. What they fail to realize is that if psychoanalysts lay less stress than they did on this aspect of theory, it is because it is now taken for granted as a generally accepted fact. Infantile sexuality, castration, transference, the Oedipus complex, etc., go to make up the common heritage, the overarching standpoint within which all psychoanalytic discussion takes place.

And it is precisely these concepts which lie at the heart of the debate, a debate that is, in fact, ideological. The Soviets still reject in psychoanalysis sexuality, individualism, and a conception founded on the idea of an

in psychotherapy; they merely reject the specifically Freudian idea that what is involved in the relation is the repetition of infantile fantasies.

Another Leningrad therapist, Svjadosč (1978, p. 366), even employs, in his psychotherapeutic method known as "causal analysis," the technique of free association, the study of dreams, and recall through hypnosis in order to enlighten the patient as to the causes of his sickness. He believes that infantile complexes are of no importance.

antagonism between drives and the restraints imposed by social intercourse. However, they no longer set themselves up as exclusive repositories of the truth; they no longer claim to have solved all the problems. On the contrary, they are now open to dialogue. This simple fact represents, in my opinion, a major step forward.

It should be pointed out, nevertheless, that PBS positions are by no means shared by all Soviet authors. Broadly speaking, we may currently distinguish between two sharply opposed groups in the Soviet Union: the "psychologists" and the "anti-psychologists." The former group was present at Tbilisi and acknowledges the existence of a psychological unconscious. It comprises the majority of psychologists and philosophers, and a certain number of psychiatrists and neuropathologists. (The term neuropathologist, designating people specializing in the nervous system, belongs to the German tradition: neurologists treat neuroses, while psychiatrists treat psychoses. Freud was a neuropathologist. Certain neuropathologists also describe themselves as psychotherapists and are open to the psychological aspects of mental illness.) Among the "psychologists" we must once again distinguish between PBS, who claim to be disciples of Uznadze, and other investigators, mostly Muscovites, working in the tradition of Vygotsky, Rubinstein, Luria, Leontiev, etc. This "psychological" group publishes in the columns of the reviews *Voprossy Filosofii* (Philosophical Questions) and *Voprossy Psikhologii* (Psychological Questions).

The "anti-psychologists" are essentially the psychiatrists, specialists in psychoses. They regard mental illness as an organic disorder, genetically determined: they publish in the journal *Zhurnal Nevropatologii i Psikhiatrii Korsakov*. In the 1980, No. 2, issue of this review they published a polemical article (Kukujev, 1980) in which they attacked the scientific character of the notion of the psychological unconscious. Essentially, they adduced three arguments:

1. It is unscientific to study the unconscious in dreams and psychopathology and to do so is a manifestation of outmoded Freudian representations.
2. To consider that a piece of information which the subject finds unpleasant never reaches consciousness but remains in the unconscious is also a Freudian viewpoint.
3. The fact of wanting to elaborate a theory of the psychological unconscious amounts to a denial of neurology.

What are we to make of all these discussions? That there is no real science of the unconscious at the present time. PBS, Gill and Wallerstein all agree on that; they themselves admit that their research is in the nascent stage. None of them refers, moreover, to any concrete study in support of their general statements. Let us, therefore, taking care not to wander off too far into the labyrinth of futurology, wait for the birth to take place. The parameters involved are so many and so difficult to pinpoint that the task will surely be an arduous one, as all fully realize. The unconscious is, in fact, a term with many levels, some better known than others, which link together and interpenetrate. Concerning psychoanalysis, we may say that it has opened up for our understanding the field of psychic causality by forging a technique founded essentially on interpretation and verbal communication, to the exclusion of all direct intervention on the somatic. This has made possible a formidable enterprise of decipherment of our psychological life and our cultural heritage, our familial behavior, our institutions and myths, our languages, art, jokes, dreams, symptoms, etc. This labor of decoding has been carried to its highest point, today, through the incorporation of models proposed by various human sciences, and by linguistics, sociology, and literary criticism in particular. We might even say, simplifying slightly, that exploration has focused chiefly on the verbal: even where dreams are concerned. Although these involve the body profoundly, the psychoanalyst has only the patient's account to go on — in other words, language once again.

Certain areas still remain unexplored: the non-verbal, affectivity, the body, everything connected with the psychosomatic dimension. It is surely here that most remains to be discovered.

Note A (see page 150, footnote 6)

Since this book was published in French, a historian of science, Frank J. Sulloway(1979), has published a remarkable book: *Freud, Biologist of the Mind.* This is a minutely detailed piece of historical research. The author has gone through all the sources, even consulting Freud's own library, to track down marginal notes and passages underlined by him.

Sulloway attempts, in his book, to rehabilitate Freud's biological ideas. Following in the footsteps of Ellenberger (1971), he sets out to demystify the legend in psychoanalytic circles that Freud was a pure psychologist who discovered everything through his self-analysis.

It is generally thought that this lay at the origin of his rejection of the seduction theory, the revelation of infantile sexuality, the Oedipus complex, the theory of dreams, the technique of free association, transference, resistances, in a word everything that goes to make up the Freudian unconscious. Sulloway tries to show that these concepts were already more or less present in the cultural climate of the period and were not the outcome of Freud's self-analysis. In his view, this legend was fostered for tactical reasons in order to accentuate the revolutionary character of Freud's discovery.

Sulloway distinguishes two periods in the work of Freud. He believes we may consider that, between 1895 and 1905, Freud did in effect gradually abandon his original neurophysiological standpoint, developing purely psychological concepts in their place. Subsequently, though. he sought to supply a biological underpinning for these concepts by drawing on the evolutionary theories of Darwin and Lamarck.

Sulloway's book is a work of remarkable precision and erudition. But, in my view, it merely underlines with still greater force the extent to which it was as a psychologist that Freud really innovated. His biological ideas, which are described here in great detail, are in fact more than debatable from a scientific standpoint. Sulloway (p. 440) mentions a particularly significant anecdote on this score, related by Jones in his biography of Freud (1957, p. 313). Jones tells how, shortly before the publication of "Moses and Monotheism," he tried to dissuade Freud from reliance on Lamarck's theory of hereditary transmission of acquired characteristics, explaining that this theory ran counter to the whole of modern genetics. But Freud stuck to his point of view, despite the absence of any scientific proof.

Sulloway himself points out, moreover: "Between 1899 and 1905, Freud set forth his basic psychoanalytic corpus of ideas in five major publications: The Interpretation of Dreams, The Psychopathology of Everyday Life, Jokes and Their Relations to the Unconscious, The 'Dora' Case History, and Three Essays on the Theory of Sexuality. Had Freud written nothing more in his lifetime, psychoanalytic theory would still have been available to the world in virtually all the essential aspects that we recognize today. These five works constitute a magnificent achievement, which certainly places Freud among the most creative scientific minds of all time" (Sulloway, 1979, p. 358).

It would, perhaps, have been more appropriate to have entitled Sulloway's book "The Biological Temptations of Freud." Is it merely a coincidence that today, in a recent issue of the *Nouvelle Revue de Psychanalyse* (1980), certain psychoanalysts should be re-examining Freud's mystical temptations?

Mysticism would certainly seem to be in fashion: the *American Journal of Psychiatry* has just devoted a special section to the use of mystical or religious experiences in psychotherapy.

Might one not also include in this trend the appearance in the USSR of "natural" medicine which presents many analogies with mesmerism, not least of which is the technique of magnetic passes and the laying on of hands? When Spirkin (1980), a corresponding member of the Academy of Sciences, published an article in a mass-circulation periodical describing the theory of the bio-field – according to which the *physical* radiation transmitted from one person to another may be curative – was there not a somewhat mystical undertone to this notion? This "natural" medicine is practiced by healers known as "extrasensors" (apparently gifted with the faculties of ESP – the most celebrated among them being the extremely attractive young woman whom even eminent public figures do not hesitate to consult...). Naturally, this trend by no means enjoys unanimity. Far from it: most scientists oppose the theory, explaining away the successful cures through the phenomenon of suggestion. This controversy may yet prove fruitful in that a commission set up by the Soviet Ministry of Health has recommended that "greater attention be paid to research into the unconscious processes of the human mind, and to the scientific elaboration of different types of psycho-therapy (including hypnosis, suggestion, and other therapeutic techniques) (*Literaturnaïa Gazeta*, 1980).

The phenomenon of suggestion, though better known than that of physical radiation, akin to Mesmer's "fluid," remains nonetheless obscure and is often relegated to a secondary position by psychiatric circles. Judd Marmor (1980b), who is making an exhaustive survey of all psychotherapeutic methods in order to discern the common denominators, ranks suggestion as a minor factor, while in our opinion it lies at the heart of the discussion.

13

Hypnosis Tomorrow

It has been the author's aim to demonstrate the importance of hypnosis in psychological research. But are hypnotic phenomena destined to remain a mere enigma, an embarrassing object which shows us the limits of our knowledge? Or is research possible, and if so, with which perspectives in mind?

In 1960 the American Psychoanalytical Association and the American Psychiatric Association organized a joint meeting on hypnosis. In the course of that meeting, Kubie (1961) stated that hypnosis could be truly understood only through interdisciplinary research, but that in his view the ground for such a collaboration was not yet laid. Perhaps, after 25 years' work by each research worker in his own particular field, another meeting might be envisaged. These 25 years will soon have elapsed. Have things changed much? What, today, is the situation of research on hypnosis?

Psychobiological Research

As we have seen in the preceding chapter, the interaction between the psychic and the biological is far from being realized. So far as hypnosis is concerned, progress will be difficult as long as the objective, physiological evidence of the hypnotic state remains unknown. On the one hand, nothing prevents our believing that the tools for measuring cerebral activity may become more refined and that we may succeed in discovering such evidence.

On the other hand, this does not mean that today collaboration between neurophysiologists and researchers on hypnosis is fruitless. The example of the author's experiments on analgesia prove that this contact can be mutually enriching, since these experiments have made it possible to confirm the neurophysiological hypotheses on the twofold character of pain. Generally speaking, hypnosis is a privileged tool for the study of psychophysiological interactions and of the relationships between the central nervous system and the autonomic system. Black's experiments, for instance, on the action of hypnotic suggestion on immunological defenses would, if they could be replicated, open up interesting vistas in immunology. Progress in neurophysiology and biology can reveal possibilities, on condition, however, that neurophysiologists bear in mind the existence of hypnosis, and are ready to make use of it. (In Paris, the author himself has vainly sought an immunologist with whom to work on the perspectives opened up by Black. He was confronted with such scepticism that this proved impossible.)

Experimental Psychology

In the last 20 years, American experimental psychologists have essentially been working in a behaviorist and neo-behaviorist perspective (stimulus-response). Interest in the subject's state of consciousness has become secondary. This trend started to become apparent around the 1930s, when scales were developed to measure the subject's hypnotizability by reducing it to a series of responses to given suggestions (motor changes, hallucinations, etc.) considered as specific to the depth of the trance. Hypnosis thus came to be confused with suggestibility. One can say that experimental psychologists adopted *de facto* a position close to that of Bernheim, even if some did acknowledge, also, the existence of an altered state of consciousness.

The author believes that this research came to a deadlock, well summed up by the famous question: How do we know that someone is hypnotized? Because he is hypersuggestible. Why is he hypersuggestible? Because he is hypnotized. This led some authors such as Barber to deny that there was any reality in the hypnotic state by showing that phenomena produced under hypnosis could also be obtained in the waking state.

Today, it is becoming increasingly clear that the problem had been badly posed (for further information, see Appendixes). It was impossible to define the specificity of the hypnotic state since, as criterion of that state, an aspect was chosen which was, at best, only a side effect. While it is true that suggestibility is, in most cases, increased under hypnosis, it cannot be dissociated from the hypnotic state. It is also present in the waking state; conversely, the degree of suggestibility is not a function of the depth of the trance.

Must we, for all that, reject altogether this research? Weitzenhoffer (1979), one of the authors of the Stanford hypnotic susceptibility scales, now tends to adopt the following view: "Speaking of only hypnotism research done during the last 45 years, I find much of it and the associated writings to have been of low scientific caliber. There has been far more pseudoscience than science in it. Except for a small minority, investigators in this area have been on the whole a pretentious and opinionated lot, basically ignorant in spite of their academic training, and frequently poorly grounded even in their very chosen field of inquiry. They have been prone to shallow thinking, the overuse of technical jargon, the abuse of statistics, and various forms of unintentional and intentional intellectual dishonesty" (Weitzenhoffer, 1979, p. 353).

He believes that such an approach is not only incapable of explaining hypnosis, but that it is also inadequate for the study of suggestibility insofar as it does not make it possible to distinguish between voluntary and involuntary reactions (the latter, in his view, are the only ones that should be attributed to suggestion). He also criticizes the quality of the research work undertaken, and its pandering to fashion and to the demands of the institutions supporting researchers. Another obstacle is the fact that, under hypnosis as in the waking state, it is impossible to make any distinction between what is attributable to hypnosis (or suggestion) and what is due to the subject's constitution. To give an example, is hypnotic anesthesia due to the action of hypnotic suggestion or to the aptitude of certain subjects to "amnesiate" pain? It is, at present, very difficult to answer this question (even if everything would seem to show that there is a correlation between this type of aptitude and the aptitude to hypnosis). This is the reason why any approach solely based on behavioral criteria runs the risk of being based on very imprecise elements, however scientific the methodology employed.

But these criticisms should not let us forget that thanks to American work it has been possible to achieve some basic progress. Three aspects of this progress may be particularly mentioned, which would seem to be of special importance: the perfectioning of scales measuring hypnotic susceptibility (from a standard context of inductions and a number of suggested exercises) has provided a common frame of reference which allows making comparison and measurement. The induction can be effected by anybody, and its effects are fairly constant. The problem of the type of hypnosis and the quality of the hypnotist can no longer be put forward to account for all the differences that can appear from one session to another. This has allowed the mystic, even mystifying, aura that surrounded hypnosis to be dissipated. It has become clear that, while hypnotic suggestibility is sometimes manifested by spectacular effects, such as hypnotic analgesia, there was no reason to expect it to produce paranormal or magical effects. On the whole, this research has made it possible to submit concepts to the trial of reality and to leave the realm of pure speculation.

In our laboratory, however, it has seemed to us important to go beyond the limits within which the experimental approach has hitherto been confined and to take into account the subjective dimension of the hypnotic experience. Field's research (1965, 1969), which draws a parallel between certain aspects of what is experienced and the score obtained on the scale, is placed in a perspective close to that of the author and his associates. Barber himself (Barber and Calverley, 1969b) introduced into one of his experiments the occurrence or non-occurrence of certain subjective indices and spontaneous behavior patterns during hypnosis. The author and his associates, for their part, have adopted the following methodology. A classical induction is first effected with the help of the scales. The subjects are then offered very detailed questionnaires concerning the various aspects of their subjective experience. This approach is completed by non-directive interviews in order to ascertain what was missed by the questionnaires. (For further details, see Appendixes.) As our laboratory is incorporated within a treatment center, it is believed that, from this point of view, the interaction between research and clinical work can prove of particular interest.

Psychoanalysis

In the author's opinion, the psychoanalytical perspective remains an essential one as far as pure clinical research is concerned. It is, in fact, the only approach in which therapeutic work is directly linked to a deepening of the relational interaction.

If we were to "play pretend" that there existed "new analysts" — that is to say analysts who had gotten rid of all their prejudices and resistances, freed once and for all from the picture of a circus-hypnotism — who would come to inquire in what way hypnosis could be of use to them, as much from the point of view of research as at a therapeutic level, what answer could we give them?

It would seem that there are two kinds of answer. On the one hand, from a theoretical point of view, the knowledge of hypnotic phenomena can enrich psychoanalytical thought by contributing a whole body of experimental material on psychological mechanisms fundamental to the knowledge of the unconscious: regressive states, alterations of the body image, dissociation phenomena, etc. The data obtained by hypnosis can constitute a stimulus to research work and can provide confirmation of certain metapsychological hypotheses – or invalidate them. Above all, hypnosis could compel psychoanalysts to take into account the psychophysiological dimension of unconscious phenomena and forbid them an isolationism which makes them *take the part for the whole* and prevents them from thinking out the interaction of their science with other spheres of knowledge. (It should be made quite clear, at the outset, that what the author has in mind is not an overall interaction giving rise to a totalizing theory of the psychic apparatus, but all the openings, the bridges that can be built between data of a different order which are nonetheless directed toward the same object.) The psychoanalysts' gain would at least be to learn at which level they are working, and at which levels they are *not* working.

These are already good enough reasons to induce analysts to seek out information and to take their place in hypnotic research laboratories. This approach, however, is in a sense outside analysis: it does not concern the analyst in his practice.

We have seen, in the preceding chapters, that hypnosis revealed the existence of a primary, archaic level of the relationship, corresponding to "obscure areas" of psychoanalytic theory, particularly with regard to affect. From this point of view, the integration of hypnosis in analytical practice could constitute a fundamental contribution, as much for the understanding of hypnosis as for psychoanalysis itself.

It remains to be seen whether such an integration is possible. The basic argument which seems to militate against this is that suggestion is so powerful in hypnosis that, by this very fact, analysis of the situation becomes difficult. This is what Freud meant when he declared that hypnosis prevented the analysis of resistances.

But this deserves closer examination. Psychoanalysts keep repeating this argument because it was the starting point for the relinquishment of hypnosis, but the question has never really been raised as to what the possibilities might be of a use of hypnosis in which these dangers were reduced to a minimum. Attempts have, in fact, already been made to combine psychoanalysis and hypnosis. Hypnoanalysts have shown that resistances were in no way abolished, but simply appeared in a different form, and that it was perfectly possible to subject them to the process of interpretation.

The question is obviously far from being settled. It is true (Wolberg, 1964) that hypnoanalysis does imply a certain relinquishment of "analytical neutrality," since the therapist performs an induction and this in part disturbs the production of analytical material. But this opposition is not so radical as some would have us believe. The analytical situation itself is not truly neutral insofar as, so we have shown, it comprises hypnogenic elements. At all events, suggestion is present in all psychotherapy. Everything depends on how it is used.

From this point of view, not enough questions have been asked about the different ways of practicing hypnosis; therefore, it is advisable to avoid being entrapped in *a priori* judgments. There have not been many hypnoanalysts, and they have been left on the fringe of analytical circles. This has prevented any more intensive inquiry into the matter. Hypnosis, moreover, has always been used with the underlying idea that it should allow us to speed up treatment while sparing us some of the therapeutic work involved. The hypnotic relationship has rarely been investigated *per se*, with the aim of thoroughly studying all its aspects.

It is certain that if we go on using hypnosis as a tool destined to eradicate conflicts and traumatic experiences in order to dispel the symptoms, we must expect to suffer the same rebuffs as Freud did. The effects produced will be just as uncertain, transient and disappointing as they were in his time. But if Freud had had the chance to return to the question of hypnosis, he would in all probability, as he proceeded to elaborate his theories, have attributed a different function to it.

The author for his part believes that it is possible to study the hypnotic relationship while retaining an analytic approach. It is simply a question of extending the analytic field so as to include a dimension that, in fact, it already contains, though in a concealed form. Psychoanalysis rests upon the technique of free association. In practice, association is rarely free. To the extent that it creates the conditions for a deep bodily regression, hypnosis promotes the emergence of a mode of mental functioning closer to the primary processes. Its integration into psychoanalytic treatment would make it possible to reach registers which usually elude verbalization. Psychoanalysts, in fact, know this well. When subjects are truly associating, they are in a state close to a light hypnotic trance: the secondary processes are partially suspended.

It is obvious that in such a relationship the therapist cannot maintain the same distance as in a classical analysis. The relationship is experienced in a far more fusional form which is a reminder of the primary relational dimension which, as we have seen, is present in all intersubjective relations. A sort of symbiosis occurs, in which the therapist provides an affective support for processes situated at very archaic levels: narcissism, constitution of the body image, etc.

Psychoanalysts are showing more and more interest in these processes, which play a central role in the understanding of psychosis, borderline cases, etc. At a theoretical level, different authors have different ways of interpreting the genesis of disorders,[1] but they all stress the fact that the therapeutic exchange is situated at a very archaic level of affective communication. This is what they call empathy.

In his theorization of narcissistic pathology, Kohut gives a central place to empathy. He works in the perspective of structural theory and developmental psychoanalysis (based on "direct observation" of the child's behavior). According to him, psychosis and borderline cases are linked to disturbances in the evolution of narcissistic structures, originating in breaches in the mother's capacity for empathy in her relationship with the child (infant). The therapist's role is to promote the development of a particular form of transference: "narcissistic transference" which makes it possible for the patient to re-experience his archaic cathexes and their evolution.

The British School of Kleinian inspiration (Winnicott, Masud Khan, Milner, etc.) also attaches great importance to this notion of empathy. The following lines would seem to provide a very vivid picture of what the practice of the empathic relationship can be. In this extract, Masud Khan relates an incident which occurred during a session with one of his patients with suicidal tendencies: "She started to cry, gently, and with the whole of her body. I could feel its reality and pain in myself. . . . It is hard to define this in words, *as in my counter-transference experience I registered it with the whole of my*

---

[1] On this subject, the reader is referred to two articles by Meissner (1978) and Shapiro (1978).

mental and body sensibility. In this phase I had to learn more and more to rely on and use my body as a vehicle of perception in the analytic setting" (M. Khan, 1974, pp. 154–155) (italics added). And he adds: "If I was not all there in my body-attention, she would register it straight away" (*ibid.*, p. 157). "There was no actual physical contact between the patient and me at any point of her treatment. It was a *way of being* she asked for (. . .). If my body-attention sagged she would *wake up*[2] into an artificial mental state or depress herself into apathy" (*ibid.*, p. 159). Such an attitude presupposes an intense emotional involvement on the therapist's part, the ability to live with his patient without allowing himself to be submerged, a narcissistic regression.

Elisabeth Hansen (1978), an American psychotherapist who has worked on borderline cases following the ideas of the British school and American authors (Kohut, Kernberg), has studied this problem in a recent article entitled "Symbiosis." She criticizes Kohut and Kernberg for not describing with sufficient precision the therapist's countertransferential experience, and relates with noteworthy honesty and attention to detail the experience of what she calls her "counter-transferential psychosis": "Certainly I was participating in the spontaneous regression initiated by my patient. I could feel tears pushing against the back of my eyeballs, at times sensing something like object loss in a preview of her completion as a person and termination of our relationship. . . . Her sessions were vital intervals in my week, providing me a sense of challenge and mastery, demand and fulfillment" (pp. 194 and 197).

She stresses that this experience was therapeutically beneficial for her and that she was changed by this treatment. Winnicott (1954, p. 17) expresses the same feeling about an analysis carried out with a psychotic: "I have therefore had a unique experience even for an analyst. I cannot help being different from what I was before this analysis started."

It may be noted that, although it arose in relation to borderline cases, the concept of empathy actually concerns psychotherapy as a whole. It is, in fact, impossible to draw a rigid line between psychosis and neurosis, and this research cannot but have repercussions on the whole of psychotherapy and analytical theory.

Of course, neither Kohut nor Masud Khan practices hypnosis. They have been quoted here because it seems to the author that the notion of empathy functions at levels similar to those that enter into play in the hypnotic relation-

---

[2] And this was not a hypnotic session . . . but who knows?

ship. It is, however, necessary to be clear on this point. Hypnosis, as we have seen, is an all but automatic behavior pattern, with an instrumental dimension. By inducing a deep regression, it creates a situation which favors the development of an empathic type of relationship. For all that, the hypnotist must be prepared to enter into such a relationship and not to take refuge in an "objectifying" attitude devoid of affectivity.

With regard to the application of hypnosis to the treatment of psychotics or borderline cases, the traditional position is that psychotics are not hypnotizable. In actual fact, this question has never been studied in depth. Rather it is an accepted idea in the same way as it has long been asserted that psychotics are unable to establish transferences.[3] According to the work of Vingoe and Kramer (1966) and Lavoie (1973), it would seem that the psychotic's hypnotic susceptibility is more nearly comparable with that of normal subjects. Clinical examples of the positive impact of hypnotic treatment can be found in the literature (Wolberg, 1948, 1964; Bowers, 1961; Abrams, 1963, 1964; Biddle, 1967; Erickson, 1970; Crasilneck and Hall, 1975). Gill and Brenman (1959, pp. 340-341) record the case of a young schizophrenic who was totally withdrawn and who, after being hypnotized, communicated normally with those around her for 24 hours. More intensive research would be required to know if and how hypnosis can be used in this type of case.

In a very different field, the example of psychoanalytical relaxation constitutes an attempt to work, more particularly, on bodily experience by

---

[3] It may be, simply, that psychotics and neurotics do not experience hypnosis in the same manner. In this connection, in the article already quoted, Rozhnov and Burno (1976) make an interesting observation. Their theoretical considerations are questionable, but their clinical experience seems appreciable. They distinguish two different forms of the hypnotic state, corresponding to mental structures of a psychasthenic, or a hysteric, nature. (The term "psychasthenic" is used by these authors in a very wide sense, and comprises obsessional patients as conceived by Janet, as well as borderline cases and certain forms of schizophrenia.) The former (psychasthenics), when placed in a light or medium trance—which Rozhnov and Burno call phases I and II, experience a state of "psychic hypesthesia" extending to the point of depersonalization and resulting in an anxiolytic action which lasts for several days after the session. In hysterics, one can observe a narrowing of consciousness (twilight state) and partial amnesias. Rozhnov and Burno recall an interesting observation made by two Soviet psychotherapists, Platonov and Konstorum, who noted that good hypnotic subjects do not as a rule pass from phases I and II to somnambulism, but enter directly into a somnambulistic state. This observation calls into question the widely accepted notion of a single hypnotic state extending along a continuous scale from a slight trance to somnambulism.

combining Schultz's "Autogenic Training" with psychoanalysis. Practitioners of this method use very light induction, and thereafter assume an analytic approach. This work seems to be yielding interesting results.

To be sure, the integration of hypnosis in psychoanalytic treatment is not without problems. The very term of hypnoanalysis is imprecise, for hypnosis can be anything from a light trance to somnambulism. The drawback with light trance is that it only operates a superficial regression which can disappear fairly rapidly. In the case of deep trance, there is a more stable state which allows such operations as induced dreaming, automatic writing, age regression, etc. On the other hand, the very fact that the material is obtained in a "dissociation state" entails the risk that it will not be truly integrated in the working-through. It is certain that hypnoanalysis poses many problems, practical as well as theoretical. But no answer can be provided beforehand, nor can one forego the adoption of certain orientations until such time as any thorough research has been undertaken.

Let us be quite clear. It is not proposed to substitute hypnoanalysis for analysis. Used with knowledge and in well-selected cases, the latter remains the more elaborated technique. Apart from its specific factors – transference and insight – its long duration makes it possible for analysis to provide, as it were "à la carte," such other components as learning, conditioning, suggestion, empathy, catharsis – and who knows what else besides, including love. Even if it should prove, as some people believe, that psychoanalysis is essentially suggestion, there are patients who need time for a change to take place.

But it is certain that, on the theoretical plane, it is today vital for psychoanalysis that research should be undertaken on the processes brought into play by the hypnotic relationship.

This assertion may seem presumptuous. One can imagine sceptical, if not indeed contemptuous, smiles that it may raise amongst those who consider hypnosis as an anachronism scarcely fit to be exhibited in the museum of pre-analytical curios. But if, for such people, the psychoanalytical theory is a dogma, established once and for all, dispensing them from facing new questions, so much the worse for them.

The Freudian revolution opened up unforeseen perspectives for the understanding of the human psyche. Everything remained to be discovered and the best minds in psychiatry and psychology used their imagination and their creativity to lay the foundations of a new science and a new therapy. In the euphoria of the early days, it may have been thought that everything that related to the unconscious had been understood. No attention was paid to the areas that remained obscure.

Time has passed. The first psychoanalysts, impelled by a spirit of adventure and non-conformity, have been succeeded by therapists settled in the "Establishment." Psychoanalytical societies have been organized. The theory has solidified and become a doctrinal corpus, an instrument for reassurance and power. This has not prevented the development of an intense theoretical activity. Many schools have sprung into life, following every orientation. New grounds have been explored: child psychoanalysis, the treatment of psychosis, psychosociology, pedagogy, etc. In spite of all this, there still remain uncertainties.

There are many signs to show that psychoanalysis is at present going through a critical phase. Treatment is becoming more and more prolonged. In France, one is no longer surprised to hear of 10-year cures. Little by little, the public is coming to believe that therapy is only effective if it lasts a long time. And we may wonder whether the expenditure of time and money is proportional to the results obtained, all the more so as these results are hard to evaluate. In this field, the utmost lack of precision prevails. Methods which, from a theoretical point of view, are simplistic sometimes turn out to be efficient in practice for reasons no one has managed to discover. We have seen with what difficulties researchers in the United States are faced in attempting to determine criteria for the measurement of the efficiency of different psychotherapies. No formal proof has been put forward to establish with any certainty the superiority of psychoanalysis. And even within the latter, one is faced with a whole range of methods (Lacanian, Kleinian, etc.) among which it is impossible to decide. More and more, the opponents of psychoanalysis are taking advantage of this situation to discredit analytical practice and theory. Simultaneously, the public is starting to show signs of disaffection and is turning to other techniques. This trend is especially to be seen in the United States, but premonitory signs are apparent in other countries.

In France, psychoanalysis reigns supreme. Since the 1950s, there has been an unprecedented theoretical development, especially under the influence of Lacan and his disciples. A vast movement, questioning and exploring the basic principles of the Freudian discovery, has made it possible to investigate new and fascinating paths in very diverse fields. But this movement also gave rise to a true theoretical inflation, which is today assuming more and more extreme forms. As always, the intuitions of the beginnings have generated a new dogmatism. Reading the numerous texts published nowadays, one is often under the impression of being confronted with the repetition of pre-established certainties, claiming to bring answers for each and every problem. The contact with clinical work is becoming increasingly vague. It is a common thing to meet psychologists and philosophers capable of producing learned dissertations on the etiology of such and such a neurosis, and who have never seen a patient. Young analysts tend to become set in an attitude of unvarying passivity, often motivated by the fact that they just do not know what to do.[4] Analytical writings are becoming essentially literary and philosophical. Their language is often abstract and incomprehensible.

According to an ironical comment by Catherine Clément (1978), one feels that the ambition of psychoanalysts is no longer to cure patients, but to become writers. Reflection on the analytical process is taking precedence over the efficiency of the analysis. Interest tends to become concentrated on the training analysis, to the exclusion of any other concern. As Maud Mannoni (1979, p. 158) writes: "would not the 'pure' dream of the analyst be no longer to have to become involved with a patient?"

At the same time, one can see that certain points receive no satisfactory answer, although they nevertheless concern basic problems: the resolution of the transference, the termination of analysis, and the training of analysts, are so many insoluble questions that have recurred painfully over many years. It is no accident that, in the discourse of analysts, fissures are increasingly revealed, and more and more are points coming to be called in question. Nor that, among the Lacanians, there are those who assert the existence of an "unanalysable nucleus," or that, in a recent article, an author such as Fédida (1977) could speak of a "blind spot" in the analyst's relationship to the psychotic. The fact that Roustang should go so far as to wonder whether psychoanalysis is anything but a "long-term suggestion" gives an idea of the questions pervading the French analytic community.

We should bow to the facts. As far as the relational process is concerned, there is more non-knowledge than knowledge. In such a situation, it is time for us to proceed with a basic reassessment of the problem, without excluding any working orientation in the name of a so-called orthodoxy. It is hard to foresee whence new light will come. The author does not believe that all the

[4]See Held, 1975, p. 121.

questions that he has posed will be answered by research on hypnosis, all the more so in that it is impossible in the present state of our knowledge to propose clearly defined working perspectives. But one thing is certain. If one small part of all the grey matter which has been, and still is, expended for the benefit of psychoanalytic theorization were devoted to hypnosis, the latter would be better known and our knowledge of the unconscious and the analytical relationship would gain thereby.

In 1964, at a conference at the Chicago Institute of Psychoanalysis, Balint invited psychoanalysts to give their attention to the psychological aspects of the doctor–patient relationship. On this occasion, he observed that, every 20 years, the analytic community had had to express its views on an extension of the applications of psychoanalysis. In the 1920s the question was whether or not psychoanalysts should tackle child psychotherapy. In the 1940s the problem concerned group psychotherapy. When, in the 1960s, he raised the problem of the psychological training of doctors, Balint's intention was to confront psychoanalysts with the pathological functioning of the body, the enigma of conversion "that mysterious leap into the organic . . . one of the oldest, and still a most attractive, concept in psycho-analysis" (Balint, 1966, p. 55). Will it be possible for us, in 1980, by using the same argument, to persuade psychoanalysts to take an interest in hypnosis? Or shall we have to await the year 2000?

Epilogue

At the end of this long peregrination, what conclusion can we reach? That we are almost totally ignorant of the mechanisms of hypnosis and suggestion. This would not be a serious matter if such ignorance did not extend to realms as varied as they are essential to the understanding of man. While the author's experiments do show that it is possible to manipulate states of consciousness, we know neither how the passage from one state to another takes place nor what are the conditions peculiar to each of these states. This variability is, in fact, the basis of our mental functioning, be it normal or pathological.

More generally, whether it is a question of the psychotherapeutic relationship, of affect, or of the changes which occur during treatment, we always come up against the problem of the interaction between the psychic and the somatic. We are still the prisoners of Cartesian dualism. Most authors nowadays speak in terms of psychosomatic oneness. Physicians observe daily the effects of the action of the psyche on the soma. A great many of the concepts underlying contemporary thought presuppose such action. But in practice, collaboration between psychologists and doctors proves difficult. Each remains entrenched in his own realm together with its categories. The physicians, for their part, often continue to adhere to a strict physico-chemical causality inherited from the nineteenth century. As for the psychologists, they refuse to take any interest in the physiological dimension of the mental processes.

To extricate us from this impasse, a veritable epistemological evolution would seem to be required. Whence will it come? That is hard to predict. The biological sciences will no doubt have a role of prime importance to play insofar as it is difficult to conceive that we might hope to understand

178

the body–mind relationship so long as we do not have a better knowledge of the circuits controlling the complex aspects of central nervous function.

It may equally be hoped that relational psychology will contribute to this synthesis. Psychoanalysts are indeed showing increasing interest in early relationships and are thus getting closer to the cross-roads where psychology and biology meet. These investigations will perhaps open up new perspectives.

Be that as it may, with regard to these problems hypnosis represents a field of choice. And this on two grounds. On the one hand, it constitutes an invaluable instrument for research inasmuch as in it psychobiological inter-actions are manifested in a manner that is constant and accessible to manipulation. On the other hand, it constitutes in itself an enigma which has yet to be solved. It is possible that this solution will result from research undertaken in entirely different fields. Unpredictable are the ways of discovery.

The understanding of the mode of action of relational psychotherapy is closely dependent on the unraveling of this mystery. This is equally true of the knowledge of mental illness, as also of the action of the psyche on the physiological systems (autonomic, endocrine, and immunological), whose role in all diseases is being increasingly emphasized. In this way, we may succeed in gaining a better insight into illnesses whose etiology is still unknown.

Hypnosis, as we have seen, relates to many fields: psychology, psychoanalysis, medicine, experimental psychology, social psychology, psychopharmacology, neurochemistry, neuropsychology, neurophysiology, and many more. It therefore calls for an interdisciplinary approach which is unfortunately but rarely achieved.

In conclusion, it can be said that this book is an appeal for humility. The author believes he has shown the extent to which the scientific understanding of the mode of action of psychotherapy remains rudimentary. Too many psychotherapists are settled in a reassuring quietude and compensate for their uncertainty by a dogmatic attitude. Hence the many disputes prevailing between schools, which use up energy and are prejudicial to the development of research.

It is almost two centuries ago that, in 1784, Mesmer's pupil, the Marquis de Puységur, was conversing with a shepherd named Victor whom he had just hypnotized. Observing to his great surprise that, on awaking, the latter remembered none of the events that had occurred during this session, he concluded that we had two independent memories. Thus did the unconscious enter the field of experimental research. A century later, Sigmund Freud gradually discovered, through the words of his hypnotized patients, the dynamics of the wish and repression. On these two occasions hypnosis had been the catalyst through which fundamental discoveries became possible. It may well be that it still holds some surprises for us.

APPENDIX I

EXPERIMENTAL RESEARCH ON HYPNOTIC ANALGESIA[1]

A great deal of work on hypnotic analgesia has been carried out in the U.S.A., principally by three large laboratories (Stanford, Philadelphia, and Boston).

Barber's work (Barber and Hahn, 1962; Barber, 1963, 1969a) seems to show that suggested analgesia is not specific to the hypnotic state, but may also be observed under certain conditions in the waking state. According to Barber, the mechanisms operating in analgesia are in fact due to psychological variables, such as the subject's suggestibility, his anxiety and the relationship between the research worker and the subject.

Other work such as that carried out under the direction of Hilgard (1967, 1969, 1971, 1974, 1975) and Orne (McGlashen, Evans, and Orne, 1969) has, on the other hand, demonstrated the superiority of hypnotic analgesia as compared with different types of analgesia, in the waking state, namely analgesia induced by suggestion and the placebo effect.

The authors' experiment, however, focused especially on the study of hypnotic analgesia, with the particular intention of determining its effectiveness and general applicability from a practical point of view.

Experiments in hypnotic analgesia generally follow a set pattern: subjects are selected according to their capacity to enter the hypnotic state. They are then subjected to the same painful stimulus (electric shock, hand plunged into cold water, ischemic pain, etc.) administered successively in states of hypnosis and consciousness.

The aim of the authors' experiment was to demonstrate hypnotic analgesia and thereby show that, under hypnosis, suggestions of analgesia are far more effective than in the waking state.

The experimental procedure chosen corresponds to that used by Lenox (1970): ischemic pain induced by the application of a tourniquet, accompanied by muscular exercises for a predetermined period of time. This method of inducing pain presents several advantages:

---

[1] This research was carried out in the author's laboratory by D. Michaux, P. Peuchmaur, and G. Bleirad.

The pressure applied by the tourniquet can be regulated and remains constant. The pain induced is progressive and increases with time.

There is no danger, provided that the experiment is not too prolonged.

The experiment was performed with the same subjects, submitted to the same suggestions of analgesia under two sets of conditions, in the waking state and under hypnosis. It did not seem worth conducting a third session under hypnosis without suggestion, since Hilgard (1967) showed that under these conditions there was no analgesia.

Two indices of the pain experienced by the subject were analyzed: on the one hand, the duration of his tolerance of the tourniquet; on the other hand, the mark he allotted to the pain he experienced, on a subjective 10-point scale.

Translated into terms of the chosen indices, the hypothesis regarding hypnotic analgesia should appear as follows:

There should be an increase in the length of time for which the pain is tolerated under hypnosis.

There should be a lessening under hypnosis of the subjective evaluation of the pain (a lowering of the marks allotted to the pain).

Description of the Experiment

1. *Apparatus*

A rubber bandage (Esmarch bandage), a pneumatic tourniquet with a pressure gauge (for precise measurement of the pressure), a dynamometer for muscular exercise (by pressing on the apparatus) to accelerate the appearance of pain, and a chronometer.

2. *Procedure*

Both parts of the experiment, in the hypnotic and the waking state, followed an identical course. There was an interval of 30 minutes between the two parts. Half the subjects began the experiment in the hypnotic state, while the other half began it in the waking state.

Pain was induced in the following manner: first, the right forearm was tightly encased in a rubber bandage up to the elbow, in order to reduce the amount of blood contained in the forearm. The experimenter then applied the tourniquet (at a pressure of 30 cm of mercury) so as to stop the circulation of blood in the right forearm.

The subject exerted pressure on the dynamometer for periods of 3 seconds alternating with 3-second rest periods. This exercise lasted 2 minutes. It was intended to accelerate the process of ischemic pain.

The subject was then asked to estimate the sensation of pain on a subjective scale from 0 to 10, 0 being defined as the absence of pain, and 10 as intolerable pain requiring the removal of the tourniquet. The score was noted every minute. In no case did the experiment last more than 15 minutes.

Under hypnosis, the procedure remained the same, except for one addition designed to verify the depth of the hypnotic state. The subject was asked to place himself on a 5-point hypnotic scale where 5 corresponded to a state of very deep hypnosis.

3. *Subjects*

Sixteen subjects were involved, all volunteers, remunerated at the rate of 30 francs per session. Of these, nine were male and seven female. The subjects were selected according to their hypnotizability. They all obtained a high score on the SHSS scales A and C (see p. 192) (Weitzenhoffer and Hilgard, 1959, 1962).

4. *Controlled variables*

(a) Subjects' degree of hypnotizability.

(b) Pressure of the tourniquet (30 cm of mercury).

(c) Duration and number of muscular exercises (20 pressures each lasting 3 seconds, alternating with 20 rest periods of 3 seconds – 2 minutes' exercises in all).

(d) Suggestions of anesthesia in the right arm were the same for both the hypnotic and waking parts of the experiment.

(e) The sequence of the two parts was reversed. Half the subjects undertook the experiment in the order Hypnosis – Waking (sequence A), and the other half in the sequence Waking – Hypnosis (sequence B).

Results

1. *Analysis of the time*

The authors' hypothesis anticipated that the tourniquet would be tolerated for a greater length of time under hypnosis than in the waking state. With Lenox's findings (1970) in mind, it was thought that under hypnosis the time would approximate 15 minutes (the maximum duration of the experiment).

Table 3 shows that the hypothesis was verified. *The subjects endured the tourniquet longer under hypnosis than in the waking state.* (The difference is significant at $p < 0.005$, $t = 3.75$.)

It can be seen that the hypothesis was verified, although not in such a clear-cut fashion as was earlier suggested. The subjects endured the tourniquet for almost 11 minutes under hypnosis and not 15 minutes. This was due to the fact (analyzed in detail later) that the subjects' behavior varied somewhat from one to another and that some did not experience a true state of *hypnotic* analgesia.

TABLE 3

Average length of time [2] for which the tourniquet was tolerated

	Hypnosis	Waking state	Average
Sequence A (8 subjects) Hypnosis — Waking	10 min 26 sec	5 min 21 sec	7 min 53 sec
Sequence B (8 subjects) Waking — Hypnosis	11 min 15 sec	7 min 35 sec	9 min 25 sec
	10 min 50 sec	6 min 28 sec	

It will also be noticed that the differences between the waking and hypnotic states were reduced by the procedure followed in the experiment. Thus, for safety reasons, the session was systematically brought to a close after 15 minutes, even if the estimated degree of pain at that point was less than 10.

It must further be recorded that, under hypnosis, ten subjects fell into this category, whereas they numbered only three in the waking state.[3]

2. *Analysis of the scores on the pain scale*

The establishment of average scores for pain, the second criterion for assessing the analgesia, also posed certain problems:

On the one hand, the score is subjective. However, it does seem possible that pain appreciation remains the same in the two states of consciousness pertaining to the experiment. The subject constructs a criterion for the assessment of pain and allocates a mark accordingly, and this criterion remains the same in the waking state as under hypnosis.

On the other hand, the process of analyzing the results presents certain difficulties.

Two different procedures were chosen for this purpose. *Mean scores for each subject* [4] were calculated for the two conditions and compared. *An average curve* was also constructed by calculating the group mean for each experimental condition, for each 1-minute period of the experiment (0--15 minutes). It was possible to take these calculations only by using an artifice: in order for there to be a score for each period, in cases where the score had reached 10 before the 15 minutes had expired (which in practice meant the removal of the tourniquet), it was assumed that the score would not have fallen below 10 between that point and the end of

[2] The average times were obtained by taking the mean of the lengths of time for which the subjects could endure the tourniquet (sum of the times over number of subjects).

[3] This difference is further accentuated if account is taken of the scores after 15 minutes. Of the ten subjects mentioned, eight had scores of less than 5 after 15 minutes, while the scores of the three subjects in the waking group reached 8.5 and 9.5 after 15 minutes.

[4] The mean scores were obtained by establishing the average of the pain ratings obtained every minute from each patient.

the full 15 minutes. This procedure seemed justifiable, compatible as it is with the principle of increasing pain which characterizes the method used.

It should finally be mentioned that the average scores for each subject and the mean curve do not correspond to any very precise psychological reality. It will be appreciated that, if valid comparisons can be made in the case of a single subject (supposing that his criterion for the measurement of pain remains the same for the whole experiment), comparisons between subjects and the establishment of average scores for the whole sample are a more hazardous undertaking, for pain thresholds vary greatly from one subject to another.

(a) *Analysis of the average scores*

The hypothesis anticipated that the average score under hypnosis would be lower than that obtained in the waking state.

TABLE 4

Average scores on the pain scale

	Hypnosis	Waking state	Average
Sequence A (8 subjects) Hypnosis — Waking	5.39	8.79	7.09
Sequence B (8 subjects) Waking — Hypnosis	5.49	8.10	6.80
	5.44	8.45	

The hypothesis was verified. *Under hypnosis, the average pain score was lower than in the waking state.* The difference is significant at $p < 0.001$ $(t = 4.48)$. Although it is fairly difficult to assess what the scores given by the subjects correspond to, the following scheme might be suggested:

From 0 to 3: slight pain.

From 4 to 6: moderate pain.

From 7 to 10: considerable pain.

According to this classification, 5.44 would be equivalent to moderate pain, a sensation which is beginning to be perceived as painful. On the other hand, the score of 8.45 corresponds to a level of pain which is approaching the intolerable. It would seem, therefore, that one passes from an unpleasant sensation to a painful one.

Furthermore, the results obtained are the same, regardless of the sequence. The slight difference between the two sets of scores (sequence A and sequence B) is not significant $(t < 1)$.

(b) *Average curve*

It was possible to obtain an average curve by establishing the mean score for each period of the experiment and for each condition (waking state and hypnosis).

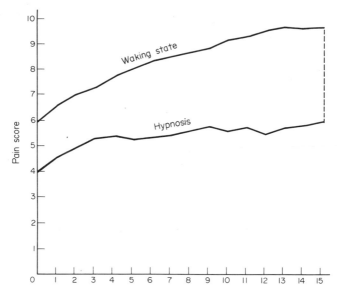

Fig. 2.   Average curve of pain as a function of time in the waking state and under hypnosis.

This procedure offers a means for observing how, on average, the pain develops during the session in each condition.

It should be remembered that the curve has no true psychological reality as it represents the average of subjective scores given by sixteen subjects. But it does indicate certain interesting tendencies. It can be seen, for example, that in the waking state the pain increases progressively; under hypnosis, however, the pain increases over the first 4 minutes, then remains more or less constant. The two curves thus "behave" in very different ways. Furthermore, they clearly confirm that the scores are lower under hypnosis than in the waking state.

3. *Study of the two groups of subjects in relation to their capacity to achieve hypnotic analgesia*

(a) *Principle of dichotomization*

Study of individual profiles revealed that there appeared to be two types of behavior in response to the noxious stimulus. Certain subjects "performed well" in the experiment, others not.

Knowing the average scores (the average of the pain scores given by each subject every minute during the 15-minute experiment) in the hypnotic and waking states, the difference between the two scores was calculated (i.e. the improvement or deterioration in the analgesia due to hypnosis).

Grouping the differences between the scores according to the size of difference, the following distribution was obtained:

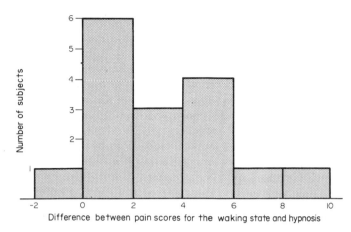

Fig. 3.   Distribution of the differences between pain scores in the waking and hypnotic states.

The distribution comprises two modalities: one at 1 and the other at 5. This enables two groups of similar size to be distinguished. In the first of these, the analgesia is non-existent or very weak (-2 to $+2$). In the second group, the analgesia is distinctly stronger ($+3$ to 10).

As none of the subjects in these two groups showed any marked analgesia in the waking state (see Fig. 3), they will be referred to in the succeeding paragraphs by the following titles in order to distinguish them from each other. The first of these groups will be called the *non-analgesic group*, and the second, the *analgesic group*, on the understanding that this distinction applies to the performance of the two groups under hypnosis.

(b) *Analysis of the evolution of the average pain curve for each group of subjects (analgesic and non-analgesic) as a function of time*

The average pain curves were established for the two groups, "analgesic" (N^1) and "non-analgesic" (N^2).

It will be observed that there is a similarity between the two curves (waking and hypnosis) for the non-analgesic patients. A slight underestimate of pain intensity is apparent along the whole length of the curve, but it is small and no conclusion can be drawn from it.

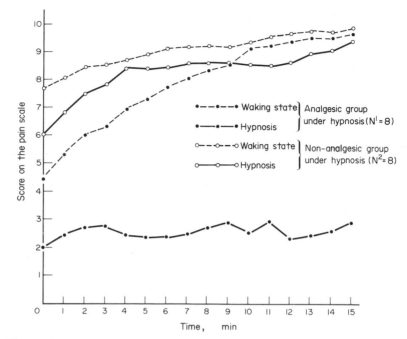

Fig. 4. Average pain curves under hypnosis and in the waking state for each group (N^1 and N^2) as a function of time.

It will be noted, on the other hand, that in the case of the strongly analgesic subjects the two curves for hypnosis and waking are completely different in shape. The graph of the pain scores under hypnosis is linear and lies between 2 and 3.

Furthermore, it seems possible to set aside the hypothesis that scores may be distorted by the subject who is anxious to conform to the suggestion, because the curve remains horizontal up to time point 15; therefore, in contrast to what happened previously, the subjects did not ask for the tourniquet to be removed (score 10) before the end of the 15-minute experiment.

In order to analyze and interpret the graph in more detail, it is important to remember that one of the characteristics of ischemic pain is its progressive nature. The pain should therefore be slight at the beginning and then steadily increase. It is therefore relevant to question the significance of the scores given at 0 minute, and more generally over the first half of the experiment. Is it really an appreciation of pain, as must be the case at the end of the experiment, or is it rather an expression of the subject's attitude toward pain?

If this second hypothesis is adopted, what emerges is as follows:

1. That the two groups have radically different attitudes toward pain in the waking state. The non-analgesic group has a quasi "aversive" response (7.5 out of 10 at 0 minute), whereas the analgesic subjects have a certain amount of tolerance of the situation (4.5 out of 10 at 0 minute). It was possible to verify this distinction from the individual curves, which showed that in the analgesic group six out of eight subjects had a pain score of less than 5 at time 0 in the waking state, and in the non-analgesic group seven out of eight subjects had a score of more than 5.

2. That hypnosis produces a slight movement in the attitude of the aversive group (since the score at 0 minute falls from 7.5 to less than 6) which affects each subsequent evaluation of pain under hypnosis throughout the experiment.

3. That in the tolerant group, hypnosis produces almost total analgesia. The linear nature of the graph seems to indicate that the pain factor did not appear, since the essential characteristic of ischemic pain is that it increases with time.

Finally, it seems that, on the basis of these results, there is evidence for the conclusion that some factor other than the aptitude for hypnosis is at work in hypnotic analgesia.

Could this factor be, as has been suggested, the subject's attitude toward pain? In this case, the achievement of analgesia would be a function of two factors: on the one hand, the subject's attitude[5] toward pain before the experiment, and on the other hand, the possibility of change introduced by hypnosis.

The effect of hypnosis seems to depend on the attitudes already held by the subject. In this respect there appears to be a threshold. Beyond the threshold, the subject is "aversive" and the suggestion has no effect on the pain[6] (the curves are identical), but produces a slight reduction in the score, a reduction which would take effect in the area of attitudes. Before the threshold is reached, the subject is "tolerant" and a double effect can be observed: as far as the subject's attitude is concerned, a slight reduction in the pain score at 0 minute, and as regards recognition of the sensation, apparently no pain; the curve does not rise.

---

[5] It would perhaps be more exact to say that the first factor can be detected in the area of attitudes. It is not possible here to determine the exact nature of the factor in question — attitudes, aptitudes, etc.

[6] It is useful to elaborate this statement in relation to the average curves, and, in six cases out of eight, in relation to the individual curves, for there are two exceptions in which acutely aversive subjects nevertheless achieved hypnotic analgesia. It does seem that there is a factor here which has to be acknowledged, a factor which could not be taken into account in this chapter, namely the subject's level of autonomy and self-control under hypnosis. This factor might in certain cases introduce some distortion into the effect described. Slight autonomy might lead to analgesia in spite of pre-existing aversive attitudes, and strong autonomy to non-analgesia in "tolerant" subjects.

(c) *Comparative study of the aptitude for hypnotic analgesia:*
ischemia and ammonia. The predictability of the capacity for
analgesia by means of the anosmia to ammonia test

It seemed interesting to see if success in the anosmia to ammonia test (administered during a previous session: scale C) would enable the subjects' performance during ischemic analgesia to be predicted.

Anosmia to ammonia is suggested olfactory anesthesia. After appropriate suggestions, the subject is asked to inhale, and the test is successful when the patient can inhale without any painful reaction or discomfort.

The breakdown of subjects according to their results in the two tests is presented in tabulated form below (see Table 5).

TABLE 5
Figures relating to the success or failure in anosmia
to ammonia and in hypnotic analgesia

	Success or failure in hypnotic analgesia		
	−	+	
Success or failure in anosmia to ammonia +	2	8	10
−	6	0	6
	8	8	N = 16

It will be observed on reading the table that all the subjects who failed in the exercise in anosmia to ammonia also failed in the experiment on hypnotic analgesia. In contrast, the subjects who succeeded in this item had a high chance of success in hypnotic analgesia, since eight out of the ten subjects who succeeded in this test performed well in the experiment, while only two failed in it. The correlation between the two variables is significant at $p < 0.01$ (χ^2 corrected: 6.66).

However, the number of subjects is very small and a much larger sample would be necessary to confirm this result.

Thus, as was supposed, there is a close relationship between the achievement of anosmia to ammonia and the subject's capacity for analgesia as demonstrated during ischemia.

Discussion and Conclusion

The results obtained during this experiment show that a high degree of analgesia can be produced under hypnosis with the aid of verbal suggestions. Similarly, they show that suggestions are not of themselves sufficient, since their effect depends on the subject's state of consciousness.

The discussion which follows bears upon two points: the reality of the analgesia observed and the role of hypnosis.

(a) *The reality of the analgesia*

In order to refute the results reported in this chapter, it could be asserted that pain induced in the laboratory cannot be compared to spontaneous pain or pain during surgery.

This criticism is itself countered by the fact that hypnotic analgesia has also been demonstrated in relation to spontaneous and severe pain (Chertok, 1957, 1975), as illustrated in considering the history of hypnotic analgesia and the authors' clinical experiments.

Nevertheless, this does not entirely dismiss criticism of the method of inducing pain (by ischemia), or of the lack of precision in the measurement of its real intensity, and therefore leaves room for objections to its validity as a means of demonstrating the appearance of analgesia.

The objection to this second criticism is that the two groups of subjects (strongly and slightly analgesic under hypnosis) produce identical average results in the waking state at 10 minutes (Fig. 4). It therefore seems that after 10 minutes the pain becomes intolerable for the majority of subjects. It was seen that, whatever their aptitude for hypnotic analgesia, the tolerance limit of the tourniquet for these subjects in the waking state stood at between 10 and 15 minutes. (There were only three exceptions, whose score at time 15 was nevertheless close to 10 in the waking state.)

This spontaneous agreement on the part of the subjects seem to confirm the algogenic value of ischemia, and thus the validity of the hypnotic analgesia observed.

(b) *The role of hypnosis*

The authors' experiment took place under two sets of conditions, under hypnosis and in the waking state, the suggestions given being identical in both. This was in order to control the variable suggestibility, an indispensable factor, for Hilgard (1967) showed that it was necessary for suggestions to accompany the hypnosis in order for the hypnotic analgesia to make its appearance.

The procedure established with these considerations in mind revealed the increased effectiveness of the suggestions when given under hypnosis, thus demonstrating the role of the state of consciousness factor in the phenomenon.

However, while it was possible by means of this procedure to establish control of the suggestion and its content, one problem nevertheless remains. This problem, subject of considerable controversy for more than a century, can be summarized as follows: has the concept of hypnosis been established, or should one rather speak only of suggestibility?

It is true that according to certain writers, the "hypnotic state" is a fiction, and in fact involves no more than an increase in one of the subject's permanent faculties, namely his suggestibility. From this point of view, hypnosis and its behavioral accompaniments would only be the subject's responses to the suggestions, and the typical induction procedures would merely reinforce the subject's aptitude for responding to suggestions, by playing on his expectations, motivations, and attitudes (Barber, 1969a).

In the authors' view, it is not possible to give an entirely satisfactory answer at present. One cannot, however, but be impressed by the exceptional value of induction and the "hypnotic" situation in modifying the subject's expectations, attitudes, and motivations, and thus rendering him hypersuggestible.

Whatever the case, whether one is inclined, like the author, toward the hypothesis that there is a change in the state of consciousness, or, like Barber, toward the hypothesis that there is an increase in suggestibility, it can nevertheless be agreed that, in the context of a "hypnotic" situation, major analgesic effects can appear.

Addendum: The Scales

One of the major problems in all experimental work is that of measurement. In the case of hypnosis this problem proves particularly difficult to resolve in the absence of any physiological indicators. The solution favored in the United States rests implicitly upon two assumptions: that the level of hypnosis induced in the subject is relatively stable and constant, and that it can be perceived at the behavioral level in the subject's response to the various suggestions.

On this basis, it has been possible to construct a certain number of scales: Scales A, B, C, Profiles I and II (Stanford), the Barber Scale, etc. They are all based on the same principle: in the first place, an induction phase in which suggestions are designed to induce the "hypnotic state"; once this has been achieved, a series of exercises in suggestion, increasing in difficulty (the degree of difficulty having first been established in the study of an earlier sample). The depth of hypnosis is then determined by the degree of success on the scale.

It follows that every experiment should in the first place include one or more trials on the scale in order to determine the depth of hypnosis induced in the subject as a result of the induction phase. The measurement obtained can then serve as a numerical reference in research for differential purposes (influence of age, sex, etc.), comparative purposes (personality and hypnosis; EEG and hypnosis, etc.), and so on.

The scales most frequently used internationally in experiments are Scale A (SHSSA) and Scale C (SHSSC).

The success of Scale A can be explained by its great ease of objectification and notation, its relative brevity, and also perhaps by the fact that it is easier from the subjects' point of view.

Scale A consists of twelve items contributing to a final score. Of these, ten suggestions are directed toward motor activity, including five inhibiting voluntary movement and one post-hypnotic compulsion. The other two items are the hallucination of a fly, and the suggestion of post-hypnotic amnesia. The hallucination is to be observed in the subject's behavior, e.g. his gestures or facial expression.

Scale C is distinctly more diverse, with items on motor activity, sensory distortion of taste, smell, hearing (the hallucination of a voice asking questions), and vision.

At another level: amnesia, temporal regression, and dreams. However, it takes much longer, is more difficult to objectify and more difficult for the subject, including certain items which may even disturb the latter (ammonia, regression) sufficiently to wake him up during the test. In the authors' view, this last disadvantage is such as to make it very difficult in fact to administer this scale directly, as a certain amount of prior habituation is required.

APPENDIX II

AN EXPERIMENTAL STUDY OF
THE HYPNOTIC EXPERIENCE[1]

Introduction

As research on hypnosis has been developed in the United States, especially in the twentieth century, there follows a brief presentation of the various streams of research and concepts which presently coexist in that country.

The association between the authors' work and this stream of "behaviorist" research on hypnosis is undeniable. Some of their research on analgesia, hypnotic recall, etc., adopts the same approach. The induction method and scales of suggestibility they use derive directly from that source. They do, however, depart considerably from the behaviorist approach by taking account of the spontaneous behavioral manifestations as a whole and the psychic experience during hypnosis.

The subject will therefore be presented as follows:
1. a rapid overview of the American research;
2. a series of answers to the principal questions about suggestibility as they arise from the results of experiments conducted in our laboratory in France;
3. the results drawn from the authors' more subjective and clinical approach to the experimental situation;
4. the authors' research perspectives.

Contemporary Experimental Research in the U.S.A.

The American research which emerged in the 1930s represents a continuation of Bernheim's work.

The first studies were undertaken by Hull (1933) who worked within a "neo-behaviorist" perspective and finally concluded after many experiments that hypnosis was a state characterized by the reinforcement of suggestibility.

Not long afterwards, Sarbin (1950), on the basis of his experiments, elaborated a theory of hypnosis in terms of "role-playing".

[1] Produced in collaboration with D. Michaux, P. Peuchmaur, and G. Bleirad, this article is a slightly modified version of the paper first published in the *Revue de Santé Mentale* (special issue 1978) under the title "Recherches expérimentales et cliniques sur l'hypnose".

The late fifties saw the creation of several laboratories, among which should above all be mentioned that of Stanford, under the direction of Professor E. Hilgard, and also those of Philadelphia under M. Orne and Boston under T. X. Barber.

The team at Stanford, aware of the paucity of methods of measurement, directed its energies toward perfecting scales on which the degree of suggestibility could be measured. Several scales were developed in succession: Scales A, B, and C, and Profiles I and II. By their diversity, these scales, proceeding in order of increasing difficulty, make it possible better to determine individual differences and areas of psychic activity affected by suggestibility.

A great deal of research has since been conducted at Stanford: research into physiological signs and effects (EEG, etc.); research correlating sex, age, etc., and hypnosis; the study of the effect of hypnosis on muscular performance, analgesic capacity, and so on.

Other experiments were carried out on personality traits as measured in numerous tests (M.M.P.I., C.P.I., M.I.A.P.S.); they proved disappointing and threw little light on the personality of hypnotizable subjects.

Finally, attention must be drawn to the research by J. Hilgard (1970, 1974), a psychoanalyst, centered upon clinical psychology, and which would seem to have demonstrated amongst other things a very significant relationship between authoritarian education and hypnotic susceptibility: subjects who had received a strict education were all highly suggestible under hypnosis.

In these experiments, which might be regarded as classic, the existence and specificity of the hypnotic state were taken for granted, and the study concentrated therefore on the comparison of the subjects' characteristics as a function of their score on the hypnotic scale. Other researchers, however (Orne, 1959; Barber, 1969a), less convinced of the reality of hypnosis, have perfected new experimental procedures[2] with the principal aim of answering the following two questions: Does hypnosis exist? If so, in what respect is the subject's behavior specific to the hypnotic state?

Though these questions represented the common starting point for both researchers, they employed very different methodologies.

Observing that the course of the experiments was influenced by the idea which the subject had of the hypnotic situation, and by the experimenter's implicit suggestions, Orne planned the creation of control groups in order to test these "parasitic" factors in the experiments.[3]

---

[2] In this connection see the very interesting book by Sheehan and Perry (1976) which studies the impact and consequences of these different methodological approaches.

[3] The question of what features if any in the attitude of the hypnotized subject actually come from the experimenter is sometimes a very difficult one, for the latter's expectations of the subject can in fact be communicated to him implicitly. Orne uses the heading *demand characteristics of the experimental situation* to denote all the means by which the hypnotist's intentions and wishes are conveyed (including implicit and non-verbal signals arising from the experiment and from the experimental procedure).

These control groups consist of simulators selected for their low level of response on the hypnotic susceptibility scales (0 to 2 out of 12). These subjects are asked to play the role of a truly hypnotized subject to the best of their ability. They are also advised that the experimenter attempting to hypnotize them will not be aware of their true status, but that if he happened to observe that they were not hypnotized, he would immediately halt the experiment.

Thus, thanks to this type of control, whose true nature is unknown to the experimenter, it is reasonable to assume that the demand characteristics of the experimental situation remain rigorously the same in all cases and therefore the differences in behavior can be attributed to hypnosis.

Barber, for his part, uses classical control groups with one difference, however. In most control groups used in hypnosis, the subjects are subjected to the same suggestions as the hypnotized subjects without undergoing hypnotic induction, or receiving any other instructions. It is in this last respect that the procedure adopted by Barber differs from the classical procedure. His control groups may be informed that they are going to take part in a test of their imagination in which they are encouraged to do their best, or that they are to undergo a test of task motivation, which Barber holds to be the essential underlying element in hypnotic induction.

These researchers reach radically different conclusions.

If Orne demonstrates that the majority of so-called characteristic phenomena of hypnosis are not really specific to it, he nevertheless highlights certain subtle and fundamental differences which emerge from his experiments and in the end validate the actual notion of hypnosis and the hypnotic trance.[4]

For his part, Barber maintains that nothing specific results from hypnotic induction. All the phenomena produced under hypnosis can be produced in the waking state by the proper manipulation of certain variables: the formulation of the instructions, the level of motivation proposed, etc. Hypnosis, the adoption of a type of behavior and a role, is but a variable depending on what has been suggested. It is not therefore a specific state characterized by a trance or an alteration of the state of consciousness. It is all suggestibility, imagination, etc., and individual differences can similarly be explained in terms of motivation, expectations, and attitude.

Experimental Research Conducted in Our Laboratory
(Centre Dejerine)

THE CLASSICAL EXPERIMENTAL APPROACH: NORMATIVE RESEARCH

The scales for the measurement of hypnosis perfected at Stanford are composed of two distinct parts. The first part, *the procedure for induction*, consists in a series

---

[4]Orne (1959, 1968) demonstrates three essential characteristics of hypnotic behavior: *Congruence*: homogeneity of behavior and its adequacy in relation to the situation (rhythm of responses, etc.): *Trance logic,* or, more precisely, the capacity to reason on a basis which would appear illogical in everyday life; *Response to hypnotic suggestions outside the experimental situation* and irrespective of whether the experimenter is present or not.

of instructions persuading the subject to concentrate his gaze and hearing, and suggestions aimed at inducing sleep and isolation. The second part, *the procedure for suggestions*, consists in instructions aimed at inducing by means of suggestions certain phenomena, such as the involuntary lowering of the hand, the hallucination of a fly, etc.

The level of hypnotic susceptibility is measured in an objective fashion as a function of the subject's behavior. If the behavior tends in the direction suggested, the subject obtains a positive score on the exercise. The total score is obtained simply by adding up the successful exercises, and is the measure of the subject's hypnotic susceptibility.

At the Centre Dejerine, the A, B, and C Scales and Profiles I and II have been translated into French. Having administered and validated Scales A and C on samples of voluntary and remunerated students, the authors felt the need to create a shorter scale whose level of difficulty would fall between these two scales and which could be administered by means of a tape recorder. To this end, they simplified and shortened the induction procedures of Scale A. In particular all the passages aiming to motivate the subjects were eliminated and the emphasis on closing the eyes was reduced.

The suggestions retained in the second part of the procedure are eight in number: four motor suggestions (eye closing, involuntarily bringing the hands together, verbal inhibition, arm rigidity), three ideational suggestions (dreaming about hypnosis, hallucinating a fly, and hallucinating music) and a post-hypnotic compulsion (removing a shoe in response to a pencil being tapped on the table).

Administering this scale to several samples of French students gave rise to the following observations:

Hypnotic susceptibility is a commonplace aptitude and relatively widely distributed

Since it was devised in 1976, the reduced scale has been administered to 104 voluntary subjects; the results obtained are reported below (Table 6, Figure 5).

As can be seen from Table 6 and Fig. 5, hypnotic susceptibility appears to be evenly distributed amongst the population studied. The distribution reveals a distinct predominance of average scores in the 3 to 6 range, whereas the low scores (0 to 2) and high scores (7 to 8) are clearly less frequent (20% and 13% respectively).

The small number of subjects who score very highly on the condensed scale demonstrates its level of difficulty and confirms the empirical observations of the reactions of hypnotized subjects since Mesmer, all of which tend to identify a small percentage of subjects who are highly suggestible under hypnosis (somnambulists), from 5% to 15% according to the literature.

The small number of subjects frankly "resistant" to suggestion under hypnosis, in the population under examination, can very probably be explained by the mode of recruitment and the nature of the subjects: volunteers, students paid for their services including a large number of psychology students (50%).

The hypnotic susceptibility, as measured on the scale, varies little according to the sample studied. Thus the overall results presented above were obtained from three distinct samples studied in 1976, 1977, and 1978.

TABLE 6
Distribution of scores

Score	Sample
0	4
1	6
2	11
3	18
4	18
5	17
6	16
7	11
8	3

The averages of these three samples were 4.21, 4.32, 4.04 respectively. Student's "*t*-test" shows that none of these slight differences is significant. If the 1977 and 1978 samples, composed of only twenty-eight subjects each, are taken together and compared to the 1976 sample consisting of forty-eight subjects, we find two averages which are to all intents and purposes identical: 4.18 and 4.21 ($t = 0.20$ not significant).

Thus even quite small samples are satisfactory for studying hypnotic susceptibility, which, contrary to the view which is widely held, is a common aptitude and occurs with great regularity.

The role of the experimenter

Here again, experimental work contradicts preconceived ideas to a considerable extent. None of the psychologists working in the Laboratory and the trainees who sometimes took part in the authors' research were hypnotists in the generally accepted sense of the word. Psychologists recruited for scientific reasons, none of them had ever had the inclination to hypnotize anyone prior to joining the laboratory.

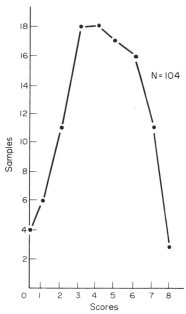

Fig. 5.   Distribution of scores
represented as a curve.

The results obtained by the various experimenters are very similar. As a statistical demonstration of this, the 1976 and 1978 results were broken down in terms of the experimenter who conducted the session. The results were as follows:

TABLE 7

Comparison of the average scores by experimenter.

Experimenter 1:   45 subjects — average score 4.22, standard deviation = 2.19
Experimenter 2:   17 subjects — average score 4.00, standard deviation = 1.41
Experimenter 3:   14 subjects — average score 4.07, standard deviation = 1.90

None of the differences in average scores is significantly different from the others according to the t-test.

Thus in spite of some differences in distribution reflected by the differences in the standard deviations, none of the subdistributions differ significantly from the others. Here again we can see the astonishing stability of the average score, even in samples as small as fourteen or seventeen subjects.

As all the hypnotists were experimenters and not "hypnotists" in the traditional sense of the term, one might ask whether their apparent equality is not a snare and does not conceal a major difference between them and the classical hypnotist. The authors cannot at this moment answer the question with numerical data, but it must be emphasized that in all cases where subjects had experienced the two types of induction, they produced equivalent levels of hypnosis in both situations. The differences between one hypnotist and another, according to the subjects, lie more in the affective and emotional dimension than in the depth of the hypnotic state. With the classical hypnotist, the subject feels a greater affective warmth but also feels under greater pressure, more under attack, when his behavior does not correspond to the hypnotist's expectations.

In fact, the main source of variability is to be sought much more in the subjects' personality than in that of the experimenters, as most hypnotists have already observed since Abbé Faria (1819).

Personality of the subject and hypnosis

Here again the results of experimentation are in conflict with certain preconceived ideas. Thus, in the early years of their research, the authors compared the results obtained by a group of pathological subjects (who had come for a consultation to the Centre for Psychosomatic Medicine seeking hypnosis) with the voluntary and remunerated subjects. The scale used was Stanford Scale A. The results in the two groups were as follows:[5]

TABLE 8

Comparison of the average scores obtained by voluntary subjects and "pathological" subjects on Scale A

	Average score	Standard deviation
Pathological subjects (= 24)	5.33	4.31
Voluntary subjects (= 52)	7.31	3.39
	$t = 2.581$	$p < 0.02$

Therefore the majority of the so-called "pathological" subjects is shown to be less suggestible[6] under hypnosis than the sample of student volunteers. It is perhaps a matter for regret that the patients were not studied in nosological groupings, but

---

[5]Scale A is scored out of 12 and not out of 8 like the condensed scale.

[6]If these results show clearly that hypnotic susceptibility should not be considered a "pathological" characteristic, they nevertheless do not authorize the conclusion that these subjects are less hypnotizable, for other studies have shown that hypnotic susceptibility decreases with age; now, as the authors' group of volunteers was distinctly younger than their "pathological" group, it seems that this may suffice to explain the difference in their success.

the smallness of the sample did not permit it. However, it is a fact that the majority of these patients were hysterics.

Finally the authors would like to make the point that it was among the hysterical patients that those most "refractory" toward hypnosis were found, even though some of them were, on the other hand, particularly suggestible.

These results seem to show clearly that hypnotic susceptibility is not the preserve of the pathological personality and that, up to the present at least, it would also seem that no research laboratory has been able to establish such a relationship. Nor is hypnosis linked, as has often been thought, to some ego weakness. If he must be characterized, the *easily* hypnotizable voluntary subject should rather be *described as a very sociable personality (attracted by the group and capable of confronting it).* That is what has emerged from a study recently begun on the authors' voluntary subjects, in which there has been an attempt to link personality traits with hypnotizability.

In order to measure the personality of the subjects, tests such as the M.M.P.I. have been deliberately avoided because of their excessive emphasis on pathological traits. The tests chosen were those of Cattell (16 P.F.) and Guilford and Zimmerman who adopt a structural approach to personality.

The results obtained are reported in Table 9.

TABLE 9

Significant correlations between hypnosis
scores and personality traits
(twenty-three subjects)

Tests	Factors	Correlation with hypnotic susceptibility
16 P.F. Cattell	A	0.52*
	E	0.43*
Guilford	A	0.47*
Zimmerman	S	0.41*

*Significant at the 0.05 level.

In the Cattell test, factor A contrasts subjects who are *open,* warm, easy to be with and co-operative with subjects who are *reserved,* detached, critical, distant, and rigid. Factor E contrasts subjects who are *modest,* gentle, and accommodating, with subjects who are *authoritative,* aggressive, and obstinate, with a highly developed sense of rivalry.

In the Guilford–Zimmerman test: factor A contrasts subjects with a strong *ascendancy* drive, used to public speaking, directing, persuading, etc., with subjects who show *submissive* behavior more or less linked to an incapacity for performing in public. Factor S contrasts *sociable subjects*: those who like and seek out the group and group activities, with *unsociable* subjects: those who have difficulty in engaging in social relationships, have few friends, etc.

As all the correlations reported in Table 9 are positive, it appears that the subjects most susceptible to hypnosis emerge on the Cattell Scale as the most OPEN and the most AUTHORITATIVE, and on the Guilford—Zimmerman as SOCIABLE subjects with a fairly high degree of ASCENDANCY.

It is noticeable that the results obtained in the two personality tests converge appreciably. The good hypnotic subject therefore seems to be one who makes easy social contact, in the authors' sample at least,[7] a subject who is open to others but can also preserve his own personality and express himself within the group, which qualities give him a dominant role in return.

These results are paradoxical when compared to the general idea of the hypnotizable subject as someone with a weak and somewhat submissive personality.

However, they are not as surprising as they seem. We can assume that the subject's attitudes toward others and to the group determine the type of relationship which he can establish with the hypnotist in the induction phase. If these attitudes are good (an open, sociable subject), the subject will be able to abandon himself to the hypnotic relationship and by extension to hypnosis.

It can also be assumed that if the subject can assert himself in the group, it is because he has sufficient confidence in himself, and does not particularly fear the criticism of the group. The subject's confidence in himself is perhaps what enables him to abandon himself to hypnosis and to accept suggestion.

We may therefore take the view that the personality test provides an indirect measure of the subject's *deep-seated attitudes* toward hypnosis, the hypnotic relationship and suggestion.

In this context it should be remembered that the subject's attitudes play an essential role in modulating the appearance of the hypnotic state. In an experimental situation, for example, the subject may effectively resist hypnosis. For the subject to be hypnotized he must give way to an acceptance of hypnosis.

If this hypothesis is valid, the relationship that has been observed between personality and hypnosis informs us not so much about the personality factors involved in hypnosis as such, but rather about the personality factors which determine the subject's acceptance of or resistance to hypnosis, that is about his attitudes.

Clinical Approach to the Experimental Situation

The clinical approach   .

In all the experiments mentioned hitherto, the sole index of hypnosis used was the subject's level of behavioral response to suggestions. This position rests upon two questionable assumptions:

1. hypnosis is a state characterized by high suggestibility;
2. suggestibility can be defined as the appearance of behavior which conforms to the suggestions.

---

[7] This experiment is at present in progress, with the aim of verifying whether the relationships observed hold true for a larger sample.

The assumptions which have dominated research on hypnosis for about the last 30 years can be contested.[8] It is clear that the aptitude for suggestibility is present in the waking state, with considerable variations, in all individuals. It is only the increase in suggestibility which has been shown by some writers to be an essential characteristic of hypnosis (Hull, Weitzenhoffer, etc.).

The measurement of hypnosis should not therefore be equated simply with that of suggestibility under hypnosis.

Furthermore, if we confine our measurement to the subject's behavior without taking account of his experience, we find ourselves having to include under the heading of "suggestion" types of behavior which can vary enormously according to whether they were experienced by the subject as voluntary or involuntary.

These major criticisms of the pseudo-objectivity of the standardized measurement of hypnosis (hypnotic susceptibility scales) have led the authors to attempt to realize a more clinical approach to the experimental hypnotic situation. To this end they have compiled a manual for the analysis of the situation to enable:

a complete view of the suggested and spontaneous behavior of the hypnotized subject;

the study of the subjective experience of the suggestions and, more generally, of the total hypnotic situation (mental functioning under hypnosis).

The completion of such a manual seems of prime importance. Indeed, apart from Charcot's description (1882b)[9] of the three "stages" of hypnosis, no systematic approach to hypnotic phenomenology has been undertaken for more than 200 years. Of course some writers with a clinical orientation (White, 1937; Shor, 1962; Gill and Brenman, 1959) have described certain aspects of hypnotic behavior and experience, but these contributions have always been partial and unsystematic. From the experimental point of view, thousands of sessions have been devoted to the study of various aspects of hypnotic suggestibility, but this enormous volume of work, from which a very precise phenomenology of hypnosis might have resulted, remains but a collection of often contradictory results on hypnotic suggestibility, without its being for all that any easier today to answer the most elementary questions about the hypnotic state and its spontaneous, subjective or behavioral, manifestations.

The detailed analysis of sessions is therefore a necessity for anyone nowadays who wants to understand what hypnosis is, and the relationship between hypnosis and suggestibility.

The authors' precise objectives in compiling their manual for such an analysis were as follows:

to make a sufficient wealth of information available to permit case studies in depth, and to enable research into the meaning of behavior or subjective

---

[8] This criticism which has lain at the base of the authors' work for the last 6 years seems to be more and more widely accepted today amongst researchers who include the creators of the hypnotic susceptibility scales (Weitzenhoffer, 1979, see p. 185).

[9] According to Charcot there were three successive stages of hypnosis, in order of increasing depth: catalepsy, lethargy, somnambulism.

manifestations (distortion of time, alteration of the body image, etc.) which
might appear in the course of a session;

to make finely detailed and precise information available in written form so that
past sessions could be re-examined in order to test any particular hypothesis,
and/or to make a retrospective comparison of the behavioral characteristics
and experience of any one subject session by session (longitudinal studies);

to make available standardized information which could be studied by existing
statistical methods: factorial analysis of correlations, automatic classification,
etc. These mathematical methods should enable us to investigate the very
essence of the phenomenon to be studied, by enabling what arises from the
subject's various individual characteristics to be classified and distinguished
from what is common to all the subjects.

First results

The systematic use of this approach on 104 subjects over a 3-year period has
already led to improved knowledge of hypnosis.

On the one hand, the authors have come to recognize the existence not of an
ideal hypnotic trance but of *many different forms of trance* varying according to
the individual, and also within the same individual depending on the conditions in
the session (greater or lesser degree of constraint, type of suggestion, etc.). On the
other hand, they have been able to verify the existence of a *division between
hypnosis and suggestibility* both in individual cases and at the statistical level.
These two principal aspects of the research will now be presented.

The hypnotic trance and the forms it takes;

   Interindividual variations

If, as the sessions proceed, the experimenter vaguely senses the existence of
broad types of trance behind the individual differences, it is but a hazy impression.
Given the multiplicity of variables involved, it is virtually impossible to pinpoint
the precise character of these different types in any concrete way. For the same
reason, it is practically impossible to distinguish the factor or factors common to
every form of hypnotic trance.[10]

Consequently, in an attempt to establish a typology of hypnotic experience, the
subjective material obtained by means of the authors' manual was submitted to
factorial analysis (Benzecri's analysis of correlations). From the entire range of
factors the analysis of fifty-two subjects distinguished five major factors structuring
the hypnotic trance.

The first of these factors contrasts the hypnotized subjects with those not
hypnotized. It is characterized by a collection of subjective evaluations around the

---

[10] Charcot's description of the three phases of hypnosis was a move in this direction, even if
the legitimacy of his distinction is questionable.

following two themes: partial loss of control,[11] and loss of contact with the environment and with reality. It can be interpreted at several levels. On a purely descriptive level, it can be understood as *"unawareness"* insofar as the subject's failure to exercise control is not due to the impossibility of self-control, but to an absence of awareness as regards the exercise of control. ("I didn't think of it" is frequently the response of subjects in support of their evaluation.) On a more theoretical level, if we turn to the various theories of ego functioning, we might say that it represents *the loss of the negativity function of consciousness,* an essential ego function acquired in the course of child development, since the result of this "unawareness" is to prevent the subject from differentiating clearly between the ego and the non-ego, as much in relation to personal control as in orientation and perception of the external world.[12] It is therefore a true "regression" of the individual to an archaic phase of his mental structure which characterizes hypnosis.

If the authors are correct in their interpretation, there is a *structural regression* to an archaic mode of functioning, in which fusion reigns and the individual as such has not yet been constituted. This structural regression is not automatically accompanied by a regression in terms of skills available to the hypnotized subject (language, writing, motor function, etc.); it is not a true return to infancy, but the reappearance in the adult of the mode of mental functioning which prevailed in early infancy, particularly in relationships to others and to the environment.

To avoid any confusion in the rest of this presentation, the authors will leave it at a descriptive level and refer to this factor as "unawareness."[13]

The four factors which follow do not, like the first factor, distinguish hypnotized subjects from non-hypnotized subjects, but reveal the different forms of trance.

These factors are, in order of importance: the modality of attention (focused or diffuse); the location of control (external or internal); the level of mental activity (activity or passivity); the level of resistance (resistances, adjuvants).

Concretely, since each of these factors may affect the subjective experience of the trance, it is the combination of factors $2 \times 3 \times 4 \times 5$ which determines a multitude of forms of trance. Some tend toward the stereotype of *autohypnosis* (internal control, mental activity, focused attention), others toward the stereotype of *hypnosis* (external control), passivity, resistance (insofar as these give rise to a loss of mental structure when they occur within the hypnotic state), or else the stereotype of a *drug state* (diffuse attention, activity, etc.).

---

[11] The impossibility of self-control corresponds to the evaluation: *"total* loss of control" which is not explained by this factor.

[12] One of the three factors suggested by Shor (1959, 1962) is entitled: *loss of generalized reality orientation,* which is, as we can see, not very far from the theoretical formulation which the authors propose in order to characterize their first factor.

[13] However, let us not lose sight of the limits of this term as applied here. Contrary to what is implied in the notion of "unawareness," the hypnotized subject undergoes a partial loss of awareness within a relationship maintained with the hypnotist at the verbal and sensori-motor levels, which distinguishes hypnosis from dreaming and sleep. Hence the interpretation in terms of regression.

It seems therefore that, in response to hypnotic induction as practiced by the authors, the alterations in the state of consciousness experienced by the non-refractory subjects assume diverse forms according to the subject. These forms cover in fact the whole range of altered states of consciousness, of which the forms approximating to the stereotye of hypnosis constitute only a fragment.

Observations carried out on drug addicts show the occurrence of a high degree of suggestibility in some of them, while in others it is negligible. In dealing with traditional forms of meditation, some writers distinguish between those which introduce an external agent (a religious symbol) to guide the meditation and those which operate without any external adjuvant. This shows clearly that certain factors which can be used to differentiate between the forms of hypnotic trance can also be used to differentiate between other types of trance. It is not possible here to set out the authors' argument point by point, but it is worth mentioning that Naranjo, in considering transcendental meditation, defines three essential forms of altered consciousness which correspond exactly to the first two of the authors' own factors.[14]

Naranjo defines three forms of meditation according to the nature of the mode of entry and the nature of the state induced (see Diagram I).

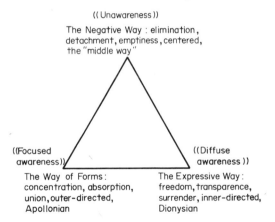

Diagram I.   Diagram comparing the three states of meditation described by Naranjo and Ornstein (1971) and the three types of hypnotic state distinguished by the factorial analysis.

Thus, if hypnosis is specific in the sense that it is induced by a third person and that it is accompanied by an attempt at interpersonal communication during the

[14]Diagram I is a table presented by Naranjo (Naranjo and Ornstein, 1971, p. 16). The double brackets contain the designations arising from the authors' factorial analysis: unawareness (factor 1, −pole), focused awareness (factor 2, +pole), diffuse awareness (factor 2, −pole).

trance, the forms of trance resulting from the induction are multiple and seem to cover the whole field of altered states of consciousness. This observation seems to be of the utmost importance: the "stereotype of hypnosis" is only one form of the hypnotic state; judging the level of hypnosis in each subject by reference to this stereotype is but an approximation which leads to the recruitment and selection of only a certain type of subject. (In this light, we can more easily understand the choice of hysterics in the eighteenth and nineteenth centuries as ideal hypnotic subjects (somnambulists).)

Variations within one individual

Since, in response to the first hypnotic induction which is highly standardized, many different forms of trance can be observed, it is justifiable to assume that the personality of the subject plays a determining role in these variations of the hypnotic experience.

Having said that, it must be asked whether the type of trance observed in any one subject is invariable, or if, on the contrary, the subject can, depending upon the circumstances, pass from one type of trance to another.

The beginnings of an answer to this question emerge from an in-depth study conducted (Michaux, 1977) with one subject, who underwent hypnotic induction three times in succession. The subject who was hypnotized three times, according to the procedure then in force, described after each session a state of consciousness under hypnosis radically different from his waking state of consciousness. But above all, he emphasized that the states of consciousness experienced during each of the three sessions were radically different from one another.

In order to further the understanding of the significance of these divergences in the state of consciousness from one session to another, an in-depth comparative analysis of the experience of the three sessions had to be carried out. Such an analysis enabled the following conclusions to be drawn: in the second session the subject showed a greater degree of relaxation and well-being than in the first session; his suggestibility tended to decrease slightly, which his depth of hypnosis increased considerably, accompanied by sleepiness. The subject spontaneously compared his new state of consciousness, in the second session, to a *state of Nirvana*. In the third session, however, whereas the depth of trance appeared the same as during the second session, radical changes in the type of trance were observed:

1. Increased motor and tonic responsiveness in the subject.
2. A feeling of total loss of control, the subject even using the word "possession."
3. Increased suggestibility at the behavior level.
4. A profound sense of unease.

If we wanted to express these differences in terms of the factors structuring the hypnotic experience, as discussed earlier, it would seem that, in the third session, the subject moves from passivity to activity, from internal to external control, from an attitude of acceptance to one of resistance under hypnosis.

This case shows clearly that radically different forms of trance can be induced in the same subjects.

As for the cause of these changes, it seems to the authors that they arise in this particular case from variations in the level of authority and pressure exercised on the subject, and variations in his level of resistance to suggestions. In the second session (the retest session), the pressure experienced by the subject was at a minimum; simultaneously a considerable deepening of the trance was observed with no increase in suggestibility; hypnosis was then experienced as Nirvana. During the third session, when hypnosis had already been induced, the experimenter increased the "pressure" by requiring the subject to talk under hypnosis; the subject, being deeply hypnotized, could no longer maintain his (passive) defences under hypnosis; he began to talk and behave according to the suggestions made,[15] all of which was accompanied by a reversal of the affective tone of the sessions: the state of passive well-being (Nirvana) in the second session was succeeded by an active state in which the subject felt ill at ease and alienated.

The division between suggestibility and hypnosis

The individual approach

The division between suggestibility and hypnosis already noted by the clinicians (Chertok, 1963, pp. 32, 81) emerged clearly in many of the subjects, even before the authors' manual for the analysis of behavior and experience had been put in its final form. It was apparent that some subjects gave the very clear impression that they were hypnotized without for all that responding to suggestions. Thus sometimes all the behavioral signs of a state of sleep were present while the subject remained insensible to suggestions. Or in other cases subjects might report very unusual sensations and phenomena upon waking, whereas their hypnotic suggestibility had proven almost nil, as in the cases mentioned previously.

The systematic use of the manual of analysis made it possible to bring out the subjects' characteristics more clearly, and to verify that there had in fact been some alteration in their mental functioning, an alteration in consciousness and therefore hypnosis.

For the purposes of greater precision and clarity, there follows a brief account of the case of one subject[16] which makes it easier to understand the value of the distinction between hypnosis and suggestibility.

---

[15] It will be noted that whereas the behavioral response to suggestions increased, the limitations observed during the preceding sessions remained (the impossibility of either positive or negative hallucination); the subject discovered a strategy for overcoming this obstacle in order to respond to the suggestions and therefore make the suggested gestures. It would therefore seem that some of the limits involved are due to the subject's mental structure and cannot be overcome even by the hypersuggestibility manifested at the behavioral level.

[16] A more detailed analysis of this case has been made by Michaux (1978).

The subject, Olivier D., presented as quite a calm, relaxed person. He had carried out the two suggestions in the waking state with relative ease. After hypnotic induction, his attitude changed. Under hypnosis he would no longer carry out the suggestions, nor the orders which were given to him. His reaction to the suggestions appeared to signify both refusal and irritation: vague grunts, deep sighs, wide circular movements of the head. When the suggestions ceased, the subject calmed down. His breathing was observed to be deep, regular, and audible, as in sleep.

Upon waking the subject obtained 5 points out of 8 on the subjective hypnosis questionnaire. It was noted that, amongst the most marked features of this hypnotic experience was an impression of total loss of control, with control under hypnosis residing neither in the subject nor in the experimenter, but, according to the subject's own words, in his limbs themselves, arms, hands, etc. What was also observed was an impression of confusion between his own body and the armchair (he could no longer distinguish his own arm from the armrest), and finally what was for the subject the cruel experience of being unable to voice his inability to carry out the suggestions.

It is obvious therefore that this subject did indeed enter an altered state of consciousness in response to hypnotic induction, even if the depth of this altered state of consciousness was limited (5/8) and even if its manifestations seemed very much colored by the underlying conflict resulting from the body's rejection of the suggestions. With this subject we are therefore clearly confronted with the problem of the division between suggestibility and hypnosis.

If it is conceivable that, because of the conflict it arouses, resistance to suggestion limits the depth of hypnosis, it is an inescapable observation that, in this subject, induction nonetheless engendered the appearance of a trance – a trance not accompanied by reinforcement of suggestibility, but on the contrary stimulating the appearance of an increased capacity to resist the suggestion (suggestibility in the waking state 2/2, hypnotic suggestibility 1/8).[17]

In this subject, therefore, hypnosis did not generate hypersuggestibility but, on the contrary, enabled him to express and give rein to his capacity for resistance.

The statistical approach

The independence of suggestibility and hypnosis illustrated by this subject, O.D., is not exceptional. The evidence from many subjects points in the same direction. Clearly, it still remains to give this finding numerical expression and to demonstrate the existence of this divergence statistically. The principal obstacle arises from the difficulty in measuring hypnosis as such.

For example, the establishment of some means of measuring the subjective aspect of hypnosis presupposes clear knowledge of the essential elements and

---

[17] The only successful exercise was the rigid arm. His success in this exercise is attributable to the fact that he did not bend his arm. But to the extent that he did not raise his arm when instructed and made no apparent effort to bend it, it is questionable whether the point was legitimately awarded.

characteristics of the hypnotic trance. At the moment, however, it is not yet possible to develop such a measure with any certainty.

It is for this reason that it was decided to use factorial analysis as a means of demonstrating the essential characteristics of hypnosis. It will be recalled that in the analysis presented above, only the first factor seemed to provide a measure of the depth of hypnosis. All the authors' subjects were classified in relation to this factor, and all of them had a hypnotic suggestibility score, and it was therefore possible to see from this factor the nature of the relationship between hypnosis (depth of trance) and hypnotic suggestibility.

If the relationship between suggestibility and hypnosis is linear, we should see an improvement in the average scores of hypnotic suggestibility as we move from the negative to the positive pole of this factor (non-hypnotized to hypnotized respectively). To simplify matters, we can study the average suggestibility scores in four successive segments and see whether the variation in the scores is regular.

As can be seen from Fig. 6, the level of suggestibility does not vary in a continuous progressive fashion as a function of the depth of hypnosis. The axis separating

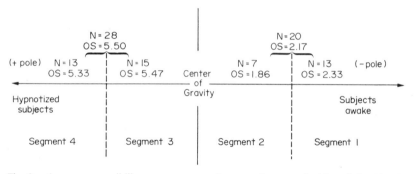

Fig. 6.   Average suggestibility scores corresponding to each group of subjects defined by the segmentation of the first factor of hypnosis.

the + and − poles of the first factor separates the suggestible subjects almost perfectly from the non-suggestible subjects (+ vector: N = 28, OS = 5.50;[18] − vector: N = 20, OS = 2.17). On the other hand, the position of the subjects on each of the vectors seems not to play an essential role. The most hypnotized subjects (segment 4) are no more suggestible than the moderately hypnotized subjects (segment 3); the slightly hypnotized subjects (segment 2) are no more suggestible than the subjects who were not hypnotized at all (segment 1).

[18] OS = Objective Score of hypnotic susceptibility.

It is therefore as if, irrespective of the depth of hypnosis, the subject's suggestibility is released all at once insofar as he feels himself to be hypnotized; insofar as he does not feel himself to be genuinely hypnotized, his suggestibility remains blocked.

To explain this phenomenon, one could put forward the hypothesis that the resistance which prevents the subject giving way to hypnosis also leads him to block his response to suggestion.

The dual role played by the subject's attitude in relation to the appearance or non-appearance of a hypnotic-like state, and the release or inhibition of suggestibility, might explain the apparent relationship which has *generally* been observed between suggestibility and hypnosis[19, 20] without such a relationship really being involved, since there is no progression in suggestibility as a function of depth of hypnosis, i.e. the passage from segment 3 (slight hypnosis) to segment 4 (deep hypnosis).

Research Perspectives

As has been shown, the detailed study of the experience of hypnotized subjects and their behavior under hypnosis may make possible a reorientation of research on hypnosis, and help us to abandon certain erroneous concepts.

The tools used for this purpose in the research previously described are in the nature of prototypes.[21] It is hoped therefore that it will be possible in the near future to restructure them in the light of the results already obtained, in order to bring them up to date, improve their descriptive value and make them more easily usable.

With the help of these tools it will be possible to explore certain essential questions more precisely:

1. The relationship between personality and hypnosis: are certain types of hypnotic trance specific to particular types of subjects?

2. The relationship between suggestibility and hypnosis: do certain forms of trance engender hypersuggestibility, whilst other forms of trance have no influence on suggestibility? Is this because there are different types of hypnosis in which different levels of mental regression can appear?

---

[19] This apparent relationship no doubt explains why, for 20 years, experimenters have been satisfied with hypnotic suggestibility as a measure of whether or not the subjects were hypnotized.

[20] For 3 years the authors have been developing an empirical scale of hypnosis based on eight subjective questions. The correlations between this score and the suggestibility score fluctuates around $r = 0.60$, depending on the sample.

[21] These tools (observation and analysis manual, grids for data processing) and the statistical processing by factorial analysis of the first collection of data and their interpretation were constructed and carried out by D. Michaux as part of his doctoral dissertation.

3. Study devoted to the possibility of modifying the type of hypnotic trance manifested by a subject by variation of the induction procedures, the degree of authority and pressure exercised, etc.

4. Study of changes of the subjects' mental functioning under hypnosis, in order to examine on the one hand the changes in mental structure produced by hypnosis in a given subject and, on the other hand, the relationship between the type of trance and mental structure under hypnosis.

5. Study of hypnotic and non-hypnotic suggestibility. Such a study would have to be directed to three aspects:

(a) Study of alterations in the state of consciousness in response to suggestions given in the waking state, or under hypnosis.

(b) Study of the role of mental structure in the appearance of any particular level of suggestion: irreversible spontaneous amnesia and schizophrenia; catalepsy and hysteria, etc.

(c) Study of the potential and limitations of suggestibility: the areas in which manipulation by suggestion is possible and impossible.

Conclusion

It can be deduced from the foregoing that hypnosis and suggestion are two phenomena present in almost all subjects and that they can be induced by any experimenter. The two phenomena:

1. the capacity for suggestion;

2. the capacity to enter an altered state of consciousness;

are certainly fundamental to an understanding of the mechanisms governing individual and group relationships.

They are very probably not related to a specific mode of induction and can appear in many situations: sensory deprivation, drug states, stress, hypnotic induction, etc. The form they take depends both on the subject's personality and on the induction situation.

The multiplicity of trance forms which appear in response to the standard induction seem to show that there is no essential division between the various altered states of consciousness.

The study of hypnosis is not therefore the study of exceptional reality but of a mechanism which plays a central role in the mental life of the subjects. It is quite certain that on the understanding of hypnosis depends the understanding of certain phenomena whose spontaneous appearance is regarded as pathological – regression, dissociation, hallucination – and which, under hypnosis, appear in the context of normality.

References

ABRAMS, S. (1963) Short term hypnotherapy of a schizophrenic patient. *Amer. J. Clin. Hypn.* **5**, pp. 237-247.

ABRAMS, S. (1964) The use of hypnotic techniques with psychotics; a critical review. *Amer. J. Psychother.* **18**, pp. 79-94.

ABRAMS, S. (1971) Panel on models of the psychic apparatus. *J. Amer. Psychoanal. Ass.* **19**, pp. 131-142.

ABRAMSON, M. and HERON, W. (1950) An objective evaluation of hypnosis in obstetrics: Preliminary report. *Amer. J. Obstet. Gynec.* **59**, pp. 1069-1074.

ALEXANDER, F. (1963) The dynamics of psychotherapy in the light of learning theory. *Amer. J. Psychiat.* (11/1963), **120**, pp. 440-448.

ALEXANDER, F. and FRENCH, P. (1948) *Studies in psychosomatic medicine.* New York, Ronald Press.

ALRUTZ, S. (1914) Die suggestive Vesikation. *J. Psychol. Neurol.* **21**, pp. 1-10.

ALTHUSSER, L. (1964) Freud et Lacan. *Nouvelle Critique,* **161–162**, pp. 88–108.

American Journal of Psychiatry (1980), **137**, 12, Special section: Modern religious experience and psychiatry, pp. 1553-1579.

APFELBAUM, B. (1965) Ego psychology, psychic energy and the hazards of quantitative explanation in psychoanalytic theory. *Int. J. Psychoanal.* **46**, pp. 169-181.

APPELBAUM, S. (1976) Book Review: *New language for psychoanalysis* by Roy Schafer. *Bull. Menninger Clin.* **40**(6), pp. 675-680.

APPELBAUM, S. (1977) *The anatomy of change.* New York, Plenum.

APPELGARTH, A. (1977) Psychic energy reconsidered: Discussion. *J. Amer. Psychoanal. Ass.* **25**(3), pp. 599-602.

APTER, I. M. (1976) O Prirodie Gipnoza i Ievo Značznijc v Peikhoferapii. (On the nature of hypnosis and its significance in psychotherapy). *Zh. Nevropat. Psykhiat.* **9**, pp.1408-1411.

APTER, I. M. (1979) O Fiziologičeskoj Sušnosti Gipnoza (On the physiological character of hypnosis). *Zh. Nevropat. Psykhiat.* **1**, pp. 115–117.

AUARD MARTINEZ DIAZ (1892) Quelques faits d'anesthésie chirurgicale sous l'influence de la suggestion. *Rev. Hypnotisme,* pp. 309-313.

AUGUST, R. (1961) *Hypnosis in obstetrics.* New York, McGraw-Hill.

AUVARD, Q. and SECHEYRON (1888) L'Hypnotisme et la suggestion en obstétrique. *Arch. Tocologie,* pp. 26-40, 78-104, 146-176.

AVTONOMOVA, N. S. (1977a) *Filosofskiic Problemy Strukturnovo Analiza v Gjmonitarnikh Naukakh (Philosophical problems of structural analysis in behavioral sciences).* Moscow, Nauka.

213

214   References

AVTONOMOVA, N. S. (1977b) [Preface]. In: FOUCAULT, M. (1966) *Slova i Vešči* (Words and things). Moscow, Progress Editions.

AVTONOMOVA, N. S. (1979) Bessoznatelnoe: Epistemologičeskije Aspekty. (The unconscious epistemological aspects.) Mimeograph.

AZAM, E. (1860). Note sur le sommeil nerveux ou hypnotisme. *Arch. gén. méd.* (Janvier 1860). pp. 5–24.

BALINT, M. (1955) Notes on parapsychology and parapsychological healing. *Int. J. Psychoanal.* **36,** pp. 31–35.

BALINT, M. (1966) Psycho-analysis and medical practice. *Int. J. Psychoanal.* **47,** pp. 54–62.

BALINT, M., ORNSTEIN, P. and BALINT, E. (1972) *Focal psychotherapy. An example of applied psychoanalysis.* London, Tavistock.

BANDLER, R. and GRINDER, J. (1975) *Patterns of the hypnotic techniques of Milton H. Erickson.* Cupertino (Calif.), Meta Publications (2 vols).

BARANOV, I. O. and NARITSIN, N. (1979) Gipnoz: Metod Bolšoi Praktičeskoi Cennosti. (Hypnosis as a method of great practical value.) *Zh. Nevropat. Psykhiat.* **1,** p. 117.

BARBER, T. X. (1963) The effects of hypnosis on pain: a critical review of experimental and clinical findings. *Psychosom. Med.* **25,** pp. 303–333.

BARBER, T. X. (1969a) *Hypnosis: A scientific approach.* New York, Van Nostrand Reinhold.

BARBER, T. X. and CALVERLEY, D. (1969b) Multidimensional analysis of hypnotic behavior. *J. Abnorm. Psychol.* **74,** 2, pp. 209–220.

BARBER, T. X. and HAHN, K. W. (1962) Physiological and subjective responses to pain producing stimulation under hypnotically suggested and waking imagined "analgesia." *J. Abnorm. Soc. Psychol.* **65,** pp. 411–418.

BARTLETT, E. E. (1971) Hypnoanaesthesia for bilateral oophorectomy. A case report. *Amer. J. Clin. Hypn.* **14,** pp. 122–124.

BASSIN, F. V. (1968) *Problema Bossoznatel'novo (Problems of the unconscious).* Mowcow, Meditsina.

BASSIN, F. V. (1971) Le conscient, "l'inconscient" et la maladie: A propos de l'approche moderne du problème psychosomatique. *Rev. Méd. Psychosom.* (1972), **3,** pp. 263–280.

BASSIN, F. V. (1978) U Predelov Rozpoznanovo. K Probleme. Prerečevoï Formy Myšlenija. (At the bounds of the cognized: the problem of the pre-speech form of thinking.) In: PRANGISHVILI, A., BASSIN, F. and SHEROZIA, A. (eds.) *The Unconscious. Nature, functions, methods of study,* Tbilisi, Metsniereba,,Tome III, pp. 735–750.

BASSIN, F. V. and PLATONOV, K. K. (1973) *Verborgene Reserven des höheren Nervensystems.* Stuttgart, Hippokrates Verlag.

BASSIN, F. V., ROZHNOV, V. and ROZHNOVA, M. (1974) Niekotorije Voprossy Emotionalnoï Naprazhënnosai. (Some problems of emotional tension.) *Komunist* (9/1974), **14,** pp. 60-70.

BASSIN, F. V. and ROZHNOV, V. (1976) [Preface] pp. 5–40. In: CLEMENT, C., BRUNO, P. and SEVE, I. *Marksistskaia Kritika Psikhoanalisa. (Marxist critic of psychoanalysis.)* Moscow, Progress.

BASSIN, F. V. and SHEROZIA, A. (1979) *The role of the category of the unconscious in the system of the present day scientific knowledge of the mind: materials for the International Symposium of the Problem of the Unconscious.* Tbilisi, Metsniereba.

BASSIN, F. and SHEROZIA, A. (1980) Les Idées de Jacques Lacan sauveront-elles la psychanalyse? *Revue de Medecine Psychosomatique,* **2,** pp. 173–189.

BEAUNIS, H. (1886) *Le Somnambulisme provoqué.* Paris. J. B. Baillière et fils.

BERGIN, A. E. (1971) The evaluation of therapeutic outcomes. In: GARFIELD, S. L. and BERGIN, A. E. *Handbook of psychotherapy and behavior change.* New York, Wiley, pp. 217–270.

BERNHEIM, H. (1884) *De la suggestion dans l'état hypnotique et dans l'état de veille.* Paris, O. Doin.

BERNHEIM, H. (1886) *De la suggestion et de ses applications à la thérapeutique.* Paris, O. Doin.

BERNHEIM, H. (1889)Valeur relative des divers procédés destinés à provoquer l'hypnose et à augmenter la suggestibilité au point de vue thérapeutique. In: BERILLON, E. (ed.) *Premier Congrès international de l'hypnotisme expérimental et thérapeutique tenu à l'Hôtel Dieu à Paris, du 8 au 12 août 1889.* Paris, Doin, pp. 79-111.

BERNSTEIN, M. (1965a) Observations on the use of hypnosis with burned children on a pediatric ward. *Int. J. Clin. Exp. Hypn.* 13, pp. 1-10.

BERNSTEIN, M. (1965b) Significant value of hypno-anesthesia: Three clinical examples. *Amer. J. Clin. Hypn.* 7, pp. 259-260.

BEXTON, W. H., HERON, W. and SCOTT, T. H. (1954) Effects of decreased variation in sensory environment. *Canad. J. Psychol.* 38, pp. 70-76.

BIDDLE, W. (1967) *Hypnosis in the psychoses.* Springfield, Thomas.

BINET, A. and FERE, CH. (1887) *Le Magnétisme animal.* Paris, Alcan.

BINET, A. (1888) *Etudes de psychologie expérimentale.* Paris, Doin.

BINET, A. (1892) *Les Altérations de la personnalité.* Paris, Alcan.

BLACK, S. (1969) Some physiological mechanisms amenable to control by direct suggestion under hypnosis. In: CHERTOK, L. (ed.) *Psychophysiological mechanisms of hypnosis.* New York, Springer, pp. 10-27.

BONILLA, K., QUIGLEY, W. and BOWERS, W. (1961) Experience with hypnosis on a surgical service. *Milit. Med.* 126, 364-370.

BORELLI, S. (1953) Psychische Einflüsse und reaktive Hauterscheinungen. *Münch. Med. Wschr.* 95, pp. 1078-1082.

BOTKIN, I. (1897) *Gipnotism v Ginekologü i Akušertvie. (Hypnotism in gynaecology and obstetrics.)* Moscow.

BOURRU, H. and BUROT, P. (1888) *Variations de la personnalité.* Paris, Baillière.

BOWEN, D. (1973) Transurethral resection under self-hypnosis. *Amer. J. Clin. Hypn.* 16, pp. 132-134.

BOWERS, K. (1961) Theoretical considerations in the use of hypnosis in the treatment of schizophrenia. *Int. J. Clin. Exp. Hypn.* 9, pp. 39-46.

BOWLBY, J. (1969) *Attachment and loss,* Vol. I. *Attachment.* London, Tavistock.

BOWLBY, J. (1973) *Attachment and loss,* Vol. II. *Separation, anxiety and anger.* London, Tavistock.

BRAID, J. (1843) *Neurypnology.* London, Churchill.

BRENMAN, M., GILL, M. and KNIGHT, R. P. (1952) Spontaneous fluctuations in depth of hypnosis and their implications for ego-function. *Int. J. Psychoanal.* 33, pp. 22-33.

BRÈS, Y. et al. (1977) La durée des analyses. *Psychanalyse à l'Université* (12/1977), pp. 147-154.

BREUGELMANN, J. (ed.) (1975) *Progress in behaviour therapy.* New York, Springer.

BROCA, P. (1859) Note sur une nouvelle méthode anesthésique. Séance du 5 décembre 1859. *Comptes rendus hebdomadaires des séances de l'Académie des Sciences,* 49, pp. 902-905.

BROCA, P. (1860) Sur l'anesthésie chirurgicale provoquée par l'hypnotisme. Société de Chirurgie. Séance du 7 Décembre 1859. *Bull. Soc. Chirurgie Paris,* pp. 247-271.

BROCA, P. (1861) Séance du 21 février 1861. *Bull. Soc. Anthropologie Paris.* Paris, Masson, 1st series, tome II, pp. 66-81.

BURTON, A. (ed.) (1976) *What makes behavior change possible?* New York, Brunner/Mazel.

CASTELNUOVO-TEDESCO, P. (1974) Toward a theory of affects. *J. Amer. Psychoanal. Ass.* **22**, 3, pp. 612-625.

CASTORIADIS, C. (1977) La Psychanalyse, projet et élucidation. Destin de l'analyse et responsabilité des analystes. *Topique,* **19,** pp. 25-75.

CHARCOT, J.-M. See also GUINON and LEVILLAIN.

CHARCOT, J. M. (1882a) Sur les divers états nerveux déterminés par l'hypnotisation chez les hystériques. *Comptes rendus hebdomadaires des séances de l'Académie des Sciences,* **94,** pp. 403-405.

CHARCOT, J. M. (1882b) Essai d'une distinction nosògraphique des divers états compris sous le nom d'hypnotisme. *Comptes rendus hebdomadaires des séances de l'Académie des Sciences,* pp. 44.

CHARCOT, J. M. (1887) *Clinical lectures on diseases of the nervous system,* vol. III. London, The New Sydenham Society, 1889.

CHARPIGNON, D. R. (1860) Etude sur l'hypnotisme. *Gaz. Hôp. Paris* (10/1/1860), **33,** 4. pp. 13/14.

CHEEK, D. B. (1959) Unconscious perception of meaningful sounds during surgical anesthesia as revealed under hypnosis. *Amer. J. Clin. Hypn.* 1(3), pp. 101-113.

CHEEK, D. B. (1964a) Surgical memory and reaction to careless conversation. *Amer. J. Clin. Hypn.* 6(3), pp. 237-240.

CHEEK, D. B. (1946b) Further evidence of persistence of hearing under chemo-anesthesia: detailed case report. *Amer. J. Clin. Hypn.* 7(1), pp. 55-59.

CHEEK, D. B. (1966) The meaning of continued hearing sense under general chemo-anesthesia: A progress report and report of a case. *Amer. J. Clin. Hypn.* 8(4), pp. 275-280.

CHEEK, D. and LE CRON, L. (1968) *Clinical hypnotherapy.* New York, Grune & Stratton.

CHERTOK, L. (1954) Sommeil hypnotique prolongé. In: NORA, G. and SAPIR, M. (eds.) *La cure de sommeil.* Paris, Masson, pp. 57-70.

CHERTOK, L. (1957) *Psychosomatic methods in painless childbirth. History, theory and practice.* London, New York, Pergamon Press, 1959.

CHERTOK, L. (1960) On the discovery of the cathartic method. *Int. J. Psychoanal.* 1961, **42,** pp. 284-287.

CHERTOK, L. (1963) *Hypnosis.* Oxford, London, New York, Pergamon Press, 1966.

CHERTOK, L. (1966a) On extra-ocular vision; a historical note. *Amer. J. Psychother.* **20,** pp. 319-322.

CHERTOK, L. (1966b) An introduction to the study of tensions among psychotherapists. *Brit. J. Med. Psychol.* **39,** pp. 237-243.

CHERTOK, L. (1969a) The evolution of research on hypnosis. Introductory remarks. In: CHERTOK, L. (ed.) (1969) *Psychophysiological mechanisms of hypnosis.* New York, Springer, pp. 1-9.

CHERTOK, L. (1969b) Psychosomatic medicine in the West and in Eastern European countries. *Psychosom. Med.* **36**(6), pp. 510-521.

CHERTOK, L. (1969c) The discovery of transference. Towards an epistemological interpretation. *Int. J. Psychoanal.* **49,** pp. 560-577.

CHERTOK, L. (1975) Hysteria, hypnosis, psychopathology. *J. Nerv. Ment. Dis.* **161**(6), pp. 367-378.

CHERTOK, L. (1979) The Unconscious and Hypnosis. Paper presented at the Tbilisi Symposium on the Unconscious. To be published.

CHERTOK, L., BONNAUD, M., BORELLI, M. R., DONNET, J. L. and REVAULT D'ALLONNES, C. (1966) *Motherhood and personality.* London, Tavistock, 1963.

CHERTOK, L., MICHAUX, D. and DROIN, M. C. (1977) Dynamics of hypnotic analgesia: some new data. *J. Nerv. Ment. Dis.* **164**, 2, pp. 88-96.

CHERTOK, L. and SAUSSURE, R. DE (1973) *The therapeutic revolution from Mesmer to Freud.* New York, Brunner Mazel, 1979.

CHONG, T. (1964) The use of hypnosis as an adjunct in surgery. *Med. J. of Malaya,* **19**, pp. 154-160.

CLAGHORN, J. (ed.) (1976) *Successful psychotherapy.* New York, Brunner/Mazel.

CLÉMENT, C. (1978) *Les Fils de Freud sont fatigués.* Paris, Grasset.

CLÉMENT, C., BRUNO, P. and SÈVE, L. (1973) *Pour une critique marxiste de la théorie psychanalytique.* Paris, Editions Sociales.

CLOQUET, J. (1829) Ablation d'un cancer du sein pendant le sommeil magnétique. *Arch. gén. Méd.* 1(20), pp. 131-134.

COHEN, J. (1966) *The man robots in myth and science.* New York, Allen & Unwin.

COTTRAUX, J. (1978a) *Les Thérapies comportementales.* Paris, Masson.

COTTRAUX, J. (1978b) Effets et résultats des psychothérapies. Problèmes posés par leur évaluation. In: GUYOTAT, J. (ed.) *Psychothérapies médicales.* Tome I. Paris, Masson, pp. 78-85.

CRASILNECK, H. and HALL, J. (1975) *Clinical hypnosis: Principles and applications.* New York, Grune & Stratton.

CRASILNECK, H. and JENKINS, M. (1958) Further studies in the use of hypnosis as a method of anesthesia. *Int. J. Clin. Exp. Hypn.* **6**, pp. 152-158.

CRASILNECK, H., MCCRANIE and JENKINS, M. (1956) Special indications for hypnosis as a method of anesthesia. *J. Amer. Ass.* **162**, pp. 1606-1608.

CROCQ, L. (1974) Stress et névrose traumatique. *Psychol. méd. (Paris),* **6**(8), pp. 1493-1531.

CUTTER, D. (1845) Traitements magnétiques. Accouchement. *J. Magnétisme,* pp. 115-116.

DARNTON, R. (1968) *Mesmerism and the end of the enlightenment in France.* Cambridge (Mass.), Harvard University Press.

DELEUZE, J. P. F. (1825) *Instruction pratique sur le magnétisme animal, suivie d'une lettre écrite à l'auteur par un médecin étranger,* Paris, Dentu.

DEMARET, A. (1974) Préliminaires d'une théorie ethnologique de l'hypnose. *Acta Psychiat. Belg.* **74**, pp. 345-356.

DEMENT, W. (1964) Part III, Research Studies: dreams and communication. In: *Science and psychoanalysis,* vol. VII. New York, Grune & Stratton.

DEUTSCH, H. (1926) Occult processes occurring during psychoanalysis. In: DEVEREUX, G. (ed.) (1953) *Psychoanalysis and the occult.* New York, International Universities Press.

DEVEREUX, G. (ed.) (1953) *Psychoanalysis and the occult.* New York, International Universities Press.

DINGWALL, E. (1967) *Abnormal hypnotic phenomena. A survey of nineteenth century cases.* 4 volumes. London, J. & A. Churchill. (Vol. I: France; vol. 2: Belgium, Netherlands, Germany, Scandinavia; vol. 3: Russia, Poland, Italy, Spain, Portugal, Latin America; vol. 4: U.S.A., Great Britain.)

DOBROVOLSKY, M. (1891) Huit observations d'accouchements sans douleur sous l'influence de l'hypnotisme. *Rev. Hypnotisme,* pp. 274-277; 310-312.

DOHRENWEND, B. P., DOHRENWEND, B. S., GOULD, M. S., LINK, B., NEUGEBAUER, R. and WUNSCH-HITZIG, R. (1979) *Mental illness in the United States: epidemiologic estimates.* New York, Praeger, in press.

DOLTO, F. (1971) *Psychanalyse et pédiatrie.* Paris, Seil.

DOSWALD, D. C. and KREIBICH, K. (1906) Zur Frage der posthypnotischen Hauptphänomene. *Mh. Prakt. Derm.* **43**, pp. 634-640.

DUMONTPALLIER, D. (1892) De l'action de la suggestion pendant le travail de l'accouchement. *Rev. Hypnotisme*, pp. 175-177.

DUNBAR, H. F. (1935) *Emotions and bodily changes.* New York, Columbia University Press.

EDWARDS, B. (1890) Quelques faits de suggestion. *Progr. Méd. Paris*, 1, pp. 500-502.

EITINGON, M. (1922) Bericht über die Berliner Psychoanalytische Poliklinik. *Int. Z. Psychoanal.* 8, pp. 506-520.

ELLENBERGER, H. (1970) *The discovery of the unconscious, the history and evolution of dynamic psychiatry.* New York, Basic Books.

ELLIOTSON, J. (1843) *Numerous cases of surgical operations without pain in the mesmeric state.* London, Elliotson.

ELLIOTSON, J. (1846) Operations without pain in the mesmeric state. *Zoist* (1845-1846), pp. 380-383.

ERICKSON, M. See also: BANDLER, R. and GRINDER, J., and HALEY, J.

ERICKSON, M. (1970) Hypnosis: its renascence as a treatment modality. *Amer. J. Clin. Hypn.* 13, pp. 71-89.

ERICKSON, M., ROSSI, E. and ROSSI, S. (1976) *Hypnotic realities. The induction of clinical hypnosis and forms of indirect suggestion.* New York, John Wiley.

ESDAILE, J. (1846) *Mesmerism in India.* London, Esdaile.

ESDAILE, J. (1852) *Natural and mesmeric clairvoyance with the practical application of mesmerism in surgery and medicine.* London, Esdaile.

EYSENCK, H. J. (1952) The effects of psychotherapy: An evaluation. *J. Cons. Psychol.* 16, pp. 319-324.

EYSENCK, H. J. (1965) The effects of psychotherapy. *J. Psychiat.* 1, pp. 97-178.

FARIA, J. C. DE (1819) *De la cause du sommeil lucide ou étude sur la nature de l'homme.* Paris, Horiac.

FÉDIDA, P. (1977) Preface. In: SEARLES, H. *L'Effort pour rendre l'autre fou.* Paris, Gallimard, pp. 11-32.

FELDMAN, E. A. and LEIZEROVICH, M. (1978) O Gipnoze i Gipnosugestivnoi Terapii. (On hypnosis and hypnosuggestive therapy.) *Zh. Nevropat. Psykhat.* 9, pp. 1410-1411.

FERENCZI, S. (1909). *Introjection and transference. First contributions to psycho-analysis.* London, Hogarth Press, 1952, pp. 35-93.

FIELD, P. (1965) An inventory scale of hypnotic depth. *Int. J. Clin. Exp. Hypn.* 13,(4), pp. 238-249.

FIELD, P. and PALMER, R. (1969) Factor analysis: hypnosis inventory. *Inst. J. Clin. Exp. Hypn.* 17(1), pp. 50-61.

FINER, B. and NYLEN, B. (1961) Cardiac arrest in the treatment of burns, and report on hypnosis as a substitute for anesthesia. *Plast. Reconstr. Surg.* 27, pp. 49-55.

FINNE, V. N. (1928) Ozhogi Vyzvanyie Vnusheniem v Gipnotičeskom Sostoianii. (Burns produced by suggestion in a hypnotic state.) *Zh. Dlia Osoveršenstovania Vračei*, 3, pp. 150-157.

FISHER, C. (1965) Psychoanalytic implications of recent research on sleep and dreaming. *J. Amer. Psychoanal. Ass.* 13, 2, pp. 197-303.

FIX, A. J. and HAFFKE, E. A. (1976) *Basic psychological therapies: Comparative effectiveness.* New York, Human Sciences Press.

FOISSAC, P. (1833) *Rapports et discussions de l'Académie Royale de Médicine sur le magnétisme animal . . . ,* Paris, Baillière.

FOREL, A. (1889) De l'hallucination négative chez les aliénés et de la différence entre l'hallucination des hypnotisés et celle des aliénés. In: BERILLON, E. (ed.) *Premier Congrès International de l'hypnotisme expérimental et thérapeutique.* Paris, O' Doin, pp. 122-128.

FORT, J. A. (1890) Extraction d'une loupe pendant le sommeil hypnotique sur un jeune homme de vingt ans. *Rev. Hypnotisme* (1889-1890), p. 142.

FRANK, J. (1978) Expectation and therapeutic outcome. The Placebo effect and the role induction interview. In: FRANK, J. *et al.* (eds.) *Effective ingredients of successful psychotherapy.* New York, Brunner/Mazel.

FRANK, J. D. (1979) The present status of outcome studies. *J. Consul. Clin. Psychol.* (in the press).

FRANKE, U. (1924) Amnesie und Anaesthesie bei der Hypnosegeburt. *Dtsch. Med. Wschr.* (24/6/1924), **26,** pp. 874-875.

FRANKEL, F. H. (1976) *Hypnosis—Trance as a coping mechanism.* New York, Plenum Medical Book Company.

FREUD, S. [*S.E.*] *The Standard Edition of the complete psychological works of S. Freud, translated from the German under the general editorship of James Strachey, in collaboration with Anna Freud, assisted by Alix Strachey and Alan Tyson, Editorial assistant: Angela Richards.* London, Hogarth Press, 1953 sq.

FREUD, S. [*G.W.*] *Gesammelte Werke* . . . London, Imago Publ. Co., 1952 sq.

FREUD, S. (1891) Hypnosis, *S.E.* **I,** pp. 105-114.

FREUD, S. (1895) Project for a scientific psychology. *S.E.* **I,** pp. 283-397.

FREUD, S. (1916) Introductory lectures on psychoanalysis. *S.E.* **XV, XVI.**

FREUD, S. (1918) Lines of advance in psycho-analytic therapy., *S.E.* **XVII,** pp. 167-168.

FREUD, S. (1921) Massenpsychologie und Ich-Analyse. *G.W.* **13,** pp. 71-161. Group psychology and the analysis of the ego. *S.E.* **XVIII,** pp. 67-143.

FREUD, S. (1933a) Dreams and occultism. Lecture XXX. New Introductory Lectures on Psychoanalysis. *S.E.* **XXII,** pp. 31-56.

FREUD, S. (1933b) Explanations, applications and orientations. Lecture XXXIV. New Introductory Lectures on Psychoanalysis. *S.E.* **XXII,** pp. 136-157.

FREUD, S. (1937) Analysis terminable and interminable. *S.E.* **XXIII,** pp. 211-253.

FREUD, S. (1938) An outline of psycho-analysis. *S.E.* **XXIII,** pp. 141-207.

FREUD, S. (1950) The origins of psycho-analysis. . . . London, Imago Publishing Co., 1954.

FREUD, S. (*F.C.*) *Letters of Sigmund Freud, selected and edited by Ernst I. Freud, translated by Tania and James Stern.* New York, Basic Books, 1960.

FREUD, S. (1963) *Psychoanalysis and faith. The letters of Sigmund Freud and Oskar Pfister.* New York, Basic Books.

FROMM, E. (1977) An ego-psychological theory of altered states of consciousness. *Int. J. Clin. Exp. Hypn.* **25,** pp. 372-387.

FROMM, E. and SHOR, R. (1979) *Hypnosis: Developments in research and new perspectives,* 2nd edition. Aldine Publishing Company, New York.

GILL, M. (1977) Psychic energy reconsidered: Discussion. *J. Amer. Psychoanal. Ass.,* **25,** (3), pp. 581-598.

GILL, M. (1979) *Psychoanalysis as science.* . . . Mimeograph.

GILL, M. M. and BRENMAN, M. (1959). *Hypnosis and related states; psychoanalytic studies in regression.* New York, International Universities Press.

GIOVACCHINI, P. (1972) Tactical approaches: An overview. In: GIOVACCHINI, P. (ed.) *Tactics and techniques in psychoanalytic therapy.* London, Hogarth Press, pp. 3-16.

GLOVER, E. (1972) Psychoanalysis and psychoanalytically oriented psychotherapy. In. GIOVACCHINI, P. (ed.) *Tactics and techniques in psychoanalytic therapy.* London, Hogarth Press, pp. 17-32.

GOLDIE, L. (1956) Hypnosis in the casualty department. *Brit. Med. J.* **2,** pp. 1340-1342.

GRAHAM, D. T. and WOLF, S. (1950) Pathogenesis of urticaria: Experimental study of life situations, emotions, and cutaneous vascular reactions. *J. Amer. Med. Ass.* **143**, pp. 1396–1402.

GRANDCHAMPS, DE (1889) Accouchement en état de fascination, insensibilité complète pendant la période de l'expulsion; régularisation des contractions, amnésie totale au réveil. *Gaz. Hôp. Paris* (20/8/1889), **94**, pp. 857-858.

GREEN, A. (1966) Les Portes de l'inconscient. In: *6ᵉ Colloque de Bonneval: L'inconscient.* Paris, Desclée de Brouwer, pp. 17-44.

GREEN, A. (1973) *Le Discours vivant. La conception psychanalytique de l'affect.* Paris, P.U.F.

GREEN, A. (1976) Préface. In: KHAN, M. (1974) *Le Soi caché.* Paris, Gallimard, 1976.

GREEN, A. (1977) Conceptions of affect. *Int. J. Psychoanal.* **58**, pp. 129-156.

GREEN, A. (1978a) La conception psychanalytique de l'affect. In: PRANGISHVILI, A., BASSIN, F. and SHEROZIA, A. (eds.) *The Unconscious. Nature, functions, methods of study.* Tbilisi, Netsniereba, Tome I, pp. 395-409.

GREEN, A. (1978b) Le Regard extérieur d'un membre fondateur. *Psychiat. Franç.* **9**(5), pp. 13-27.

GREEN, E. and GREEN, A. (1973) The ins and outs of mind-body energy. In: *Science Year, 1974.* Chicago, World Book Science Annual Field Enterprises Educational Corporation, pp. 137-147.

GREENE, R. J. and REHYER, J. (1972) Pain tolerance in hypnotic analgesic and imagination states. *J. Abnorm. Psychol.* **79**. pp. 29-38.

GUINON, G. (ed.) and CHARCOT, J. M. (1892) *Clinique des maladies du système nerveux, publié sous la direction de Georges Guinon.* Paris, Progrès Médical et Babé.

HADFIELD, J. A. (1917) The influence of hypnotic suggestion on inflammatory conditions. *Lancet*, **2**, pp. 678-679.

HADLEY, S. and STRUPP, H. (1976) Contemporary views of negative effects in psychotherapy. *Arch. Gen. Psychiat.* **33**, pp. 1291-1302.

HALEY, J. (1973) *Uncommon therapy. The psychiatric techniques of Milton H. Erickson.* New York, W. W. Norton & Co.

HANN-KENDE, F. (1933) On the role of transference and countertransference in psychoanalysis. In: DEVEREUX, F. *Psychoanalysts and the occult.* New York, International Universities Press, 1953, pp. 158-167.

HANSEN, E. (1978) Symbiosis. An aspect of psychotherapy. *Bull. Menninger Clin.* **42**, (3), pp. 191-202.

HARTMANN, H., KRIS, E. and LOEWENSTEIN, R. (1946) Comments on the formation of psychic structure. *Psychoanal. Stud. Child.* **2**, pp. 11-38.

HEBERER, H. (1922) 50 Geburten in Hypnose. *Zbl. Gynäk.* **19**, pp. 749-751.

HECAEN, H. and LANTERI-LAURA, G. (1977) *Evolution des connaissances et des doctrines sur les localisations cérébrales.* Paris, Desclée de Brouwer.

HELD, R. (1968) *Psychothérapie et psychanalyse.* Paris, Payot.

HELD, R. (1975) *Problèmes de la cure psychanalytique aujourd'hui. Us et abus de la psych-analyse.* Paris, Payot.

HELLER, F. and SCHULTZ, J. H. (1909) Über einen Fall hypnotischerzeugter Blasenbildung. *Münch. Med. Wschr.* **56**, p. 2112.

HILGARD, E. (1965) *Hypnotic susceptibility.* New York, Harcourt Brace, Jovanovich.

HILGARD, E. (1967) A quantitative study of pain and its reduction through hypnotic suggestion. *Proc. Nat. Acad. Sci. Wash.* **57**, pp. 1581-1586.

HILGARD, E. (1969) Pain as puzzle of physiology and psychology. *Amer. Psychologist,* **24,** pp. 103-113.

HILGARD, E. (1971) Pain: its reduction and production under hypnosis. *Proc. Amer. Philosophical Soc.* **115,** pp. 450-473.

HILGARD, E. (1974) Toward a neo-dissociation theory: Multiple cognitive controls in human functioning. *Perspect. Biol. Med.* **17**(3), pp. 301-316.

HILGARD, E. (1977) *Divided consciousness. Multiple controls in human thought and action.* New York, John Wiley & Sons.

HILGARD, E. and HILGARD, J. (1975) *Hypnosis in the relief of pain.* Los Altos (Calif.), W. Kaufmann.

HILGARD, J. R. (1970) *Personality and hypnosis: A study of imaginative involvement.* Chicago, University of Chicago Press.

HILGARD, J. R. (1974) Imaginative involvement: Some characteristics of the highly hypnotizable and the non-hypnotizable. *Int. J. Clin. Exp. Hypn.,* **22,** pp. 138-156.

HOLT, R. R. (1965) Ego autonomy re-evaluated. *Int. J. Psychoanal.* **46,** pp. 151-167.

HOLT, R. R. (1976) Drive or wish? A reconsideration of the psychoanalytic theory of motivation. In: GILL, M. and HOLTZMANN, P. (eds.) *Psychology versus metapsychology. Psychoanalytic essays in memory of George S. Klein.* New York, International Universities Press (Psychological Issues no. 36), pp. 158-197.

HOME, H. (1966) The concept of mind. *Int. J. Psychoanal.* **47,** pp. 42-49.

HONORTON, C. and KRIPPNER, S. (1969) Hypnosis and E.S.P. performance. A review of the experimental literature. *J. Amer. Soc. Psychical Research,* **63,** pp. 214-252.

HONORTON, C. and STUMP, J. (1969) A preliminary study of hypnotically induced clairvoyant dreams. *J. Amer. Soc. Psychical Research* **66,** pp. 86-102.

HULL, C. L. (1933) *Hypnosis and suggestibility: An experimental approach.* New York, Appleton-Century Crofts, 1968.

JACOBSON, E. (1954) Transference problems in the psychoanalytic treatment of severely depressive patients. *J. Amer. Psychanal. Ass.* **2,** pp. 595-606.

JANET, P. (1885) Notes sur quelques phénomènes de somnambulisme. *Bull. Soc. Physchol. Physiol.* **1,** pp. 24-32.

JANET, P. (1886) Deuxième note sur le sommeil provoqué à distance et la suggestion mentale pendant l'état somnambulique. *Bull. Soc. Psychol. Physiol.* **2,** pp. 70-80.

JANET, P. (1887) L'anesthésie systématisée et la dissociation des phénomènes psychologiques. *Rev. Philosoph. Fr. étranger,* **1,** pp. 449-472.

JANET, P. M. F. (1898) *Névroses et idées fixes. I. Etudes expérimentales sur les troubles de la volonté, de l'attention, de la mémoire, sur les émotions, les idées obsédantes et leur traitement.* Paris, Alcan (Travaux du Laboratoire de psychologie de la clinique de la Salpêtrière, 1st series).

JANET, P. M. F. (1889) *L'Automatisme psychologique, essai de psychologie expérimentale...* Paris, Alcan.

JANET, P. M. F. (1919) *Psychological healing. An historical and clinical study.* New York, Macmillan. London, Allen & Unwin, 1925.

JANET, P. M. F. (1923) *Principles of psychotherapy.* New York, Macmillan, 1924. London, Allen & Unwin, 1925.

JASPERS, K. (1923) *General Psychopathology.* Chicago, University of Chicago Press, 1975.

JENDRASSIK, E. (1888) Einiges über Suggestion. *Neurol. Zbl.* **7,** pp. 281-283, 321-330.

JOHNSON, R. F. Q. and BARBER, T. X. (1976) Hypnotic suggestions for blister formation: Subjective and physiological effects. *Amer. J. Clin. Hypn.* **18**(3), pp. 172-181.

JONES, E. (1957) *The life and work of Sigmund Freud* Vol. 3. *The last phase, 1919-1939.* New York, Basic Books.

JONG, DE (1889) cited in: BERILLON, E. (éd.) *Premier Congrès International de l'hypnotisme expérimental et thérapeutique tenu à l'Hôtel Dieu de Paris du 8-12 août 1889.* Paris, Doin, p. 205.

Journal of the American Psychoanalytic Association (1977), **25**(3), *passim.*

JOURNÉE, D. R. (1891) Grossesse, hypnose pendant la première partie du travail. *Rev. Hypnotisme,* pp. 18-20.

KALAŠNIK, I. (1927) K Voprossu o Primenienii Gipnoza Pri Beremiennosti v Rodakh. (On the question of using hypnosis in pregnancy and delivery.) *Odesskii Med. J.* **8-10,** pp. 85-89.

KAPLAN, D. M. (1977) Differences in the clinical and academic points of view on metapsychology. *Bull Menninger Clin.* **41**(3), pp. 207-228.

KARASU, T. B. (1977) Psychotherapies: An overview. *Amer. J. Psychiat.* **134**(8), pp. 851-863.

KERNBERG, O. (1975) *Borderline conditions and pathological narcissism.* New York, J. Aronson.

KERNBERG, O., BURSTEIN, E., COYNE, L., APPELBAUM, A., HORWITZ, L. and VOTH, H. (1972) Psychotherapy and psychoanalysis: Final report of the Menninger Foundation's psychotherapy research project. *Bull. Menninger Clin.,* **36,** pp. 1-278.

KESTENBERG, E. and KESTENBERG, J. (1965) *Contribution à la psychanalyse génétique.* Paris, P.U.F.

KHAN, M. (1974) *The privacy of the self.* London, Hogarth Press.

KINGSBURY, G. O. (1891) Accouchement pendant le sommeil hypnotique. *Rev. Hypnotisme,* **5,** pp. 298-300.

KIRSTEIN, F. (1922) Ueber Hypnosegeburten und Hypnonarkosen. *Zbl. Gynäk.* **21,** pp. 843-850.

KLEIN, G. (1973) Two theories or one? *Bull. Menninger Clin.* **37**(2), pp. 102-132.

KLEMPERER, E. (1969) Techniques of hypnosis and hypnoanalysis. *Int. J. Clin. Exp. Hypn.* **17**(3), pp. 137-152.

KLINE, M. (1975a) Sensory hypnotherapy and regression during psychological stress. *Clin. Social Work J.* **3**(4), pp. 298-308.

KLINE, M. (1975b) Sensory hypnotherapy in the management of crises and emergencies during the course of psychotherapy. In: ANTONELLI, F. (ed.) *Therapy in psychosomatic medicine.* Rome, Pozzi, vol. 2, pp. 415-425.

KOHNSTAMM, O. and PINNER (1908) Blasenbildung durch hypnotische Suggestion und Gesichtspunkte zu ihrer Erklärung. In: HERXHEIMER, K. (ed.) *Verh. Dtsch. Derm. Ges.* (Zehnter Kongress — Frankfurt — 8-10/6/1908). Berlin, Springer, pp. 342-347.

KOHUT, H. (1971) *The analysis of the self.* New York, International Universities Press.

KRAFFT-EBING, R. VON (1889) *Eine experimentelle Studie auf dem Gebiete des Hypnotismus.* Stuttgart, F. Enke.

KREIBICH, K. (1907) Vasomotorische Phänomene durch hypnotischen Auftrag. In: JADASSOHN, J. (ed.) *Verh. Dtsch. Derm. Ges.* (Neunter Kongress, Bern, second part, 12-14/9/1906). Berlin, Springer, p. 508.

KROGER, W. (1959) [Film:] *Thyroidectomy under hypnoanesthesia.* Wexler Film Co., 802 Seward, Hollywood, California, U.S.A.

KROGER, W. (1962) *Psychosomatic obstetrics, gynecology and endocrinology.* Springfield, Thomas.

KROGER, W. (1963) *Clinical and experimental hypnosis.* Philadelphia, Lippincott.

KROGER, W. (1977) *Clinical and experimental hypnosis in medicine, dentistry and psychology,* 2nd edition. Philadelphia, J. B. Lippincott Company.

KROGER, W. S. and DELEE, S. T. (1957) Use of hypno-anaesthesia for caesarean section and hysterectomy. *J. Amer. Med. Ass.* (1957), **163**, pp. 442-444.

KUBIE, L. (1953a) The distortion of the symbolic process in neurosis and psychosis. *J. Amer. Psychoanal. Ass.* **1**, pp. 59-86, republished in: SCHLESINGER, H. (ed.) *Symbol and neurosis. Selected papers of Lawrence S. Kubie.* New York, Int. Universities Press, 1978, pp. 87-114.

KUBIE, L. (1953b) Some implications for psychoanalysis of modern concepts of the organization of the brain. *Psychoanal. Quart.* **22**(1), pp. 21-68.

KUBIE, L. (1961) Hypnotism. A focus for psychophysiological and psychoanalytic investigations. *Arch. Gen. Psy.* **4**, pp. 40-54.

KUBIE, L. (1972) Illusion and reality in the study of sleep, hypnosis, psychosis and arousal. *Int. J. Clin. Exp. Hypn.* **20**(4), pp. 205-223.

KUBIE, L. (1975) The language tools of psychoanalysis. A search for better tools drawn from better models. *Int. Rev. Psychoanal.* **2**(1), pp. 11-24.

KUBIE, L. and MARGOLIN, S. (1942) A physiological method for the induction of states of partial sleep, and for securing free associations and early memories in such states. *Trans. Amer. Neurol. Ass.* **63**, pp. 136-139.

KUBIE, L. and MARGOLIN, S. (1944) The process of hypnotism and the nature of the hypnotic state. *Amer. J. Psychiat.* (3/1944), **100**, pp. 611-622.

KUKUJEV, L. (1980) O Niekotorikh Teoreticheskikh Aspektakh Nevropatologii i Psikhiatrii. (Some theoretical aspects of neuropathology and psychiatry.) *Z. Nevropat. Psykhiat.* **1**, pp. 3-8.

LACAN, L. (1953) Fonction et champ de la parole et du langage en psychanalyse. *Ecrits.* Paris, Seuil, 1966. Tome 1, pp. 111-208 (coll. Points No. 5).

LACAN, L. (1964) *The four fundamental concepts of psychoanalysis.* New York, Norton, 1978.

LACAN, L. (1966) *Ecrits. A selection.* New York, Norton, 1977.

LAPONTAINE, C. (1843) *L'Art de magnétiser ou le magnétisme animal,* 3rd edition. Paris, Baillière, 1860.

LAMAZE, F. and VELLAY, P. (1952) L'Accouchement sans douleur par la méthode psychophysique. Premiers résultats portant sur 500 cas. *Gaz. Méd. Fe.* **23**(59), pp. 1445-1460.

LAMAZE, F. and VELLAY, P. (1956) *L'Accouchement sans douleur par la méthode psychoprophylactique. Ses principes, sa réalisation, ses résultats.* Paris, Savoir et Connaître.

LAVOIE, G., SABOURIN, M. and LANGLOIS, J. (1973) Hypnotic susceptibility, amnesia and I.Q. in chronic schizophrenia. *Int. J. Clin. Exp. Hypn.* **21**, pp. 157.

LECLAIRE, S. (1980) Le mouvement psychanalytique animé par Jacques Lacan. *Confrontation,* **3**, pp. 69-76.

LE MENANT DES CHESNAIS (1894) Avantage du sommeil suggéré contre certaines douleurs et en particulier contre celles de l'accouchement. *Rev. Hypnotisme,* **5**, pp. 324-330.

LENOX, J. R. (1970) Effect of hypnotic analgesia on verbal report and cardiovascular responses to ischemic pain. *J. Abnorm. Psychol.* **75**, pp. 199-206.

LESHAN, L. (1977) *You can fight for your life: Emotional factors in the causation of cancer.* M. Evans.

LEVILLAIN, DR. (ed.) and CHARCOT (1890) Oedème bleu des hystériques reproduit expérimentalement par la suggestion hypnotique. . . Notes recueillies par M. le Dr Levillain. *Rev. Hypnotisme,* **4**(12), pp. 353-355.

LEVINSON, B. W. (1967) States of awareness during general anesthesia. In: LASSNER, J. (ed.) *Hypnosis and psychosomatic medicine. Proceedings of the International Congress for Hypnosis and Psychosomatic Medicine.* New York, Springer, pp. 200-207.

LÉVI-STRAUSS, C. (1958) *Structural anthropology.* New York, London, Basic Books, 1963.

LIBIKH, S. (1979) O Sodierzhanii i Forme Psikhoterapii. (On the content and form in psychotherapy.) In: 3 Mezndunarodnyj Simpozium Socialističeskih stran po Psikhoterapii. (*3rd International Symposium of Psychotherapists from Socialist Countries.*) Leningrad, Ministry of Health, pp. 154-166.

LICHTSCHEIN, L. (1898) Hypnotism in pregnancy and labor. *Med. News* (3/9/1898), **73**, pp. 295-298.

LIČKO, A. (1977) Psikhologija Otnošennii kak Teoretičeskaia Konceptsia v Medicinskoi Psikhologii i Psikhoterapii. (Psychology of relations in medical psychology and psychotherapy.) *Zh. Vevropat. Psykhiat.* **12**, pp. 1835-1838.

LIÉBEAULT, A. A. (1866) *Du sommeil et des états analogues considérés surtout au point de vue de l'action du moral sur le physique.* Paris, Masson.

LIÉBEAULT, A. A. (1885) Anesthésie par suggestion. *J. Magnétisme* **10**, pp. 64-67.

LIÉBEAULT, A. A. (1887) Emploi de la suggestion hypnotique en obstétrique. *Rev. Hypnotisme,* **5**, pp. 328-332.

LIÉGEOIS, J. (1889) *De la suggestion et du somnambulisme dans leurs rapports avec la jurisprudence et la médecine légale.* Paris, Doin.

LILLY, J. C. (1958) Mental effects of reduction of ordinary levels of stimuli on intact healthy persons. *Psychiatr. Res. Rep. Am. Psychiat. Ass.* **5**, pp. 1-9.

Literaturnaia gazeta (8/28/1980), 35. Vokrug tainstvenovo "fenomena". (Round Table on mysterious "phenomena".)

LOYSEL, A. (1846a) *Recueil d'opérations chirurgicales pratiquées sur des sujets magnétisés.* Cherbourg, Beaufort et Lecauf.

LOYSEL, A. (1846b) *Observation concernant une jeune fille de 17 ans, amputée d'une jambe, à Cherbourg, le 2 octobre 1845 pendant le sommeil magnétique.* Cherbourg, Beaufort et Lecauf.

LUBORSKY, L., SINGER, B. and LUBORSKY, L. (1975) Comparative studies of psychotherapies. Is it true that "Everybody has won and all must have prizes"? *Arch. Gen. Psychiat.* **32**, pp. 995-1008.

LUBORSKY, L. *et al.* (1979) Predicting the outcomes of psychotherapy: findings of the Penn Psychotherapy Project. *Arch. Gen. Psychiatr.* (in press).

LUGEOL (1893) Accouchement dans le sommeil hypnotique. *Mem. Bull. Soc. Méd. Chir. Bordeaux,* 1894 (année 1893), pp. 552-555.

LUYS, J. (1890a) Deux cas nouveaux d'accouchement sans douleur. *Rev. Hypnologie,* pp. 49-55.

LUYS, J. (1890b) Accouchement en état de fascination; amnésie complète au réveil. *Rev. Hypnologie,* pp. 321-323.

MABILLE, M. and RAMADIER, S. (1887) Anesthésie chirurgicale par suggestion post-hypnotique. *Rev. Hypnotisme* (1886-1887), pp. 111-112.

MACALPINE, I. (1950) The development of the transference. *Psychoanalytic Quarterly,* **19**, pp. 501-539.

McGLASHEN, T. H., EVANS, F. J. and ORNE, M. T. (1969) The nature of hypnotic analgesia and placebo response to experimental pain. *Psychosom. Med.* **31**, pp. 227-246.

McLAUGHLIN, J. (1978) Primary and secondary process in the context of cerebral hemispheric specialization. *Psychoanal. Quart.* **47**(2), pp. 237-266.

MAHLER, M. (1968) On human symbiosis and the vicissitudes of individuation. New York, International Universities Press.

MALAN, D. (1963) *A study of brief psychotherapy.* London, Tavistock.

MALAN, D. (1976) *Toward a validation of dynamic psychotherapy. A replication.* New York, Plenum.

MALAN, D. H., HEATH, E. S., BACAL, H. A. and BALFOUR, F. H. G. (1975) Psychodynamic changes in untreated neurotic patients. II. Apparently genuine improvements. *Arch. Gen. Psychiat.* **32**, pp. 110-126.

MANNONI, M. (1979) *La Théorie comme fiction. Freud, Groddeck, Winnicott, Lacan.* Paris, Seuil.

MARMER, M. (1959) Hypnoanalgesia and hypnoanaesthesia for cardiac surgery. *J. Amer. Med. Ass.* **171**, pp. 512-517.

MARMOR, J. (1975) The nature of the psychotherapeutic process revisited. *Canad. Psychiat. Ass. J.* **20**(8), pp. 557-565.

MARMOR, J. and WOODS, S. (1980a) *The interface between the psychodynamic and behavioral therapies.* New York Plenum.

MARMOR, J. (1980b) Recent trends in psychotherapy. *Amer. Jour. Psychiatry*, **137**(4), pp. 409-416.

MARTI, J. (1976) La psychanalyse en Russie et en Union Sovietique de 1909 à 1930. *Critique*, **346**, pp. 199-236.

MASON, A. (1955) Surgery under hypnosis. *Anaesthesia*, **10**, pp. 295-299.

MATVEEV, G. (1902) Narcose et hypnose au cours de la grossesse et de l'accouchement. Résumé in: WIAZEMSKY, J. Cas d'application de l'hypnose pendant l'accouchement. *Rev. Hypnotisme*, **8**, pp. 80-82.

MAYMAN, M. (1976) Psychoanalytic theory in retrospect and prospect. *Bull. Menninger Clin.* **40**(3), pp. 199-210.

MEDAWAR, P. B. (1977) The crab. *New York Review of Books* (9/6/1977), pp. 10-14.

MEEHL, P. (1955) Psychotherapy. *Ann. Rev. Psychol.* **6**, pp. 357-378.

MEICHENBAUM, D. (1977) *Cognitive behavior modification.* New York, Plenum Press.

MEISSNER, W. W. (1978) Theoretical assumptions of concepts in the borderline personality. *J. Amer. Psychoanal. Ass.* **26**(3), pp. 559-598.

MELZACK, R. and CASEY, K. L. (1968) Sensory motivational and central control mechanisms of pain: A new conceptual model. In: KANSHELO, D. (ed.) *The skin senses.* Springfield, Charles C. Thomas, pp. 423-439.

MENZIES, R. (1937) Conditioned vasomotor responses in human subjects. *J. Psychol.* **4**, pp. 75-120.

MENZIES, R. (1941) Further studies of conditioned vasomotor responses in human subjects. *J. Exp. Psychol.* **29**, pp. 457-482.

MESMER, F. A. (1781) *Précis historique des faits relatifs au magnétisme animal, jusqu'en Avril 1781 . . . , Ouvrage traduit de l'allemand.* A Londres.

MESMER, F. A. (1971) *Le magnétisme animal. Oeuvres. Publiées par Robert Amadou avec commentaires et notes de Frank A. Pattie et Jean Vinchon.* Paris, Payot.

MESNET, E. (1888) De l'accouchement dans le somnambulisme provoqué. *Rev. Hypnotisme*, **1**, pp. 33-42.

MICHAUX, D. (1977) *Etude longitudinale sur un cas: 3 séances d'hypnose* (unpublished text, 70 pp.).

MICHAUX, D. (1978) *Hypnose et libération des résistances: une étude de cas* (unpublished text, 13 pp.).

MILLER, G. (1977a) Sur le discours du Maitre et l'hypnose. *Lettres de l'Ecole*, **21**, pp. 297-310.

MILLER, G. (1977b) L'Evénement-Nassif. *Ornicar?* **12-13**, pp. 68-73.

MODELL, A. H. (1963) The concept of psychic energy. *J. Amer. Psychoanal. Ass.* **11**, pp. 605-618.

MOLL, A. (1924) *Der Hypnotismus mit Einschluss der Psychotherapie und der Hauptpunkte des Okkultismus.* Berlin, Fischers medicinische Buchhandlung H. Kornfeld.

MONTASSUT, M., CHERTOK, L. and GACHKEL, V. (1953) A propos d'une amnésie hystérique traitée par hypnose. *Ann. Méd. Psychol.* **2**, pp. 1-6.

MOREAU, C. (1975) *Parapsychologie en psychiatrie et psychanalyse. A propos de quelques recherches cliniques et expérimentales contemporaines.* Faculté de Médecine de Tours. Mémoire pour le C.E.S. de Psychiatrie.

MOREAU, C. (1976) *Freud et l'occultisme.* Toulouse, Privat.

MOREAU, C. and ROGEZ, R. (1977) Phénomènes télépathiques dans l'imagerie mentale hypnotique. *Evolut. Psychiat.* **47**(2), pp. 287-303.

MULLER, J. and RICHARDSON, W. (1978a) Toward reading Lacan. Pages for a workbook [Introduction, Chap. 1. The mirror stage]. *Psychoanalysis and Contemporary Thought,* **1**(3), pp. 323-372.

MULLER, J. and RICHARDSON, W. (1978b) Toward reading Lacan. Pages for a workbook [Chap. 2: Aggressivity in psychoanalysis]. *Psychoanalysis and Contemporary Thought,* **1**(4), pp. 503-529.

NARANJO, C. and ORNSTEIN, R. E. (1971) *On the psychology of meditation.* London, Allen & Unwin, 1972.

NASSIF, J. (1977) *Freud l'Inconscient.* Paris, Galilée.

NEMIAH, J. (1975) Denial revisited: Reflections on psychosomatic theory. *Psychother. Psychosom.* **26**, pp. 140-147.

NICOLAEV, A. (1927) *Teorija i Praktika Gipnoza v Fiziologičeskom Osveščenii. (Physiological perspectives in the theory and practice of hypnosis.)* Kharkov, Nauinaia Mysl.

Nouvelle Revue de Psychanalyse (Autumn 1980), p. 22 (Resurgences et dérivés de la lystique).

OETTINGEN, VON. (1921) Zur Frage der schmerzlosen Geburt. *Münchener Med. Wschr.* **51**, pp. 1654-1655.

ORNE, M. T. (1959) The nature of hypnosis: Artifact and essence. *J. Abnorm. Soc. Psychól.* **58**, pp. 277-299.

ORNE, M., SHEEHAN, P. and EVANS, F. (1968) Occurrence of posthypnotic behavior outside the experimental setting. *Journal of Personality and Social Psychology,* **9**, pp. 189-196.

ORNE, M. T. (1972) On the simulating subject as a quasi-control group in hypnosis research: What, why and how? In: FROMM, E. and SHOR, R. (eds.) *Hypnosis: Research developments and perspectives.* Chicago, Aldine-Atherton, pp. 399-443.

[OUDET] (1837) Séance du 24 janvier 1837. *Bull. Acad. Roy. Médicine Paris* (1836-1837). Paris, Baillière, pp. 343-347.

Painless childbirth, Discourse delivered by Pius XII before the International Assembly of Gynaecologists and Obstetricians at Rome, January 1956. *Osservatore Romano,* 9-10 January (1956).

PALACI, J. (1975) Réflexions sur le transfert et la théorie du narcissisme de Heinz Kohut. *Rev. Franç. Psychanal.* **39**(1-2), pp. 279-294.

PARLOFF, M. (1975) *Twenty-five years of research in psychotherapy.* New York, Albert Einstein College of Medicine, Department of Psychiatry. 10/17/1975 (cited in KARASU, 1977).

PASCHE, F. (1967) Société Psychanalytique de Paris: Colloque sur investissement et contre-investissement. Introduction à la discussion. *Rev. Franç. Psychanal.* **31**, pp. 231-235.

PATTIE, F. A. (1941) The production of blisters by hypnotic suggestion: A review. *J. Abnorm. Soc. Psychol.* **36**, pp. 62-72.

PATTON, I. B. (1969) Report on thyroidectomy performed under hypnosis. *J. Med. Ass. Ala.* **38**, pp. 617-619.

PAUL, G. (1963) The production of blisters by hypnotic suggestion: Another look. *Psychosom. Med.* **25**, pp. 233-244.

PAVLOV, I. (1921) O Tak Nazyvajemom Gipnoze Zhvvotnykh. (On the so-called animal hypnotism.) In: PAVLOV, I. *Dvacatiletnii Opyt Objektivnovo Izučenija Vysšei Niervoi Dejatielnosti. (Twenty years' experience of study of the higher nervous activity.)* Moscow, Medgiz, 1951 (7th edition), pp. 231-232.

PAVLOV, I. (1934) *Pavlovskije Kliničeskije Sredys (Pavlov clinical Wednesday.)* Moscow, U.S.S.R. Academy of Sciences Editions. Vol. II.

PAVLOV, I. (1951) [22nd Lesson] *Polnoie Sobranie Sočinenii. (Complete Works.)* Vol. IV, Moscow, U.S.S.R. Academy of Sciences Editions.

PITRES, A. (1886) Anesthésie chirurgicale par suggestion. *J. Méd. Bordeaux* (6/6/1886), pp. 502-503.

PLATONOV, K. (1959) *The word as a physiological and therapeutic factor.* Moscow, Foreign Languages Publishing House.

PLATONOV, K. and SHESTOPAL, M. (1925) *Vnušenie i Gipnoz v Akušerstvie i Ginekologii. (Suggestion and hypnosis in obstetrics and gynecology.)* Gosizdat Ukraini.

PLATONOV, K. and VELVOVSKY, I. (1924) K Voprossu O Primienenii Gipnoza v Khirurgii, Akušerstviei Ginekologii. (On the use of hypnosis in surgery, obstetrics and gynecology.) *Vratčebnoie Dielo,* **7,** pp. 353-356.

PODIAPOLSKI, P. (1909) O Vasomotornikh Rasstroitsvakh Vizyvaiemykh Gipnotičeskim Vnušeniem. (Vasomotor disturbances produced by hypnotic suggestion.) *Zh. Nevropat. Psykhiat.* **9,** pp. 101-109.

POPPER, K. and ECCLES, J. (1977) The self and its brain. An argument for interactionism. New York, Springer-Verlag.

POSTOLNIK, G. (1930) Opyty Primienenia Gipnoza i Vnušeniia Pri Rodakh. (Use of hypnosis and suggestion in delivery.) *Zh. Akučertsva i Jenskikh Bolezni.* **41,** pp. 73-82.

PRANGISHVILI, A., BASSIN, F. and SHEROZIA, A. (eds.) (1978a) *The Unconscious Nature, functions, methods of study.* Tbilisi, Metsniereba. 3 vols.

PRANGISHVILI, A., SHEROZIA, A. and BASSIN, F. (1978b) K Isstorii i Sovriemiennoi Postanovke Voprossa. (Toward the history and the modern statement of the problem). In: PRANGISHVILI, A., BASSIN, F. and SHEROZIA, A. (eds.) (1978a) *The Unconscious. Nature, functions, methods of study.* Tbilisi, Metsniereba. Tome I, pp. 23-36.

PRANGISHVILI, A., SHEROZIA, A. and BASSIN, F. (1978c) Problema Aktivnosti Bessoznatelnovo Pri Sne i Gipnoze. (The problem of the activity of the unconscious in sleep and hypnosis.) In: PRANGISHVILI, A., BASSIN, F. and SHEROZIA, A. (eds.) *The Unconscious. Nature, functions, methods of study.* Tbilisi, Metsniereba. Tome II, pp. 27-41.

PRANGISHVILI, A., SHEROZIA, A., and BASSIN, F. (1978d) Metodologičeskije Aspekty Sovremennikh Diskussi o Statuse Naučnoï Teorii Bessoznatelnovo. (Methodological Aspects of the Current Controversy Over the Scientific Status of the Theory of the Unconscious.) In: PRANGISHVILI, A., BASSIN, F. and SHEROZIA, A. (eds.) *The Unconscious. Nature, functions, methods of study.* Tbilisi, Metsniereba. Tome III, pp. 711-734.

PRESIDENT'S COMMISSION ON MENTAL HEALTH (1978) *Report to the President,* Washington, U.S. Government Printing Office. Vol. I.

PRIBRAM, K. and GILL, M. (1976) *Freud's project re-assessed.* London, Hutchinson.

PRITZL, E. (1885) Un accouchement dans l'hypnose. Revue de l'hypnotisme (1886-1887). pp. 157-158 (analyse). *Wien. Med. Wschr.* (7/11/1885), pp. 1365-1368.

PUYSÉGUR, A. M. J. DE (1785) *Mémoires pour servir l'histoire et à l'établissement du magnétisme animal.* S.l.n.d., 1784, *Suite des mémoires...* A Londres, 1785. 2 vols.

PUYSÉGUR, A. M. J. DE (1811) *Recherches, expériences et observations physiologiques sur l'homme dans l'état du somnambulisme naturel, et dans le somnambulisme provoqué par l'acte magnétique.* Paris, Dentu.

228   *References*

RAMON CAJAL, S. (1889) Hypnotic suggestion in labour. *Brit. Med. J.* (9/11/1889), p. 1053.
RAUSKY, F. (1977) *Mesmer et la révolution thérapeutique.* Paris, Payot.
Recueil général et complet de tous les écrits pour et contre le magnétisme animal. Vol. 14, no. 159. Recueil Bibliothèque Nationale, Paris.
RICHET, C. (1875) Du somnambulisme provoqué. *J. Anat. Paris,* 11, pp. 348-378.
RICHET, C. (1887) *L'Homme et l'intelligence.* Paris, Alcan. .
ROAZEN, P. (1975) *Freud and his followers.* New York, A. A. Knopf.
ROSENBLATT, A. and THICKSTUN, J. (1977) Energy, information and motivation: A revision of psychoanalytic theory. *J. Amer. Psychoanal. Ass.* 25(3), pp. 537-558.
ROUDINESCO, E. (1978) *Pour une politique de la psychanalyse.* Paris, Maspero.
ROUSTANG, F. (1976) *Un destin si funeste.* Paris, Editions de Minuit. (English: in press by Routledge, London.)
ROUSTANG, F. (1978) Suggestion au long cours. *Nouv. Rev. Psychanal.* 18, pp. 169-192.
ROUSTANG, F. (1980) *Elle ne le lache plus.* Paris, Editions de Minuit. (English: in press by Routledge, London.)
ROZHNOV, V., and BURNO, V. (1976) Gipnoz Kak Isskusstvienno Vyzvannaia Individualnaïa Psikhologičeskaïa Zaščita. (Kliničeskoïe Issledovanie Isteričeskikh i Psikhasteničeskikh Bessoznatielnikh Mekhanizmov v Gipnoze i v Stressovoï Situaĉii.) [Hypnosis as an artificially evoked individual psychological defence. (A clinical study of hysterical and psychasthenic unconscious mechanisms in hypnosis and stress situations.)] *Zh. Nevropat. Psykhiat,* 9, pp. 1406-1408.
ROZHNOV, V. and BURNO, V. (1978) Uĉenie o Bessoznatelnom i Kliniĉeskaia Psikhoterapija. (The unconscious and clinical psychotherapy: The problem posed.) In: PRANGISHVILI, A., BASSIN, F. and SHEROZIA, A. (eds.) *The Unconscious. Nature, functions, methods of study.* Tbilisi, Metsniereba, Tome II, p. 346-353.
RUIZ, O. and FERNANDEZ, A. (1960) Hypnosis as an anesthetic in ophthalmology. *Amer. J. Ophthal.* 50, p. 163.
RYBALKIN, J. (1890) Brùlure du second degré provoquée par suggestion. *Rev. Hypnotisme,* 4, pp. 361-362.
SAKUN, N. (1977) Po Povodu Statii I. M. APTERA: "O Prirodie Gipnoza i Ievo Znaĉenii v Psikhoterapii" (Apropos of APTER's article: "The nature of hypnosis and its role in psychotherapy.) *Zh. Nevropat. Psykhiat.* 9. p. 1416.
SALLIS (1888) Der Hypnotismus in der Geburtshilfe. *Frauenarzt* (1/1888), pp. 9-42 and (2/1888), pp. 72-80.
SANDLER, J. and JOFFÉ, W. (1969) Toward a basic psychoanalytic model. *Int. J. Psychoanal.* 50, pp. 79-90.
SAPIR, M., REVERCHON, F., PREVOST, J. J., CANET-PALAYSI, C., PHILIBERT, R., CORNIER, A., COHEN-LEON, S. and FEDIDA, P. (1975) *La Relaxation, son approche psychanalytique.* Paris, Dunod.
SARBIN, J. R. (1950) Contributions to role-taking theory. 1. Hypnotic behaviour. *Psychol. Rev.* 57, pp. 255-270.
SARDZHVELADZE, I. J. (1978) O Balanse Projekcii i Introjekcii v Procese Empatiĉeskogo Vzaimodejsvija. (Concerning the balance of projection and introduction in process of empathic interaction.) In: PRANGISHVILI, A., BASSIN, F. and SHEROZIA, A. (eds.) (1978a) *The Unconscious. Nature, functions, methods of study.* Tbilisi, Metsniereba, Tome III, pp. 485-489.
SAUNDERS, S. D. (1852) Accouchement en état magnétique. *J. Magnétisme,* p. 337.
SAUSSURE, R. DE (1968) La cure magnétique. *Inform. Psychiat.* 4(10), pp. 903-909.
SCHAFER, R. (1976a) Emotion in the language of action. In: GILL, M. and HOLZMANN, P. (eds.) *Psychology versus Metapsychology—Psychoanalytic essays in memory of Georges*

Klein. New York, International Universities Press (Psychological Issues no. 36), pp. 106-133.

SCHAFER, R. (1976b) *A new language for psychoanalysis.* New Haven, Yale University Press.

SCHILDER, P. (1922) *Über das Wesen der Hypnose.* Wien, Berlin, J. Springer.

SCHILDER, P. and KAUDERS (1926) *Lehrbuch der Hypnose.* Wien, Berlin, J. Springer.

SCHINDLER, R. (1927) *Nervensystem und spontane Blütungen.* Berlin, Karger.

SCHMALE, A. (1974) The sensory deprivations: An approach to the study of the induction of affects. *J. Amer. Psychoanal. Ass.* **22**(3), pp. 626-642.

SCHNECK, J. (1954) *Studies in scientific hypnosis.* Baltimore (Md), Williams & Wilkins.

SCHNECK, J. (1965) *The principles and practice of hypnoanalysis.* Springfield (Ill.), Charles C. Thomas.

SCHRENCK-NOTZING, A. FREIHERR VON (1893) Eine Geburt in der Hypnose. *Z. Hypnotismus,* **I**, pp. 49-52.

SCHRENCK-NOTZING, A. FREIHERR VON (1896) Ein experimenteller und kritischer Beitrag zur Frage der suggestiven Hervorrufung circumscripter vasomotorischer Veränderungen auf der aüsseren Haut. *Z. Hypnotismus,* **4**, pp. 209-228.

SCHRENCK-NOTZING, A. FREIHERR VON (1898) Zur Frage der suggestiven Hauterscheinungen. Eine Erwiderung an Herrn Prof. Dr A. Forel. *Z. Hypnotismus,* **7**, pp. 247-249.

SCHULTZE-RHONHOF, F. (1922) Der hypnotische Geburtsdämmerschlaf. *Zbl. Gynäk.* **7**, pp. 247-257.

SCHULTZE-RHONHOF, F. (1923) Zum Kapital Hypnosegeburten. *Zbl. Gynäk.* **12**, pp. 476-483.

SCHUR, M. (1958) The ego and the id in anxiety. *Psychoanal. Stud. Child.* **13**, pp. 190-220.

SCHUTZENBERGER, A. and SAURET, M. J. (1977) *Le Corps et le groupe.* Toulouse, Privat.

SCHWARCZ, B. (1965) Hypnoanalgesia and hypnoanesthesia in urology. *Surg. clin. N. Amer.* **45**, pp. 1547-1555.

SCOTT, D. (1973) Hypnoanalgesia for major surgery: A psychodynamic process. *Amer. J. Clin. Hypn.* **16**, pp. 84-91.

SEITZ, P. (1953) Experiments in the substitution of symptoms by hypnosis. I. *Psychosom. Med.* (1951), **13**(4), II. *Ibid.* (1953), **15**(5). Republished in: KLINE, M. (ed.) *Clinical correlations of experimental hypnosis.* Springfield, C. Thomas, 1963, pp. 275-284 and 285-318.

SHAPIRO, A. K. (1976) The behavior therapies: therapeutic breakthrough or latest fad? *Amer. J. Psychiat.* **133**(2), pp. 154-159.

SHAPIRO, E. (1978) The psychodynamics and developmental psychology of the borderline patient: A review of the literature. *Amer. J. Psychiat.* **135**(11), pp. 1305-1315.

SHEEHAN, P. and PERRY, C. W. (1976) *Methodologies of hypnosis: A critical appraisal of contemporary paradigms of hypnosis.* Hillsdale, Lawrence Eribaum Associated Publishers.

SHEROZIA, A. (1969) *K Probleme Soznania i Bessoznatelnovo Psikhičeskovo. (A contribution to the problem of the conscious and the unconscious.* Vol. I.) Tbilisi, Metsniereba.

SHEROZIA, A. (1973) *K Probleme Soznania i Bessoznatelnovo Psikhičeskovo. (A contribution to the problem of the conscious and the unconscious.* Vol. 2.) Tbilisi, Metsniereba.

SHEROZIA, A. (1978) Psikhoanaliz i Teorija Neosozavaiemoi Psikhologičeskoï Ustanovki: Itologi i Perspektivi. (Psychoanalysis and the theory of unconscious psychological set: Findings and prospects.) In: PRANGISHVILI, A., BASSIN, F. and SHEROZIA, A. (eds.) *The Unconscious. Nature, functions, methods of study.* Tbilisi, Metsniereba, Tome I, pp. 37-68.

SHEVRIN, H. (1976) Rapaport's contribution to research: A look to the future. *Bull. Menninger Clin.* **40**(3), pp. 211-228.

SHLIFER, R. (1930) K Slovesnomu Obezbolivanïu Rodovovo Akta. (Verbal analgesia in delivery.) In: *Psykhoterapia,* Kharkov, pp. 307-318.

230 References

SHOR, R. E. (1959) Hypnosis and the concept of the generalised reality orientation. *Amer. J. Psychother.* **13**, pp. 582-602.

SHOR, R. E. (1962) Three dimensions of hypnotic depth. *Int. J. Clin. Exp. Hypn.* **10**, pp. 23-38.

SHTERNBERG, I. (1978) Progres Poviedientscheskoï Terapii. (Progress in behavior therapy.) *Zh. Nevropat Psykhiat.* **3**, p. 460.

SIFNEOS, P. (1972) *Short-term psychotherapy and emotional crisis.* Cambridge (Mass.), Harvard University Press.

SMIRNOV, D. (1912) Zur Frage der durch hypnotische Suggestion hervorgerufenen vasomotorischen Störungen. *Z. Psychother. Med. Psychol.* **4**, pp. 171-175.

SMITH, M. L. and GLASS, G. V. (1977) Meta-analysis of psychotherapy outcome studies. *Amer. Psychologist*, **32**, pp. 752-760.

Société Neurologique de Paris (1908a) Séance du 9 avril 1908. *Rev. Neurol.*, pp. 375-404.

Société Neurologique de Paris (1908b) Séance du 14 mai 1908. *Rev. Neurol.*, pp. 494-519.

SPIRKIN, A. (1930) Poznanie psiho-bio-fizičeskoï real'nosti. (Understanding psycho-biophysical realities.) *Tekhnika Molodiozhi*, **3**, pp. 50-52.

SPITZ, R. A. (1945) Hospitalism: An inquiry into the genesis of psychiatric conditions in early childhood. *Psychoanal. Stud. Child*, **1**, pp. 53-74.

SPITZ, R. (1965) *The first year of life. A psychoanalytic study of normal and deviant development object relations.* New York, International Universities Press.

STEWART, H. (1969) The nature of the controlling forces in the hypnotic relationship, p. 201. In: CHERTOK, L. (ed.) *Psycho-physiological mechanisms of hypnosis.* New York, Springer, pp. 199-202.

STRUPP, H. (1973) Toward a reformulation of the psychodynamic influence. *Int. J. Psychiat.* **11**, pp. 263-354.

STRUPP, H. (1978) Psychotherapy research and practice: An overview. In: GARFIELD, S. and BERGIN, A. E. (eds.) *Handbook of psychotherapy and behavior change.* New York, J. Wiley, pp. 3-22.

Suggestion and allergic responses (1964) *Brit. Med. J.* (2/5/1964), **5391**, pp. 1129-1130 (editorial).

SULLOWAY, F. (1979) *Freud, biologist of the mind. Beyond the psychoanalytic legend.* New York, Basic Books.

SUMBAIEV, I. (1928) K Voprossu o vasomotorhikh Rastroistvakh Vyzyvaiemykh|Gipnotičeskim Vnušenium. (Vasomotor disturbances produced by hypnotic suggestion.) *Sibriski Arkhiv Kliničeskoi Meditsini*, **4**, pp. 332-342.

SVJADOŠČ, A. (1978) Rol'Neosoznavaemyh Motivov v Klinike Nevrozov. (The role of unconscious motives in the clinical picture of neurosis.) In: PRANGISHVILI, A., BASSIN, F. and SHEROZIA, A. (eds.) (1978a) *The Unconscious. Nature, functions, methods of study.* Tbilisi, Metsniereba, Tome III, pp. 361-367.

SWANSON, D. (1977) A critique of psychic energy as an explanatory concept. *J. Amer. Psychoanal. Ass.* **25**(3), pp. 603-634.

SYRKIN, M. (1950) Dosvid Raboti Kiivskovo Miskovo Akušerkovo Gipnoitaii za 2 Roki. (Three years' results of the works of a hypnotarium in obstetrics.) *Pediatrya Akušertvo, Ginekologia*, **I**, pp. 23-30.

TASK FORCE REPORT 5 (1973) *Behavior therapy in psychiatry.* Washington, Amer. Psychiat. Ass.

TAŠLYKOV, V. (1979) Vlijanii ossobennostiej sistemy otnošenii "Bolnoj bolezn'i vrač" na psikhoterapeutičeskij proces pri nevrozah. (Influence of doctor-patient relationship in psychotherapeutic process in neuroses.) In: *3 Meždunarodnii simpozium socialističeskih stran po psikhoterapii. (3rd International Symposium of Psychotherapists from Socialist Countries.)* Leningrad, Ministry of Health, pp. 43-51.

References 231

TATZEL (1893) Eine Geburt in der Hypnose. *Z. Hypnotismus*, **I**, pp. 245-247.

TAUGHER, V. J. (1958) Hypnoanaesthesia. *Wis. Med. J.* **57**, pp. 95-96.

TINTEROW, M. M. (1960) The use of hypnotic anaesthesia for major surgical procedures. *Amer. Surg.* **26**, pp. 732-737.

TOULMIN, S. (1978) The Mozart of psychology. *New York Review of Books* (28/9/1978). pp. 51-58.

TURKLE, S. (1978) *Psychoanalytic politics: Freud's French revolution.* New York, Basic Books.

ULLMAN, M. (1947) Herpes simplex and second degree burns induced under hypnosis. *Amer. J. Psychiat.* **103**, pp. 828-830.

UZNADZE, D. (1966a) *The psychology of set* [edited by Joseph Wortis]. New York, Consultants Bureau.

UZNADZE, D. (1966b) Psikhologičeskiie Issledovanija. (Research in psychology.) Moscow, Nauka.

VAN DYKE, P. (1970) Some uses of hypnosis in the management of the surgical patient. *Amer. J. Clin. Hypn.* **12**, pp. 227-235.

VANNES, D. DE (1826) *Traité de l'acupuncture d'après les observations de M. Jules Cloquet.* Paris, Bechet Jeune.

VELANDER (1890) Un cas de mutisme mélancolique guéri par suggestion. *Rev. Hypnotisme*, pp. 175-176.

VIDERMANN, S. (1970) *La Construction de l'espace analytique.* Paris, Denoël.

VIGDOROVIČ, M. (1938) Kollektivnoïe vnušenie Kak Metod Massovoï Podgotovki Beriemennikh K Boleznienim Rodam. (Collective suggestions as a method of pregnant women for painless delivery.) *Tezissi dokladov na II Oukrainskom Siezdie Akušersva i Ginekologii,* Kiev, pp. 34-36.

[VILLERS, CHARLES DE] (1787) *Le Magnétiseur amoureux, par un membre de la société harmonique du régiment de Metz.* Genève [Besançon].

VINGOE, F. and KRAMER, E. (1966) Hypnotic susceptibility of hospitalized psychotic patients: A pilot study. *Int. J. Clin. Exp. Hypn.* **14**, pp. 47-54.

VOISIN, A. (1896) Un accouchement dans l'état d'hypnotisme. *Rev. hypnotisme,* **6**, pp. 360-361.

VOLOSHINOV, V. (1927) *Freudianism. A Marxist critique.* New York, Academic Press, 1976.

VYGOTSKY, L. (1971) *The psychology of art.* s.1., M.I.T. Press.

VYGOTSKY, L. (1978) *Mind in society: The development of higher psychological processes.* Harvard University Press.

WACHTEL, P. (1977) *Psychoanalysis and behavior therapy.* New York, Basic Books.

WALLERSTEIN, R. S. (1976) Psychoanalysis as a science: Its present status and its future tasks. In: GILL, M. and HOLZMANN, P. (eds.) *Psychology versus Metapsychology. Psychoanalytic essays in memory of George S. Klein.* New York, International Universities Press, pp. 198-228.

WATKINS, J. G. (1949) *Hypnotherapy of war neuroses.* New York, Ronald Press.

WATKINS, J. G. (1978) *The therapeutic self. Developing resonance. Key to effective relationships.* New York, Human Sciences Press.

WEITZENHOFFER, A. M. (1953) *Hypnotism· An objective study in suggestibility.* New York, Wiley.

WEITZENHOFFER, A. M. (1979) Hypnotism and altered states of consciousness. In: SUGERMAN, A. A. and TARTER, R. E. (eds.) *Expanding dimensions of consciousness.* New York, Springer Publications, in press.

WEITZENHOFFER, H. and HILGARD, E. (1959) *Stanford Hypnotic Susceptibility Scale. Forms A and B.* Palo Alto (Calif.), Consulting Psychologists Press.

WEITZENHOFFER, H. and HILGARD, E. (1962) *Stanford Hypnotic Susceptibility Scale. Form C.* Palo Alto (Calif.), Consulting Psychologists Press.

WETTERSTRAND, O. G. (1891) *Der Hypnotismus und seine Anwendung in der praktischen Medizin.* Wien and Leipzig, Urban und Schwarzenberg.

WHITE, R. W. (1937) Two types of hypnotic trance and their personality correlates. *J. Psychol.* **3,** pp. 279-289.

WIDLÖCHER, D. (1979) L'hystérie de conversion. *Psychologie Médicale* (in press).

WINNICOTT, D. (1954) Metapsychological and clinical aspects of regression within the psychoanalytical set-up. *Int. J. Psychoanal.* **36,** pp. 16-26.

WOHLHEIM, R. (1979) The cabinet of docteur Lacan. *New York Review of Books* (25/1/1979), pp. 36-45.

WOLBERG, L. (1948) *Medical hypnosis,* vols. I-II. New York, Grune & Stratton.

WOLBERG, L. R. and KARDINER, A. (1964) *Hypnoanalysis,* 2nd edition. New York, Grune & Stratton.

WOLFF, G. VON (1927) Der geburtshilfliche Dämmerschlaf in Hypnose, mit besonderer Berücksichtigung seiner Technik. *Arch. Gynäk.* **129,** pp. 23-65.

WOLFF, P. (1959) Observations on the neonate. *Psychosom. Med.* **21,** p. 110.

WOOD, E. (1890) Opération chirurgicale pratiquée dans l'état hypnotique. *Rev. Hypnotisme,* pp. 246-247.

ZACHEPITSKI, R. (1976) O Terapii Poviedienia. (On behaviour therapy.) *Zh. Nevropat. Psykhiat.* **9,** pp. 1400-1405.

ZACHEPITSKI, R. (1979) Kompleksnaia Sistema Patogenetičeskoj Psikhoterapii Pri Nevrozah. (Pathogenic psychotherapy of neuroses.) *3 Meždunarodnij Simpozium Socialističeskih stran po Psikhoterapii. (3rd International Symposium of Psychotherapists from Socialist Countries.)* Leningrad, Ministry of Health, pp. 113-115.

ZACHEPITSKI, R. and KARVASARSKY, B. (1978) Voprossy Sootnošenija Osoznavajemyh i Neosoznavajemyh Form Psikhičeskoj Dejatelnosti v Svietie Opyta Patogeničeskoj Psikhoterapii Nevrozov. (Concerning the relationship between conscious and unconscious forms of mental activity in the light of pathogenic psychotherapy of neuroses.) In: PRANGISHVILI, A., BASSIN, F. and SHEROZIA, A. (eds.) *The Unconscious. Nature, functions, methods of study.* Tbilisi, Metsniereba, Tome II, pp. 354-360.

ZDRAVOMYSLOV, V. (1956) *Obezbolivanie Rodov Vnušeniem.* (Obstetric analgesia through suggestion.) Moscow. Medgiz.

Name Index

Subject Index

239

Books by Dr. Léon Chertok

1959 Psychosomatic Methods of Painless Childbirth
(Pergamon Press, Oxford)
(Also published in French, Spanish, Italian, German and Czech)

1966 Hypnosis (Pergamon Press, Oxford)
(Also published in French, Spanish, Italian, Portuguese, German, Polish, Russian
Serbo-Croat)

1969 Motherhood and Personality (Harper & Row, New York)
(Also published in French)

1979 The Therapeutic Revolution, From Mesmer to Freud
(Brunner/Mazel, New York)
(Also published in French, Italian and Spanish)

1981 Sense and Nonsense in Psychotherapy (Pergamon Press, Oxford)
(Also published in French; in press in Italian, Portuguese, Spanish and Russian)